# THE Data Model Resource Book

## A LIBRARY OF LOGICAL DATA MODELS AND DATA WAREHOUSE DESIGNS

*Len Silverston*
*W.H. Inmon*
*Kent Graziano*

WILEY COMPUTER PUBLISHING

D1534532

John Wiley & Sons, Inc.
New York • Chichester • Weinheim • Brisbane • Singapore • Toronto

Executive Publisher: Katherine Schowalter
Editor: Robert M. Elliott
Managing Editor: Micheline Frederick
Electronic Products, Associate Editor: Michael Green
Text Design & Composition: Publishers' Design and Production Services, Inc.

This text is printed on acid-free paper.

*Library of Congress Cataloging-in-Publication Data:*

Silverston, Len, 1958–
    The data model resource book : a library of logical data models and data warehouse designs / Len Silverston, W.H. Inmon, Kent Graziano.
        p.   cm.
    Includes bibliographical references.
    ISBN: 0471-15364-8 (alk. paper). — ISBN 0-471-15367-2 (pbk./CD-ROM). — ISBN 0-471-15366-4 (CD-ROM)
    1. Database design.   2. Data structures (Computer science).
3. Management information systems.   I. Inmon, William H.
II. Graziano, Kent, 1960–     .   III. Title.
QA76.9.D26S53   1997
650'.0285'5756—dc21                                    96-39996
                                                        CIP

Printed in the United States of America

10 9 8 7 6 5 4 3

# CONTENTS

# FOREWORD

Throughout my years of data modeling, I have often wished for a template, a proven prototype from which I could begin my work. Such a generic, adaptable model would have saved hundreds of hours of labor, representing a tremendous cost reduction and boost in productivity.

This is not another "How To" book on data modeling; there are hundreds of those. This original work of Len Silverston, Kent Graziano, and Bill Inmon answers the industry-wide need for generic data models that can be adapted immediately and effectively. Usage of these models will provide corporations with a practical guide for standardizing their entities and attributes.

The authors of this book are acknowledged experts in the field. Several years ago, I had the pleasure of designing models with Len Silverston. I am extremely impressed with the depth of his knowledge and the clarity and precise logic of his modeling skills. During his years of constructing models, Len has often combined his knowledge with the insight of Kent Graziano. Together, they have produced solid data models for numerous and diverse industries that rely on data modeling.

The models in this book combine the experience of Len and Kent, with the brilliant insight of Bill Inmon on data warehousing. Len, Kent, and Bill have done us all a favor by creating these adaptable models. I am certain that you will find the wisdom contained in these pages as valuable as I have.

*Claudia Imhoff*
*Intelligent Solutions, Inc.*
*November 18, 1996*

# ACKNOWLEDGMENTS

We are especially grateful to Claudia Imhoff of Intelligent Solutions for her comprehensive and insightful review of the data warehousing chapters.

Thank you to Ken Haley from Trinidad Benham Corporation, Mike Brightwell from FM Software and Angela Pearce for their thorough review of the logical data models and their suggestions which enhanced the models. Thanks to Arlene Graziano for her assistance with technical editing and overall support.

We would also like to thank the staff at Quest Database Consulting, Inc. who assisted in reviewing this book. In particular, thank you to Bruce Bacon, Rob Williams, and Luz Cofresi-Howe for their business analysis skills and book content reviews. Thanks to Larry Gombos and the administrative staff for assisting with the preparation of the many review copies which were sent out.

Finally, we want to thank Bob Elliott and Brian Calandra from John Wiley & Sons who were so helpful in making this book a reality.

# 1

# INTRODUCTION

## WHY IS THERE A NEED FOR THIS BOOK?

On many of our data modeling consulting engagements, our clients ask us the same question: "Where can we find a book showing a standard way to model this structure? Surely, we are not the first company to model company and address information."

Based upon our consulting experiences, most companies develop their data models or data warehouse designs with very little outside reference materials. There is a large cost associated with either hiring experienced consultants or using internal staff to develop this critical component of the system design. Often there is no objective reference material which they can use to validate their data models or data warehouse designs, or seek alternate options for database structures.

In general, one third of a data model (corporate or logical) consists of common constructs that are applicable to most organizations and the other two thirds of the model are either industry- or enterprise-specific. This means that most data modeling efforts are recreating data modeling constructs that have already been created many times before in other organizations.

With this in mind, doesn't it make sense to have a source upon which to get a head start on your data model so you are not "reinventing the wheel" each time a company develops a new system? Organizations can save time and money by leveraging the use of common or universal database structures. Even if a company has data models from its previous systems development efforts, it is very helpful to be able to check the designs against an unbiased source in order to evaluate alternative options.

Although there are a large number of publications which describe how to model data, there are very few compilations of data model examples in published form. This book provides both a starting point and a source for validating data models. It can assist data modelers to minimize design costs and develop more effective database designs.

## WHO CAN BENEFIT FROM READING THIS BOOK?

This book can assist many different systems development professionals: data administrators, data modelers, data analysts, database designers, data warehouse administrators, data warehouse designers, data stewards, and corporate data integrators. Systems professionals can use the database constructs contained within this book to increase their productivity and provide a checkpoint for quality designs.

## THE NEED FOR UNIVERSAL DATA MODELS

Data modeling has been an art that first gained recognition since Dr. Peter Chen's 1976 article which illustrated his new-found approach called "Entity-Relationship Modeling." Since then it has become the standard approach used towards designing databases. By properly modeling an organization's data, the database designer can eliminate data redundancies which are a key source for inaccurate information and ineffective systems.

Currently, data modeling is a well-known and accepted method for designing effective databases. Therefore, there is a great need to provide standard templates to enterprises (the term enterprise is used to describe the organizations for whom the models and systems are being developed) so they can refine and customize their data models instead of starting from scratch.

Although many standards exist for data modeling, there is a great need to take data modeling to the next step: providing accessibility to libraries of common data model examples in a convenient format. These libraries of models should be able to be used across many different organizations and industries.

Such *universal data models* can help save tremendous amounts of time and money in the systems development process.

## A HOLISTIC APPROACH TO SYSTEMS DEVELOPMENT

One of the largest challenges to building effective systems is integration. Systems are often built separately since there are particular needs at different times within each enterprise. Enterprises have needs to build many systems: contact management systems, sales order systems, project management systems, accounting systems, budgeting systems, purchase order systems, and human resources systems, to name a few.

When systems are built separately, there are separate pools of information for each system. Many of these systems will use common information about organizations, people, geographic locations, or products. This means that each separate system will build and use its own source of information. A huge problem with this approach is that it is almost impossible to maintain accurate up-to-date information since the same type of information is stored redundantly across many systems. In large organizations, it is not uncommon to see information about customers, employees, organizations, products, and locations stored in dozens of separate systems. How is it possible to know which source of information is most current or accurate?

Another way to approach systems development is from a perspective that an enterprise's systems are connected and, in fact, may be viewed as one interconnected system. From this perspective, there are tremendous benefits to building an enterprise-wide framework so that systems can work together more effectively. Part of this enterprise-wide framework should include a corporate data model which can assist the enterprise in maintaining one of its most valued assets: information. Since each system or application may use similar information about people, organizations, products, and geographic locations, a shared information architecture can be invaluable.

The IS (information systems) industry has recognized the need for integrated designs and this is why many corporate data modeling and corporate data warehouse modeling efforts have taken place. Unfortunately, the IS track record for building and implementing corporate data models has been very poor. Enterprises have realized that it takes a tremendous amount of time and resources to build these models.

Enter CASE (Computer-Aided Systems Engineering) tools. These tools claimed tremendous productivity and time savings when used for corporate-wide modeling efforts. While these tools help document the models, unfortunately they do not reduce the time to develop good corporate models.

Many enterprises have stopped building corporate data models because of their time constraints. They are looking at the track record of corporate data modeling and CASE efforts and choosing other alternatives.

Enter *data warehousing*. Finally, here is an approach to provide executives with the management information they need, without all the time and expense of corporate data modeling. Enterprises are now extracting the various pieces of information they need directly from their operational systems in order to build decision support systems.

The only problem with this approach is that *the same problem exists!* First of all, the information in the data warehouse may be extracted from several different, inconsistent sources. If there are multiple places that customer information is being held, which system represents the most accurate source of information?

According to data warehousing principles, the transformation routines are responsible for consolidating and *cleansing* the data. However, if different departments have different needs for various pieces of data, then each department may build its own extracts from the operational systems. One department may transform the information using one algorithm while a different department may use another algorithm. For example, if two departments are extracting sales analysis information, one department may use the order entry system as its source and another department may use the invoicing system as its source. A high-level manager may view information from both data warehouses and see inconsistent results, thus questioning the credibility of *any* of the information. This type of scenario actually compounds the initial problem of many data sources by creating even more *slices of data*.

This is not to say that data warehousing is the wrong approach. It is an ingenious approach which can be used extremely effectively not only to create decision support systems but also to build a migration path to an integrated environment. The data warehouse transformation process helps to identify where there are data inconsistencies and data redundancies in the operational environment. However, it is imperative to use this information to migrate to new integrated data structures.

The answer is still to build integrated data structures in order to provide good, accurate information. It is also necessary to understand the nature of the data in order to build effective systems. Instead of saying that corporate data modeling or CASE is the wrong approach because it just takes too long, the IS community needs to find a way to make it work effectively. By building common reusable data structures, the IS community can produce quicker results and move toward integrated structures in both the transaction processing and data warehouse environments.

## WHAT IS THE INTENT OF THIS BOOK AND THESE MODELS?

Most data modeling books focus on the techniques and methodologies behind data modeling. The approach behind this book is dramatically different. This book assumes that the reader knows how to model data. Data modeling has been around long enough that most information systems professionals are familiar with this concept and will be able to understand this book. Therefore, this book makes no efforts to teach data modeling principles, except by example. Data modelers can use this book, and their previous experience, to build upon and refine the data model examples contained within the book in order to develop more customized data models. Essentially, it is providing the modeler with fundamental tools and building blocks which can be reused. Therefore, the modeler can be more productive and save a great deal of time by starting with standard data models instead of building data models from scratch.

Furthermore, the reader can also benefit from the data warehouse models which are applicable to decision support environments. This book not only presents examples of data warehouse designs, but also explains in detail how to convert the logical data models to an enterprise-wide data warehouse, then to departmental data marts. The logical data models and data warehouse models presented here are applicable across a wide variety of enterprises.

These models are intended to be a *starting point* for developing logical and data warehouse data models for an enterprise. Each enterprise will have its own detailed requirements; the models will need to be modified and customized in order to be implemented for a specific enterprise. Since the data warehouse data models reflect actual database designs (as opposed to logical data models), they are even more dependent on the business needs of the specific enterprise wishing to use these models. In addition, the models in this book can be used to validate an enterprise's existing data models.

The models presented in the first part of this book (Chapters 2 through 8) are logical data models, not physical database designs. Therefore, these models are normalized and may require some denormalization when designing the physical database. Methodologies for physical database design are not discussed in this book. Consistent with this point, the logical data models do not include any derived attributes since derived attributes do not add anything to the information requirements of a business. They merely serve to enhance performance of the physical database.

These logical data models represent possible data requirements for enterprises. They do not include many of the business processing rules that may accompany data models. The data models generally provide all the information needed to enforce business rules; however, the reader is advised in many cases that additional business rules may need to be developed to supplement the data models. Examples of the need for business rules are provided throughout this book.

These data models were designed to benefit many different industries and enterprises. They were picked specifically because they represent very common data constructs that appear in most organizations. Within these models, whenever there was a data modeling decision which may have been dependent on a specific enterprise, the most flexible data modeling option was chosen in order to accommodate many different enterprises.

## CONVENTIONS AND STANDARDS USED IN THIS BOOK

The following section describes the naming standards and diagramming conventions used for presenting the models within this book. Details are described for entities, sub-types, attributes, relationships, foreign keys, physical models, and illustration tables.

### Entities

An *entity* is something of significance about which the enterprise wishes to store information. Whenever entities are referenced throughout the book, they are shown in capital letters. For example, ORDER represents an entity which stores information about a commitment between parties to purchase products. When the name of an entity is used in a sentence in order to illustrate concepts and business rules, it may be shown in normal text. For example, "Many enterprises have mechanisms such as a sales order form to record sales order information."

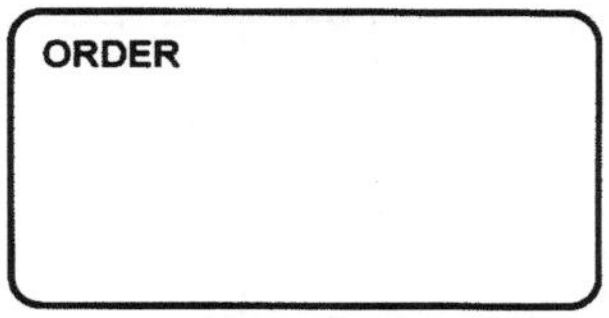

**FIGURE 1.1**

*An entity.*

The naming conventions for an entity include using a singular noun that is as meaningful as possible to reflect the information it is maintaining. Additionally, the suffix TYPE is added to the entity name if the entity represents a classification of information such as an ORDER TYPE (i.e., sales versus purchase order) rather than a specific instance of a real thing such as an ORDER ("order #23987").

The data models in this book include TYPE entities on the diagrams, even though they usually only have a **code** and **description.** These entities are included for completeness and to show where allowable values or look-ups are stored.

Entities are included in the data model if it is a requirement of the enterprise to maintain the information included in the entity. For example, if an enterprise doesn't really care about tracking the tasks associated with a shipment, then, even though this information exists in the real world, the data model should not incorporate this information since it does not add value.

Entities are represented by rounded boxes. Figure 1.1 shows an example of the entity ORDER.

## Sub-types and Super-types

A *sub-type,* sometimes referred to as a sub-entity, is a classification of an entity which has characteristics such as attributes or relationships in common with the more general entity. INTERNAL ORGANIZATION and EXTERNAL ORGANIZATION are for example, sub-types of ORGANIZATION.

Sub-types are represented in the data modeling diagrams by entities inside other entities. The common attributes and relationships between sub-types are shown in the outside entity which is known as the *super-type.* The attributes and relationships of the super-type are therefore inherited by the sub-type. Figure 1.2 shows the super-type ORGANIZATION and its sub-types INTERNAL ORGANIZATION and EXTERNAL ORGANIZATION. Notice that the **name** and **fed-**

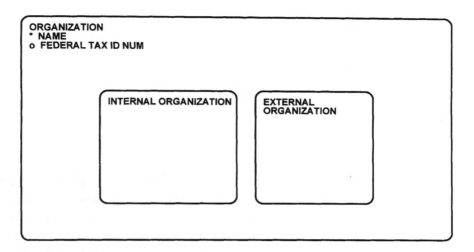

**FIGURE 1.2**

*Sub-types and super-types.*

**eral tax ID** apply to both sub-types and are therefore shown at the super-type level of ORGANIZATION. Anything specific to an internal organization would be tied to only that sub-type.

The sub-types within an entity should represent a complete set of classifications (meaning that the sum of the sub-types covers the super-type in its entirety) and at the same time be mutually exclusive of each other. Many times the data model includes an OTHER . . . sub-type to provide for other possible classifications of the entity which may be defined by the enterprise using the model.

While the sub-types represent a complete set of possible classifications, there may be more detailed sub-types which are not included in the data model; instead, they may be included in a TYPE entity. In this case, sub-types are shown in two places on a model: as a sub-type and in a TYPE entity which shows the domain of allowed types for the entity.

## Attributes

An *attribute* holds a particular piece of information about an entity, such as the **order date** on an order. Attributes are identified in the text of the book by boldface, lowercase letters such as the previous **order date** example.

Attributes may be either part of the unique identifier of an entity (also referred to as a primary key), mandatory, or optional. The primary key attribute(s)

```
ORDER
#  ORDER ID
*  ORDER DATE
o  ENTRY DATE
o  SHIPPING INSTRUCTIONS
```

**FIGURE 1.3**

*Attributes.*

is identified by a '#' sign preceding the attribute name on the diagram. Mandatory attributes are signified by a '*' before the attribute name. Optional attributes have a 'o' before the attribute. Figure 1.3 shows that the ORDER entity has **order ID** as a primary key attribute, **order date** as a mandatory attribute, and **entry date** and **shipping instructions** as optional attributes.

Certain strings included in an attribute's name have meanings based upon the conventions in Table 1.1.

**TABLE 1.1**   *Conventions Used in Attribute Naming*

| String within Attribute Name | Meaning |
| --- | --- |
| ID | System-generated sequential unique numeric identifier (i.e., 1, 2, 3, 4, . . .) |
| seq | System-generated sequence within a parent ID (e.g., order line item sequence number) |
| code | Unique pneumonic—used to identify user-defined unique identifiers which may have some meaning embedded in the key (i.e., state code = "CO") |
| name | A proper pronoun such as a person, geographical area, organization |
| description | The definition of a unique code or identifier |
| flag | A binary choice for values (i.e., yes/no, or male/female) |
| from date | Attribute specifies the beginning date of a date range and is inclusive of the date specified |
| thru date | Attribute specifies the end date of a date range and is inclusive of the date specified (**to date** is not used since **thru date** more clearly represents an inclusive end of date range) |

## Relationships

*Relationships* define how two entities are associated with each other. When relationships are used in the text, they are usually shown in lowercase as a normal part of the text. In some situations, where they are specifically highlighted, they are identified by boldface lowercase letters. For example, **manufactured by** would be the way a relationship may appear in the text of this book.

Relationships may be either optional or mandatory. A dotted relationship line means that the relationship is optional and a continuous line means that the relationship is mandatory (the relationship is present in all occurrences of each entity). Figure 1.4 shows a relationship that "each PRODUCT *must be* **manufactured by** one and only one ORGANIZATION." This means that the manufacturer for each product must be specified. The same relationship has an optional aspect when read in the other direction: "Each ORGANIZATION *may be* **the producer of** one or more PRODUCTs."

Relationships may be one-to-one, one-to-many, or many-to-many. This is generally known as the cardinality of the relationship. The presence of a *crowsfoot* (a three-pronged line which looks like a crow's foot) defines if an entity points to more than one occurrence of another entity. Figure 1.5 shows that "each ORDER may be **composed of** *one or more* ORDER LINE ITEMs," since the crowsfoot is at the ORDER LINE ITEM side. The other relationship side states that "each

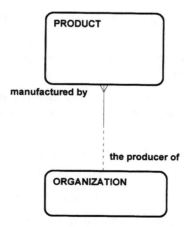

FIGURE 1.4

*Mandatory versus optional relationships.*

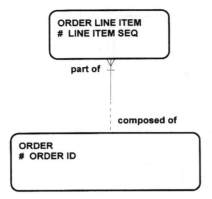

FIGURE 1.5

*One-to-many relationship.*

ORDER LINE ITEM must be **part of** *one and only one* ORDER." A one-to-one relationship doesn't have any crowsfeet on the relationship and a many-to-many relationship has crowsfeet at both ends of the relationship. Sometimes, one-to-many relationships are referred to as parent-child relationships.

Sometimes the term "over time" needs to be added to the relationship sentence to verify whether the relationship is one-to-many. For instance, an ORDER may only appear to have one ORDER STATUS. However, if status history is required, then each ORDER may be described by one or more ORDER STATUS, *over time.*

The data models in the book have very few one-to-one relationships, since most of the time one-to-one relationships can be grouped together into a single entity when normalized. The data model diagrams show very few many-to-many relationships, since most of the time many-to-many-relationships are broken out into *intersection* entities.

Intersection entities are also known as associative entities or cross-reference entities. They are used to resolve many-to-many relationships by cross-referencing one entity to another. Often they include additional attributes which may further delineate the relationship. Figure 1.6 shows a many-to-many relationship between a PRODUCT and an ORGANIZATION which is resolved in this way. The diagram indicates that a PRODUCT may be supplied through *more than one* ORGANIZATION and an ORGANIZATION may be the seller of *more than one*

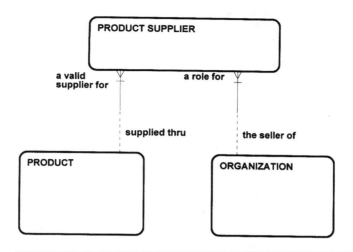

**FIGURE 1.6**

*Many-to-many relationships.*

PRODUCT. This many-to-many relationship is resolved by the intersection entity PRODUCT SUPPLIER.

Notice that in all the examples given, each relationship has two relationship names associated with it that describe the relationship in both directions. The relationship names should be combined so that they read as a complete sentence, as shown in the following format: "Each ENTITY {must be/may be} relationship name {one and only one/one or more} ENTITY, over time," where the appropriate choices are filled in.

In the models presented, the crowsfeet on the relationships generally point up and to the left in order to provide a consistent mechanism for reading the diagrams. This tends to organize the data models in a more understandable format.

Exclusive arcs are relationships where an entity is related to two or more other entities, but only one relationship can exist for a specific entity occurrence. The exclusive arc is represented by a curved line going through two or more relationship lines with little circles identifying the relationships it covers. Figure 1.7 shows an example of an exclusive arc. The relationships are read as "Each AGREEMENT LINE ITEM PRICE may be *either* a price specified for one and only one PARTY ADDRESS *or* a price specified for one and only one GEOGRAPHIC BOUNDARY, *but not both.*"

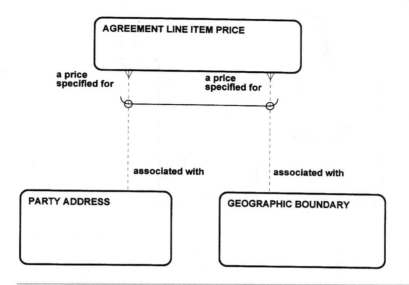

FIGURE 1.7

*Exclusive arcs.*

Recursive relationships are either modeled via a relationship pointing from an entity to itself or via a many-to-many-relationship. Figure 1.8 shows an example of a one-to-many recursion around the PRODUCT entity and a many-to-many recursion which is resolved by the intersection entity PRODUCT COMPONENT.

## Foreign Key Relationships

A *foreign key* is defined as the presence of another entity's (or table's) primary key in an entity (or table). For example, in Figure 1.5 the **order ID** from the ORDER entity is part of the ORDER LINE ITEM entity; therefore, it is a foreign key. Any one-to-many relationship indicates that the primary key of the entity on the *one* side of the relationship is brought into the entity on the *many* side of the relationship. Some data modelers show this foreign key as an attribute of the entity (this is sometimes known as key migration). *The data models in this book do not show the foreign keys of entities as attributes since this is redundant.* Instead, the relationship itself identifies the foreign key. In Figure 1.5, the **order ID** is not

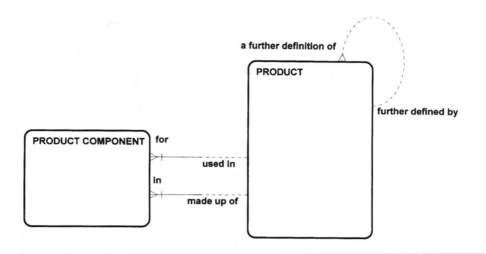

**FIGURE 1.8**

*Recursive relationships.*

shown as an attribute in the ORDER LINE ITEM entity since the one-to-many nature of the relationship reveals it is a foreign key.

Another diagramming convention in this book is to use a crossed relationship line to indicate that the inherited foreign key is part of the primary key of the child entity. The small horizontal line across the relationship in Figure 1.5 indicates that the horizontal **order ID** is part of the ORDER LINE ITEM entity primary key.

## Physical Models

The data warehouse models and diagrams (Chapters 9 through 12) represent physical database designs for decision support environments; therefore, the notation is slightly different. Since these models represent physical database designs, each square (not rounded as in the entity) box represents a table and the field names are columns. All the lines connecting tables in the model are solid lines and the foreign keys of the relationships are now shown in each appropriate table as columns since these columns will ultimately be implemented.

The naming convention for tables is to keep them plural and the column names have underscores instead of blanks between them. (The entities had singular names and attributes allowed blank spaces between the names.)

**TABLE 1.2**   *Order Line Item*

| Order ID | Order Date* | Line Item Seq | Comment |
|---|---|---|---|
| 12930 | April 30, 1995 | 1 | Need this item urgently |
| | | 2 | There's no time pressure at all on this item |

## Conventions Used for Illustration Tables

Many parts of the data models are illustrated via tables which contain possible values for attributes. Each illustration table is normally defined to show a specific entity and the relevant information from related entities. For instance, there may be a table illustrating the ORDER LINE ITEM entity as shown in Table 1.2.

In order to illustrate the details of an ORDER LINE ITEM, Table 1.2 brings in some attribute information from the ORDER entity. Notice that there is an asterisk on the **order date** column of the table. The asterisk indicates that even though the table is designed to illustrate ORDER LINE ITEM information, the **order date** information resides in an entity other than the main entity being illustrated and is included for context.

Whenever data from each illustration table is referenced in the text of this book, it is surrounded by double quotes. For instance, the text may refer to specific order "12930", line item seq "1" which has a comment of "Need this item urgently".

## THE COMPANION CD-ROM

Within this book and its appendices, are very detailed descriptions of the models discussed. The diagrams lay out all the relationships, the mandatory attributes and columns, the primary keys, and even include some optional attributes. The appendices include the physical details for the attributes and columns, such as the datatype and size. With this information, it would be possible for a data modeler or database designer to recreate these models in the tool of their choice or write the SQL code to build them in a database.

This, however, would take a substantial amount of time and opens the possibility of data entry errors. To assist those interested in quickly implementing the models discussed in the following pages, a companion CD-ROM is available for sale separately. On the CD-ROM is a series of SQL scripts derived directly from the models in the book. All the entities, attributes, tables, and columns discussed are implemented with this code. Scripts are provided for Oracle, Informix, Sybase SQL Server, and Microsoft SQL Server. Each of these scripts has been tested and verified against the above databases. Since these are standard SQL scripts, they should work with not only the current versions of these database management systems but also with future versions (i.e. Oracle8). There are also ANSI standard SQL scripts which could be used with other ANSI compliant databases.

Since the CR-ROM includes standard SQL scripts, they should work with not only the current versions of these databse management systems but also with future versions. This includes object-relational databases (i.e. Oracle8, Informix Universal Server) which should continue to support relational designs. The constructs in the book are, of course, also generally applicable to any relational or object-relational database.

Use of the scripts on the CD-ROM will allow an enterprise to more rapidly deploy the models presented in this book. In addition to the time savings, there is obviously a cost savings as well (nobody has to type in all the definitions or write SQL scripts). Once the scripts have been run, the models could be reverse-engineered into the enterprise's favorite CASE tool (most popular CASE tools provide a reverse engineering feature). Once the models have been brought into a repository, they are easily accessible and may be customized for a specific enterprise's needs. Additionally, they can be used to jump-start the development of corporate data models, new applications, data warehouse designs, or decision support systems.

The remainder of this book will provide many examples of universal data models and data warehouse designs which can assist in increasing the productivity of system development efforts.

# PEOPLE AND ORGANIZATIONS

## INTRODUCTION

The most frequent business information need is to ask questions about people and organizations and to be able to rely on accurate information. For instance:

- What are the attributes or characteristics of the people and organizations that are involved in the course of conducting business?
- What relationships exist between various people, between various organizations, and between people and organizations?
- What are the addresses of people and organizations, and how can they be contacted?
- What types of communication or contacts have occurred between various parties?

Almost all business applications track information about people and organizations, recording information about customers, suppliers, subsidiaries, departments, employees, and contractors, redundantly in many different systems. For this reason, it is very difficult to keep key information such as client contact data consistent and accurate. Examples of applications that store information about people and organizations include sales, marketing, purchasing, order entry, invoicing, project management, and accounting.

The data model within this chapter can be used for most organizations and applications. Subsequent chapters use this data model as a basis upon which to add more detail. This chapter includes data models on:

- Organization definition
- Person definition
- Party definition
- Party relationship
- Address definition
- Contact mechanism definition
- Contact information

## Organization Definition

Most data models maintain organizational information in various entities. For instance, there may be a customer entity, a vendor entity, and a department entity. Each application within an enterprise has its own needs; therefore, the data modeler will often base the model upon the needs of a particular application. For example, when building an order entry application, the customer information is crucial; therefore, the data modeler shows a separate entity for customer. Likewise, the supplier information is critical when building a purchasing application; hence there is normally a supplier entity. For a human resources system, the data modeler might show an entity called a department within which the employees work.

The problem is that an organization may play many roles, depending on the particular circumstance. For instance, in larger companies, internal organizations sell to each other. The property management division may be a supplier to the product sales division. The property management division may also be a customer of the product sales division. In this case, there would normally be both a customer and supplier record, with redundant data, for each of these divisions. Not only could there be a customer and supplier record, but there could also be many additional records for the organization depending on how many roles the organization plays within the enterprise.

When an organization's information changes—such as a change in address—the information might be updated in only one of the many systems where organization information is stored. This, of course, results in inconsistent information within the enterprise. It may also result in major frustration on the part of managers, customers, suppliers, and anyone who might want to get out a correct mailing list!

The solution to this redundancy problem is to model an entity called ORGANIZATION which stores information about a group of people with a common purpose such as a corporation, department, division, government agency, or nonprofit organization. Basic organizational information such as its **name** and **federal tax ID** is stored once within this entity, reducing redundancy of information and eliminating possible update discrepancies.

Figure 2.1 shows the data model for organization information. The ORGANIZATION entity is sub-typed into INTERNAL ORGANIZATION and EXTERNAL ORGANIZATION. An INTERNAL ORGANIZATION is one that is part of the enterprise for whom the data model is being developed and an EXTERNAL ORGANIZATION is not part of that enterprise.

This model reduces redundancy since the organization name is stored only once, as opposed to storing this information redundantly in a customer entity, supplier entity, department entity, or any other entity storing organization information.

Table 2.1 gives examples of data in the ORGANIZATION entity. Notice that organizations include not only businesses but also other groups of individuals such as departments. For example, the accounting and information systems departments are included as organizations.

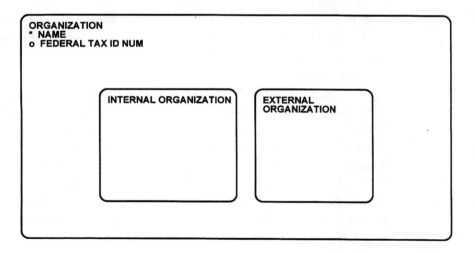

FIGURE 2.1

*Organization definition.*

TABLE 2.1   *Organizations*

| Organization ID | Name |
| --- | --- |
| 100 | ABC Corporation |
| 200 | ABC Subsidiary |
| 300 | Accounting |
| 400 | Information Systems |

For the remainder of this book, the term "enterprise" will be used to refer to all the internal organizations for whom the data model is being developed. For instance, each enterprise will have its own specific needs and business rules which will determine how the enterprise will customize these models for its own use.

## PERSON DEFINITION

Just as most data models show separate entities for various types of organizations, they also show separate entities for various types of people such as employees, contractors, supplier contacts, and customer contacts. The problem with keeping this information in separate entities is that people may also have different jobs and roles which change over time. Most systems will record redundant information about a person since they store a record each time the person's role changes.

For example, John Smith was a good customer of ABC Corporation. John then decided to perform contract labor for ABC Corporation. The people at ABC Corporation liked his work so much that they then hired him as an employee. For most systems, there would be a separate record for John Smith as a customer contact, then as a contractor, then as an employee. However, much of John Smith's information has remained the same, such as his name, sex, birth date, skills and other demographics. Because John Smith's information is stored in several locations, many systems would have trouble keeping his information accurate and consistent.

Another problem is that the same person may have many different roles *at the same time*. For instance, ABC Corporation is a large company with many divisions. Shirley Jones is an employee and manager of the transportation division. She is also considered a customer for the supplies division. At the same time, she is the supplier for the publishing division which needs her services to transport catalogues. Therefore, Shirley is an employee of yet one division, a customer contact of yet another division, and a supplier contact of another division. Rather than have three separate records for Shirley with redundant information, there should only be one record.

To address this issue, Figure 2.2 shows a PERSON entity which stores a particular person's information, independent of his or her jobs or roles. Attributes of the PERSON entity could include sex, birth date, height, weight, and any other characteristics which describe the person.

Just as the ORGANIZATION entity is sub-typed, the PERSON entity is sub-typed into EMPLOYEE and NON-EMPLOYEE. An EMPLOYEE is a person who is employed by the enterprise for whom the data model is being developed and a NON-EMPLOYEE is not employed by that enterprise.

Table 2.2 shows some example data for the PERSON entity. This model has again helped reduce redundancy since the person's base information is only maintained once, even though the person may play many different roles. The Party Relationships section later in this chapter will describe how to model the various roles each person and organization can play.

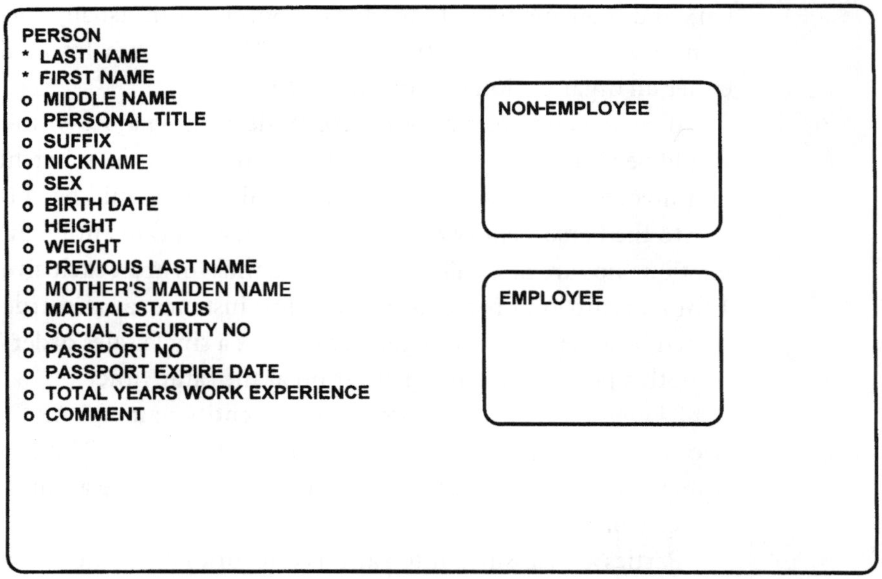

```
PERSON
* LAST NAME
* FIRST NAME
o MIDDLE NAME
o PERSONAL TITLE            NON-EMPLOYEE
o SUFFIX
o NICKNAME
o SEX
o BIRTH DATE
o HEIGHT
o WEIGHT
o PREVIOUS LAST NAME
o MOTHER'S MAIDEN NAME      EMPLOYEE
o MARITAL STATUS
o SOCIAL SECURITY NO
o PASSPORT NO
o PASSPORT EXPIRE DATE
o TOTAL YEARS WORK EXPERIENCE
o COMMENT
```

FIGURE 2.2

*Person definition.*

TABLE 2.2    *Person Data*

| Person ID | Last Name | First Name | Sex | Birth date | Height | Weight |
|-----------|-----------|------------|-----|------------|--------|--------|
| 5000 | Smith | John | Male | 1/5/49 | 6' | 190 |
| 6000 | Jones | Shirley | Female | 4/12/59 | 5'2" | 100 |
| 7000 | Cunningham | Barry | Male | 3/14/65 | 5'11" | 170 |
| 8000 | Johnson | Harry | Male | 12/9/37 | 5'8" | 178 |

# PARTY DEFINITION

Organizations and people are similar in many respects. They both have common characteristics which describe them, such as their credit rating, address, phone number, fax number, or e-mail address. Organizations and people can also serve in similar roles as parties to contracts, buyers, sellers, responsible parties, or members of other organizations. For example, membership organizations (like a computer users group) may keep similar information on their corporate members and their individual members. Contracts can usually specify an organization or a person as a contracted party. The customer for a sales order may be either an organization or a person.

If person and organization were modeled as separate entities, the data model would be more complex. Each contract, sales order, membership, or transaction that involved either a person or an organization would need two relationships: one to the person entity and one to the organization entity. Furthermore, these relationships are mutually exclusive and thus form an exclusive arc (see Chapter 1 for a discussion on exclusive arcs). For instance, a sales order could either be placed by a person or an organization, but a single sales order cannot be placed by both a person and an organization at the same time.

Therefore, Figure 2.3 shows a super-entity named PARTY which has as its two sub-types, PERSON and ORGANIZATION. This PARTY entity will enable storage of some of the common characteristics and relationships which people and organizations share.

Parties are classified into various categories using the entity PARTY DEFIN-ITION which stores each category into which parties may belong. The possible values for categories are maintained in the PARTY TYPE entity. For example, a

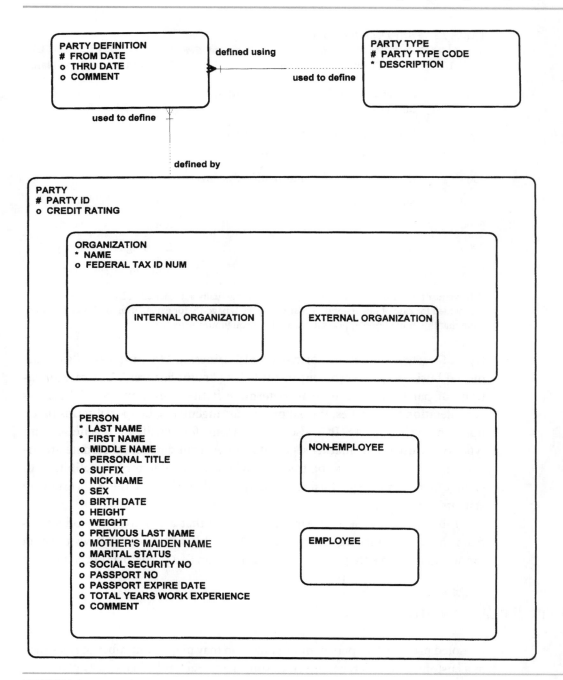

FIGURE 2.3

*Party definition.*

TABLE 2.3   *Party Definition Data*

| Party ID | Party Type* | Name | Last Name | First Name |
|----------|-------------|------|-----------|------------|
| 100 | Minority-owned business | ABC Corporation | | |
| 200 | Subsidiary | ABC Subsidiary | | |
| 300 | Department | Accounting | | |
| 400 | Department | Information Systems | | |
| 5000 | Shareholder | | Smith | John |
| 6000 | | | Jones | Shirley |
| 7000 | Minority | | Cunningham | Barry |
| 8000 | | | Johnson | Harry |

*The value of this attribute in the entity described is actually a numeric ID. Instead, a description is provided for ease of understanding—see Chapter 1, page 15 for explanation of this convention. Note that this convention appears in the tables throughout the text.

type of party may be "minority-owned business", "8A business", "woman-owned business", "government institute", or "manufacturer". The categorizations of parties can be used to determine if there are any special business considerations for parties, special pricing arrangements, or special terms based upon the type of party. It is also a mechanism for classifying businesses into types of industries for market segmentation. A **from date** and **thru date** are included so history can also be tracked, since it is possible for the definition to change over time [e.g., businesses may "graduate" from the 8A (minority startup) program].

Table 2.3 shows several party occurrences that are merely consolidations from the person and organization examples. This single entity allows the data models to refer to either a person or organization as a party to a transaction.

## PARTY RELATIONSHIP

As noted previously, a person or organization may play any number of roles such as a customer, supplier, employer, or subsidiary. Each role that a party plays only makes sense in relation to another party. If ACME Company is a customer, is it a customer of ABC Subsidiary or a customer of the parent company, ABC Corporation? Maybe it is a customer of the widgets division or the gadgets division.

Instead of modeling just the roles of the party, there is a need to model the relationship between parties. For example, there is a need to know not only that ACME Company is a customer, but that ACME Company is a customer of ABC Subsidiary. By default, this fact also implies that the ABC Subsidiary is a supplier of the ACME Company.

A relationship is comprised of two parties and their respective roles. For example, customer/supplier, parent/subsidiary, and division/department are possible organization relationships. The PARTY RELATIONSHIP entity shown in Figure 2.4 allows parties to be related to other parties and maintains the respective roles in the relationship. The PARTY RELATIONSHIP entity has attributes of **from date** and **thru date** in order to show the valid time frames of the relationship.

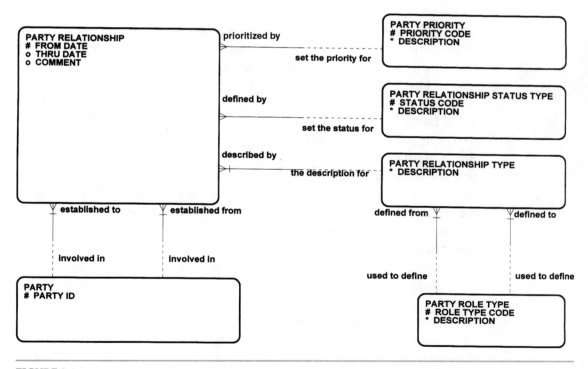

FIGURE 2.4

*Party relationship.*

The PARTY RELATIONSHIP TYPE entity in Figure 2.4 consists of a pair of roles which are used to define the nature of a PARTY RELATIONSHIP. Customer/Supplier is a valid pair of roles, while the combination of Customer/Sales Agent roles would not be valid because these roles do not complement each other (Authorizor/Sales Agent would make more sense). The **description** attribute describes the nature of a specific relationship. For example, a customer/supplier relationship description may be "where the customer has purchased or is planning on purchasing items or services from the supplier."

The PARTY ROLE TYPE entity is a list of possible roles that can be played by the parties within a PARTY RELATIONSHIP TYPE. The two relationships from PARTY ROLE TYPE to PARTY RELATIONSHIP TYPE define the nature of the relationship. To form a "customer/supplier" PARTY RELATIONSHIP TYPE, there would be two relationships: one to the "customer" instance in the PARTY ROLE TYPE entity, and another to the "supplier" instance.

The PARTY RELATIONSHIP STATUS entity defines the current state of the relationship. Examples include "active", "inactive", or "pursuing more involvement". The PARTY PRIORITY entity establishes the relative importance of the relationship to the enterprise. Examples may include "very high", "high", "medium", and "low". Alternatively, an enterprise may choose to use "first", "second", "third", and so on to prioritize the importance of various relationships.

Figure 2.5 illustrates the relationships for the organization, ABC Subsidiary. Table 2.4 shows the data which is stored in the PARTY RELATIONSHIP entity to represent these relationships. The internal organizations within the table are ABC Corporation, ABC Subsidiary, and ABC's Customer Service Division. The first row shows that ABC Subsidiary is a subsidiary of the parent corporation, ABC Corporation. The second row shows that the Customer Service Division is a division of ABC Subsidiary. The third row shows that ACME Company is a customer of ABC Subsidiary. Notice that the fifth row shows that ABC Subsidiary is a customer of Fantastic Supplies, or in other words, Fantastic Supplies is a supplier for ABC Subsidiary. If Fantastic Supplies was a supplier for all of ABC Corporation, there would be a relationship to the parent company, ABC Corporation, instead of to the subsidiary.

Just as organizations have relationships with other organizations, people have relationships with other people. Examples of person-to-person relationships include people's mentors, people's family structures, and people's business contacts. Table 2.5 shows person-to-person relationship examples. These relationships are stored in the same entity (PARTY RELATIONSHIP) as organiza-

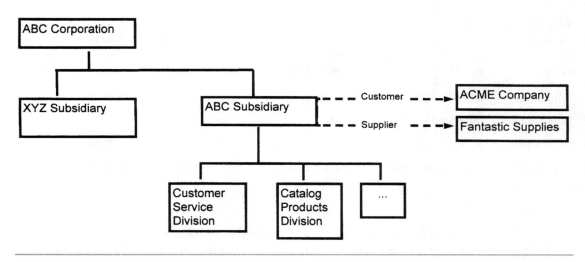

**FIGURE 2.5**

*Party relationship hierarchy example.*

TABLE 2.4   *Organization-to-Organization Party Relationships*

| From Party* | To Party* | From Relationship* | To Relationship* | From Date | Thru Date |
|---|---|---|---|---|---|
| ABC Subsidiary | ABC Corporation | Subsidiary | Parent Corporation | 3/4/88 | |
| Customer Service Division | ABC Subsidiary | Division | Corporation | 1/2/92 | |
| ACME Company | ABC Subsidiary | Customer | Supplier | 1/1/94 | |
| Sellers Assistance Corporation | ABC Subsidiary | Sales Agent | Authorizing Corporation | 6/1/95 | 12/31/95 |
| ABC Subsidiary | Fantastic Supplies | Customer | Supplier | 4/5/93 | |

tion-to-organization relationships; however, Table 2.5 breaks out the person-to-person relationships for ease of understanding.

In Table 2.5, John Smith has Barry Goldstein as a mentor. Judy Smith is John Smith's daughter. Joe Schmidt is the customer representative whom Nancy Barry calls upon to sell her company's products. John Smith is Barry Cunningham's customer (contact).

TABLE 2.5  *Person-to-Person Party Relationships*

| From Party* | To Party* | From Relationship* | To Relationship* | From Date | Thru Date |
|---|---|---|---|---|---|
| John Smith | Barry Goldstein | Apprentice | Mentor | 9/2/95 | |
| Judy Smith | John Smith | Child | Parent | 4/5/92 | |
| Joe Schmidt | Nancy Barry | Customer Contact | Supplier Contact | 3/15/93 | |
| John Smith | Barry Cunningham | Customer Contact | Supplier Contact | 5/10/94 | |

Finally, a person may play any number of roles within an organization: an employee, a supplier contact, a customer contact, and so on. Table 2.6 shows examples of people's roles within organizations. For example Nancy Barry, John Smith, and William Jones are all employees of ABC Subsidiary. William Jones is not only an employee of ABC Subsidiary but also contracts to Hughes Cargo. Barry Cunningham is a supplier representative for Fantastic Supplier; therefore, people can contact him to purchase items from Fantastic Supplies. Joe Schmidt is the customer representative for ACME Company and represents its interests as a customer.

TABLE 2.6  *Person-to-Organization Party Relationships*

| From Party* | To Party* | From Relationship* | To Relationship* | From Date | Thru Date |
|---|---|---|---|---|---|
| Nancy Barry | ABC Subsidiary | Employee | Employer | 7/19/82 | |
| John Smith | ABC Subsidiary | Employee | Employer | 12/31/89 | 12/01/92 |
| William Jones | ABC Subsidiary | Employee | Employer | 5/07/90 | |
| William Jones | Hughes Cargo | Contractor | Contracting Firm | 1/31/95 | 12/31/95 |
| Barry Cunningham | Fantastic Supplies | Supplier Representative | Supplier | 2/31/95 | |
| Joe Schmidt | ACME Company | Customer Representative | Customer | 8/30/95 | |

## ADDRESS DEFINITION

Figure 2.6 shows the data model for address-related information. The GEO-GRAPHIC BOUNDARY entity stores the COUNTY, CITY, STATE, and COUNTRY of an ADDRESS. The ADDRESS entity maintains all addresses used by the enterprise in a central place. The PARTY ADDRESS entity shows which ADDRESS is related to which PARTY. The PARTY ADDRESS ROLE entity defines the roles that a PARTY ADDRESS may have and is primarily used to validate that the address is used for its intended purpose. PARTY ADDRESS ROLE TYPE maintains the possible values of the roles which addresses may play.

### Address

Each ADDRESS has geographic boundaries in which it resides. These could include counties, cities, states, territories, provinces (Canada), prefectures (Japan), regions, and countries; they will vary by country. As an example, the model in Figure 2.6 includes the sub-types COUNTY, CITY, STATE, COUNTRY, and the super-type GEOGRAPHIC BOUNDARY with appropriate relationships between them.

The ADDRESS entity stores attributes to identify the specific location within the geographic boundary. The **address1** and **address2** attributes provide a mechanism for two text lines of an address. There may be a need for more address line attributes depending on the needs of the enterprise. The **postal code** identifies the mailing code that is used for delivery. In the United States, the postal code is referred to as the zip code. The **directions** attribute provides instructions on what roads to travel and what turns to take in order to arrive at that address.

### Party Address

An organization may have many addresses or locations. For instance, a retailer might have several outlets at different addresses. In this instance, there is only one ORGANIZATION or PARTY but many locations or addresses. Additionally, the same address might be used by many organizations. For instance, many subsidiaries of an organization might share the same address. Also, different organizations might share the same address if they are in a shared office facility. Therefore, there is a many-to-many relationship between ORGANIZATION and ADDRESS.

There is also a many-to-many relationship between PERSON and ADDRESS. A particular address may have many people residing there, such as when many

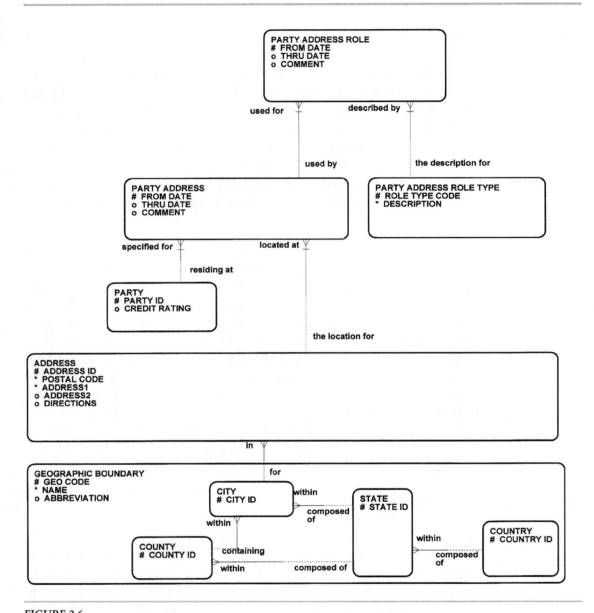

**FIGURE 2.6**

*Address definition.*

TABLE 2.7    *Address Data*

| Address ID | Address1 | Address2 | City |
|------------|----------|----------|------|
| 2300 | 100 Main Street | Suite 101 | New York |
| 2400 | 255 Fetch Street | | Portland |
| 2500 | 234 Stretch Street | | Minneapolis |

TABLE 2.8    *Party Address Data*

| Party* | Address ID |
|--------|-----------|
| ABC Corporation | 2300 |
| ABC Subsidiary | 2300 |
| ABC Subsidiary | 2400 |
| ACME Company | 2500 |

employees work at the same facility. And, of course, people generally have many addresses: their home address, work address, vacation address, and so forth.

Instead of two separate relationships for people and organizations, the model shows a many-to-many relationship between PARTY and ADDRESS that is resolved via an intersection entity (sometimes referred to as an associative or cross-reference entity) named PARTY ADDRESS, as shown in Figure 2.6. Notice that PARTY ADDRESS has a **from date** and **thru date** which allows the ability to track the address history of parties.

Tables 2.7 and 2.8 give examples of party addresses. Table 2.7 lists the individual address records, while Table 2.8 cross-references parties to addresses. With this model, addresses are only stored once—thus eliminating redundant data problems—and can be reused many times in relationship to many parties. For instance, in Tables 2.7 and 2.8, the same address, address ID 2300, is used by ABC Corporation and ABC Subsidiary. Additionally, ABC Subsidiary has more than one address as illustrated by its two entries in Table 2.8.

## Address Role

For each party located at an address, or PARTY ADDRESS, there may be many purposes or roles for the address. The address might be a mailing address, a

TABLE 2.9    *Party Address Role*

| Party* | Address ID | Address Role* |
|---|---|---|
| ABC Corporation | 2300 | Corporate Headquarters |
| ABC Corporation | 2300 | Central Mailing Address |
| ABC Corporation | 2300 | Legal Office |
| ABC Subsidiary | 2400 | Sales Office |
| ABC Subsidiary | 2400 | Warehouse |

headquarters address, a service address, and so on. Most systems have a separate record for the mailing address, headquarters address, and service address, even though the address information may be exactly the same. Therefore, the data model in Figure 2.6 shows that each PARTY ADDRESS must have one or more PARTY ADDRESS ROLEs. The PARTY ADDRESS ROLE stores the roles a party address may play. A list of possible values is available in the PARTY ADDRESS ROLE TYPE entity.

Another way this could be modeled is to include the role in the PARTY ADDRESS entity and have additional cross-reference records for each of the address' roles. For example, if the same party's address served as a mailing, headquarters, and service address, it would be stored as three instances in the PARTY ADDRESS entity. Each instance would have the same party and address ID but would have a different role. The disadvantage of this model is that the PARTY ADDRESS entity has significance on its own. For instance, each PARTY ADDRESS may have telephone and fax numbers associated with it. For this reason, our model shows separate PARTY ADDRESS and PARTY ADDRESS ROLE entities.

Table 2.9 illustrates that ABC Corporation's address can be used as the corporate headquarters, central mailing address, and legal office. The PARTY ADDRESS ROLE entity provides for the storage of a party address only once with many roles for that party's address.

## CONTACT MECHANISM DEFINITION

In many data models, phone numbers are shown as attributes of the organization or person. Usually, there are also fields for fax numbers, modem numbers, pager numbers, cellular numbers, and electronic mail addresses. This often leads to limitations in the systems built. For instance, if someone has two business phone numbers and there is only one business phone number field for a person, where is the other business phone number entered? In this new world where there are many methods for contacting parties, more flexible data structures are needed.

The CONTACT MECHANISM entity in Figure 2.7 stores access numbers for parties. Each CONTACT MECHANISM may be the way to contact either a particular PARTY or PARTY ADDRESS. The intersection entity PARTY CONTACT MECHANISM shows which contact mechanisms are related to which parties or addresses. The model also shows valid roles available via the relationship from PARTY CONTACT MECHANISM to PARTY CONTACT MECHANISM ROLE. The CONTACT MECHANISM TYPE and PARTY CONTACT MECHANISM ROLE TYPE are entities which maintain allowable values.

## Contact Mechanism

CONTACT MECHANISMs are sub-typed to include TELECOM NUMBER and ELECTRONIC ADDRESS. TELECOM NUMBER includes any access via telecommunications lines such as phones, faxes, modems, pagers, and cellular numbers. ELECTRONIC ADDRESS includes any access via services like the Internet or other electronic mail services.

The CONTACT MECHANISM TYPE entity shows all the possible values for types of contact mechanism. Examples include office phone, home phone, office fax, modem, cellular, Internet address, and other electronic addresses. With technology growing so quickly, it is very likely that there will be many ways to get in touch with someone. The data structure in Figure 2.7 provides an easy method for adding any new contact mechanisms by simply inserting and using new CONTACT MECHANISM TYPEs.

## Contact Mechanism Relationships to Party and Party Address

A contact mechanism could be tied to particular physical locations (namely, PARTY ADDRESS) such as the telephone number for a retailer's store location, or it might be tied to a particular PARTY, such as a person's cellular telephone number. There is a many-to-many relationship from CONTACT MECHANISM to both PARTY ADDRESS and PARTY. For example, a contact mechanism may be used to contact more than one party, such as a joint telephone number for a family. The contact mechanism may also be for more than one party address,

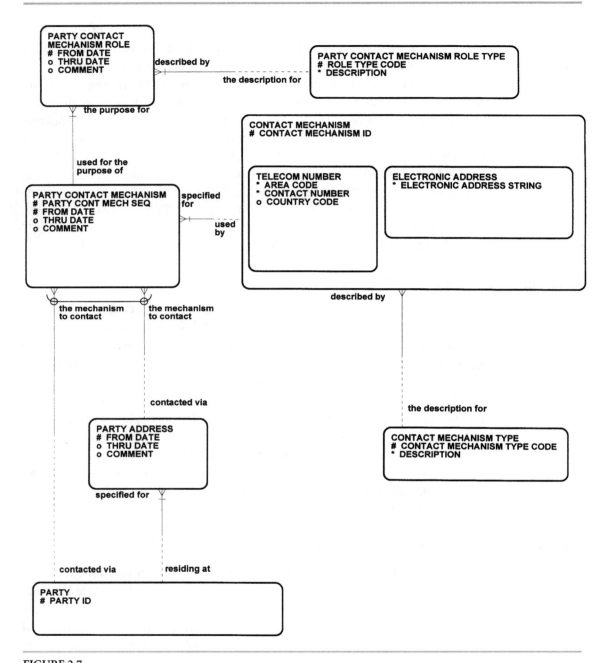

FIGURE 2.7

*Contact mechanism definition.*

TABLE 2.10   *Party Contact Mechanism*

| Party* | Party Address* | Contact Mechanism * | Contact Mechanism Type* |
|--------|----------------|---------------------|--------------------------|
| ABC Corporation | 100 Main Street | (212) 234 0958 | Office Phone |
| ABC Corporation | 100 Main Street | (212) 334 5896 | Office Fax Number |
| John Smith | 100 Main Street | (212) 234 9856 | Office Phone |
| John Smith | 345 Hamulet Place | (212) 748 5893 | Office Phone |
| John Smith | | (212) 384 4387 | Cellular |
| Barry Goldstein | 100 Main Street | (212) 234 0045 | Office Phone |
| Barry Goldstein | 2985 Cordova Road | (203) 356 3984 | Home Phone |
| Barry Goldstein | | bgoldstein@abc.com | Internet Address |

such as a roaming telephone number that covers more than one location. Therefore, the PARTY CONTACT MECHANISM is used as the intersection entity and represents the combination of a CONTACT MECHANISM used by either a PARTY or PARTY ADDRESS.

Table 2.10 gives examples of party contact mechanisms. The first two entries show the phone and fax numbers which are tied to the PARTY ADDRESS for ABC Corporation at 100 Main Street. The third and fourth rows show that John Smith's number at 100 Main Street is (212) 234-9856, but he has another office phone at 345 Hamulet Place. These are both tied to a PARTY ADDRESS. John Smith also has a cellular number which is tied directly to his PARTY instance. Barry Goldstein has an office phone which is tied to one PARTY ADDRESS (his work address) and a home phone which is tied to a different PARTY ADDRESS (his home address). He also has an Internet address which is tied directly to his PARTY instance, since he can access his e-mail from any location that is properly equipped.

## Contact Mechanism Role

Furthermore, just as addresses are intended for specific purposes, so are party contact mechanisms. A single contact mechanism may have more than one purpose. For example, business people sometimes have a single number for both their phone and fax needs. Therefore, the PARTY CONTACT MECHA-

NISM ROLE defines the designated purposes for each PARTY CONTACT MECHANISM. The valid roles are described in PARTY CONTACT MECHANISM ROLE TYPE.

An example of a party contact mechanism role is that a telephone number may be playing roles as the "primary business contact number" and the "general information number". Other possible party contact mechanism roles include "customer service number" or "invoicing questions line".

In the complex world of today, in which there are usually many contact mechanisms, it is very useful to identify the purposes of each contact mechanism. Since the purposes of various contact mechanisms change over time, the **from date** and **thru date** identify when the purposes are valid.

## Party Location

Think of a party address as a physical location and a party contact mechanism as a virtual location. Therefore, the term *party location* is used throughout this book to mean the location of the party, whether it's a physical location such as the address of a retail store or a virtual location such as an Internet address. Although this model defines physical locations and virtual locations as very different and separate entities, it is conceivable to model a super-type PARTY LOCATION which has as its sub-types PARTY CONTACT MECHANISM and PARTY ADDRESS. This could be useful, for example, in identifying where an order came from—it could have been from a physical location or a virtual location such as an Internet address.

## CONTACT INFORMATION

It is important in many applications to track information regarding with whom and when contact was made during a business relationship. For instance, sales or account representatives often need to know who was called for what purpose and when in order to properly follow up with their customers. The contact might have been via a telephone call, an in-person sales meeting, a conference call, a letter, or through any other method of encounter.

In Figure 2.8, the entity CONTACT NOTE provides a history of the various encounters or contacts made within a particular PARTY RELATIONSHIP. The CONTACT NOTE maintains the date of contact, a note describing the contact,

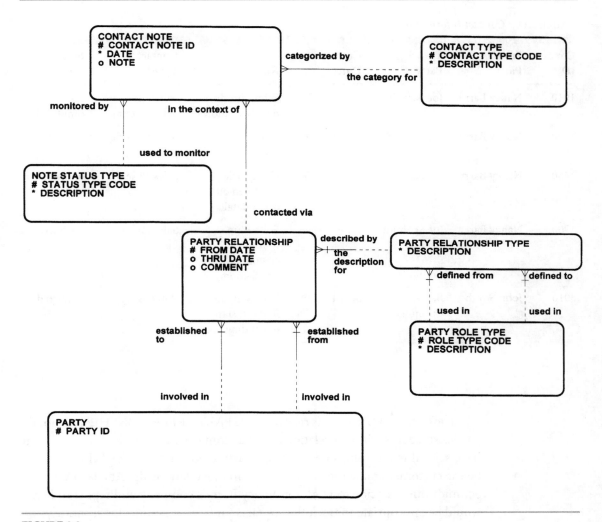

**FIGURE 2.8**

*Contact information.*

and the type of contact. The status of the contact is maintained through the NOTE STATUS TYPE entity. Example statuses include "scheduled", "in progress", and "completed". The CONTACT TYPE entity is used to define the possible types of contacts such as "initial sales call", "service repair call", "demonstration", "sales lunch appointment", or "telephone solicitation". Table 2.11 gives other examples of types of contacts.

**TABLE 2.11**   *Contact Information*

| Contact ID | From Party* | To Party* | Contact Date | Note | Contact Type* | Contact Note Status Type* |
|---|---|---|---|---|---|---|
| 1010 | Nancy Barry | Joe Schmidt | Jan 12, 1996 | Set up product demonstration | Schedule Sales meeting | Completed |
| 1300 | Nancy Barry | Joe Schmidt | Jan 30, 1996 | Demo of product | Sales meeting | Completed |
| 1450 | Nancy Barry | Joe Schmidt | Feb 12, 1996 | Closed sale and filled out order details | Sales close | Completed |
| 1900 | Nancy Barry | Joe Schmidt | June 1, 1996 | Follow-up to find out customer satisfaction | Sales follow-up | Scheduled |
| 3010 | John Smith | Barry Cunningham | Sept 12, 1995 | Follow-up to find out status of pending order | Purchasing follow-up | Completed |

The CONTACT NOTE is related to the PARTY RELATIONSHIP and not the parties since it is within a relationship that contacts make sense. It is possible to have several relationships between two parties. For instance, Joe Schmidt might be the customer contact for Nancy Barry in one relationship. At a later date, Joe Schmidt might decide to work for Nancy Barry's company and report to her. It would be appropriate to track the contacts for these relationships separately.

Table 2.11 gives examples of possible contacts. Nancy Barry, a sales person for ABC Corporation, has made several sales contacts with Joe Schmidt, the customer representative for ACME Corporation. The first four entries in Table 2.11 show the date and the nature of these calls. Notice that contacts have a status to indicate if the activity has been completed or if it is just scheduled. The fifth entry shows a contact initiated by John Smith in accounting to Barry Cunningham who is a supplier representative. This data structure provides a mechanism for tracking contacts for any type of relationship and is a very powerful business tool.

## Summary

Most data models and database designs unnecessarily duplicate information regarding people and organizations. As a result, many organizations have a very difficult time maintaining accurate information. This chapter has illustrated how to build a very flexible and normalized data model for people, organizations, party relationships, addresses, contact mechanisms, and contacts made between parties. Figure 2.9 shows the key entities discussed in this chapter and their relationship to each other.

Please refer to Appendix A for more detailed attribute characteristics. SQL scripts to build tables, columns, and constraints derived from this logical model can be found on the accompanying CD-ROM that is sold separately.

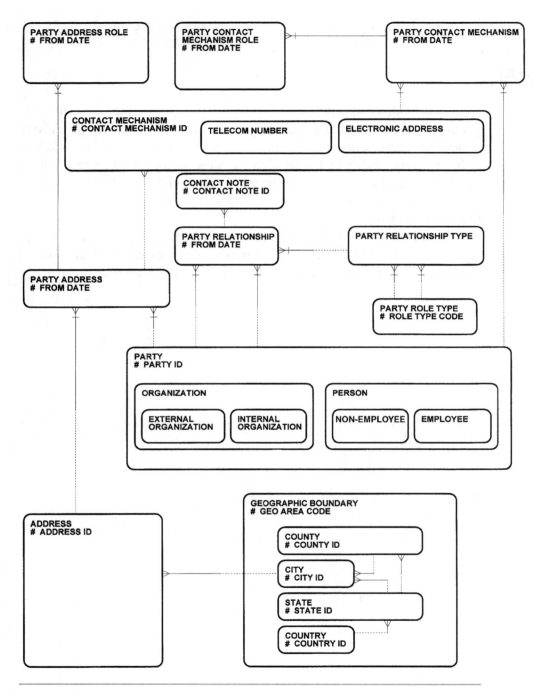

FIGURE 2.9

*People and organizations.*

40

# 3

## PRODUCTS

### INTRODUCTION

Having established the models for parties and their relationships, this chapter focuses on the products produced and used by parties. Products are defined as tangible physical *items* or nontangible *services* that are provided by parties. Every organization needs to know product information on a regular basis, such as:

How does the enterprise's services or items compare in quality and price to its competitors?

What inventory is needed at each location to meet the needs of customers?

What are the prices, costs, and profitability for the services or items that are offered?

Where can the enterprise purchase the best services and items at the best prices?

Just as the party model shows information about parties regardless of their roles, the product model is also independent of whose products they are. The product model is therefore more flexible, stable, and understandable since product information is modeled only one time, regardless of whether it is the enterprise's products, competitors' products, or suppliers' products. This chapter models information on:

- Product definition
- Product suppliers and manufacturers
- Inventory item storage
- Product pricing
- Product costing
- Product components

## PRODUCT DEFINITION

Just as parties include both internal and external parties, the product model includes products that the enterprise provides, products from suppliers, and products that competitors provide. Some of the information is independent of the supplier, such as the description, category, and characteristics of the product. Some of the information about the products, such as the availability and pricing of products, depends on the product's supplier.

### Product

Figure 3.1 shows an entity called PRODUCT which models all products including the products the enterprise sells, products from suppliers, and competitors' products. The model shows that the key is **product code** which is a mnemonic or a meaningful code for the product. Since product definitions are relatively stable, the mnemonic helps in looking up a specific product. The attributes of PRODUCT are **name,** which uniquely describes a product; **introduction date,** stating when the product was first available to be sold; **sales discontinuation date,** which documents when the product will not be sold any more by the manufacturer; **support discontinuation date,** which states when the product will no longer be supported by the manufacturer; the **manufacturer suggested retail price,** which says what the standard price is for the product; and a **comment** which documents particular descriptions or notes relating to the product.

Products include *both* tangible goods which are called ITEMs and nontangible offerings which are called SERVICEs. For example, an ITEM may include specific types of pens, furniture, equipment, or anything that can be physically stored. The ITEM sub-type in Figure 3.1 has an attribute of **reorder level** which states the quantity at which the item needs to be reordered or reproduced. The attribute **reorder quantity** states the recommended amount of the item to order.

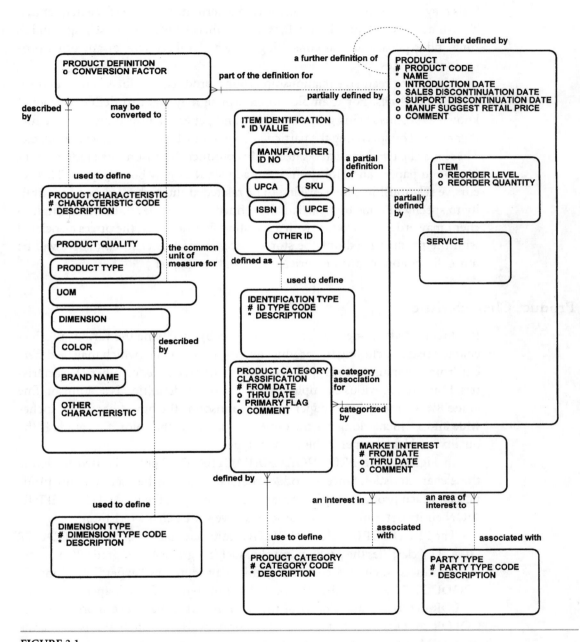

**FIGURE 3.1**

*Basic product definition.*

This may have been derived by analysis to determine the most efficient quantity. The alternate sub-type, SERVICE, is for products which involve selling people's time and expertise such as consulting services, legal services, or any other professional services.

Notice the recursive relationship around product. Products can be defined at multiple levels. For example, an enterprise may want to define a product known as "Johnson fine grade $8\frac{1}{2} \times 11$ bond paper". This product may be further defined by specifying the particular colors for which the product is available. There may be two products related to this product: "Johnson fine grade $8\frac{1}{2} \times 11$ *blue* bond paper" and "Johnson fine grade $8\frac{1}{2} \times 11$ *gray* bond paper". This recursive relationship allows pricing to be related at the higher level and the ability to specify options to a particular product at a lower level. In the example, a client may order the product with a specific color; however, the prices associated with the product need only be stored once, at the higher level. (There will be more discussion on product pricing later in this chapter.)

## Product Characteristic

Product records are defined at a precise level by specifying the various product characteristics including the product quality, brand name (which may be different from the manufacturer), the color, dimensions, style, or other characteristics. Using the previous example, a sample product definition is a "Johnson fine grade $8\frac{1}{2} \times 11$ gray bond paper" where Johnson is the brand name, $8\frac{1}{2}$ inches wide and 11 inches long are the dimensions, gray is the color, fine grade is the quality, and bond paper is the product type.

In Figure 3.1, a PRODUCT CHARACTERISTIC entity is used to define these characteristics. Since a product characteristic may be used in many products and each product may have many characteristics, the PRODUCT DEFINITION entity determines which products have which characteristics.

The PRODUCT CHARACTERISTIC entity has many sub-types. PRODUCT QUALITY classifies the product by value such as "grade A" or "grade B". For service products, such as a consultant, this may represent "expert" or "junior". PRODUCT TYPE describes the basic kind of item such as "paper" or "pen". COLOR describes the color(s) of the item. An item may have more than one COLOR characteristic but a different color may also denote that it is a separate item. DIMENSION describes the various numeric descriptions of the item such as "$8\frac{1}{2}$-inch width", "11-inch length", or "10 pound". The DIMENSION TYPE has a description attribute which specifies whether the measurement is "width", "length", "weight", and so on. UOM (unit of measure) determines how the product will be inventoried and sold, such as by the "box" or "each". For service products, the unit of measure values may be "hours" or "days". BRAND NAME describes the marketing name tied to the item, such as "Buick" for a General Motors vehicle. Notice that the brand name may be different from the manufacturer's name.

Table 3.1 shows examples of possible products and their characteristic definitions. Notice that the product name uniquely describes the product so it may be ordered by name. The details behind the product definition are actually stored in PRODUCT CHARACTERISTIC, but are shown in this table to clarify the characteristics of the product.

The attribute **conversion factor** in PRODUCT DEFINITION and the relationship to the UOM sub-type are provided to allow an enterprise to specify a common unit of measure conversion for products which may be defined as having multiple units of measure. For example, "Henry #2 pencils" may be defined with multiple units of measure such as "each", "small box", and "large box". In many cases, organizations need to show total inventories, costs, and sales for all of a product regardless of its unit of measure. By defining a common unit of

**TABLE 3.1**  *Product*

| Product Code | Name | Quality* | Type* | Color* | Dimension* | UOM* | Brand Name* |
|---|---|---|---|---|---|---|---|
| PAP192 | Johnson fine grade 8½ × 11 blue bond paper | Fine grade | Paper | Blue | 8½" wide 11" length | Ream | Johnson |
| PEN202 | Goldstein Elite Pen | Fine point | Pen | Black | | Each | Goldstein |
| DSK401 | Jerry's box of 3½ inch diskettes | | Diskette | Red | 3½" | Box | Jerry's |
| CNS109 | Office supply inventory management consulting service | Expert | Consulting | | | | ABC Corporation |

measure, such as "each" and including a conversion factor (e.g., 12 for "small box" and 24 for "large box"), it is possible to determine the total amount of "Henry #2 pencils" there are in inventory and how many have been sold.

In the latter example, the conversion factor depends on the specific products involved. In some businesses, the conversion factors between units of measures are independent of the products. For example, process manufactures are often dealing with liters, gallons, tons, and other metric conversion factors. It is often necessary to provide a common unit of measure to determine inventory levels. If this type of unit of measure conversion is required, then a UOM CONVERSION entity could be added with two relationships to the UOM entity. This would show the many-to-many recursion between different units of measures, independent of the specific products involved. A **conversion factor** attribute would be required in the UOM CONVERSION entity to provide for a conversion to common units of measure. For example, the conversion factor would be 4 in the relationship between "quarts" and "gallons".

There are other characteristics of products, many of which are dependent on the enterprise's type of business. Shoe manufacturers may be interested in styles, clothing organizations characterize products by lines, commodities organizations have varieties, and so on. This model is useful as the baseline model, but the sub-types of the PRODUCT CHARACTERISTIC may need to be customized for the enterprise.

## Product Category

A product is grouped into one or more categories in order to list various types of products together, such as in catalogues. A product may have more than one PRODUCT CATEGORY (see Figure 3.1) and vice versa. The PRODUCT CATEGORY CLASSIFICATION describes which products are in which category. For example, all pens, pencils, paper, notebooks, desk sets, and diskettes are classified into the category of office supplies.

Table 3.2 illustrates examples of product categories. Notice that diskettes are categorized into both office supplies and computer supplies. This categorization may be useful for showing different types of products under various product catalogues. The enterprise needs to be careful when classifying a product into multiple categories, as it can result in misleading results when performing certain queries. For instance, if products were grouped into multiple categories and there was a sales analysis report by category, the total sales amount for the report

TABLE 3.2    *Product Category Classification*

| Product* | Product Category* | Primary Flag |
|---|---|---|
| Johnson fine grade 8½ × 11 bond paper | Office Supplies | Yes |
| Goldstein Elite Pen | Office Supplies | Yes |
| Jerry's box of 3½ inch diskettes | Office Supplies | No |
| Jerry's box of 3½ inch diskettes | Computer Supplies | Yes |
| Office supply inventory management consulting service | Consulting Services | Yes |

would be overstated since some product sales would be counted numerous times for each of their categories. The model has a **primary flag** to indicate which is the primary category for the product in order to avoid this situation. Notice that in Table 3.2 the diskettes are classified into two categories; however, one category is flagged as the primary category to avoid duplication of results when analyzing sales. The enterprise needs to enforce a business rule that only one category for the product may be primary.

Product categories may change over time; therefore, the PRODUCT CATEGORY CLASSIFICATION has the attributes **from date** and **thru date** which state when the product was classified into its grouping.

## Market Interest

To assist in sales forecasting and prospecting, the entity MARKET INTEREST is included in this model. It is an intersection entity joining information about PARTY TYPE and PRODUCT CATEGORY that allows an enterprise to record the category of products that particular types of parties (i.e., organizations) may be interested in. If the PARTY TYPE includes specific industries or industry segments as types and these have been associated with actual parties, then an enterprise can easily identify organizations within segments of a target industry that may be interested in types of products or services. These organizations could then be the focus of a new sales campaign for those types of products. Because interests change over time, the attributes **from date** and **thru date** are also included.

## Item Identification Codes

Items have various codes which are used as a standard means of identifying the item. The ITEM IDENTIFICATION entity has an attribute of **ID value** to store the various identification codes that an item may have. The sub-types of ITEM IDENTIFICATION designate the types of codes that may be given to an item. The MANUFACTURER'S ID NO is an item code designated by the manufacturer. The **SKU** (Stock-keeping Unit) is a very standard product code which distinctly identities various products. The sub-type **UPCA** stands for Universal Product Code—American and is a mechanism for identifying products within America. **UPCE** (Universal Product Code—European) is a mechanism for identifying products in Europe. **ISBN** (International Standard Book Number) is a mechanism to identify specific books throughout the world. A single item may have more than one standard code. For instance, a certain office supply product may have a manufacturer ID number designated by the manufacturer and also a UPCA number identified by the industry.

## PRODUCT SUPPLIERS AND MANUFACTURERS

Figure 3.2 shows which suppliers and manufacturers are associated with each product. Since products may be sold by more than one organization and organizations sell more than one product, the entity PRODUCT SUPPLIER shows which products are sold by which organizations. The **available from date** and **available thru date** state when the product is offered by that supplier. This information is important because it provides the capability to find out where and when specific products may be purchased, what products competitors sell, and which products the enterprise sells. Another important consideration for product suppliers is **lead time** which indicates the average amount of time it takes for a supplier to deliver the product to the customer location from the time of order. This attribute is not shown on the data model since it can be derived from information stored in orders and shipments; this will be covered in later chapters.

Since there may be many suppliers from which the enterprise can order products, the PRODUCT SUPPLIER PREFERENCE entity provides information to track the priority of whom to order from first, second, third, and so on. This priority is the information which would be stored in the **description** attribute and related back to the PRODUCT SUPPLIER entity. In addition to pref-

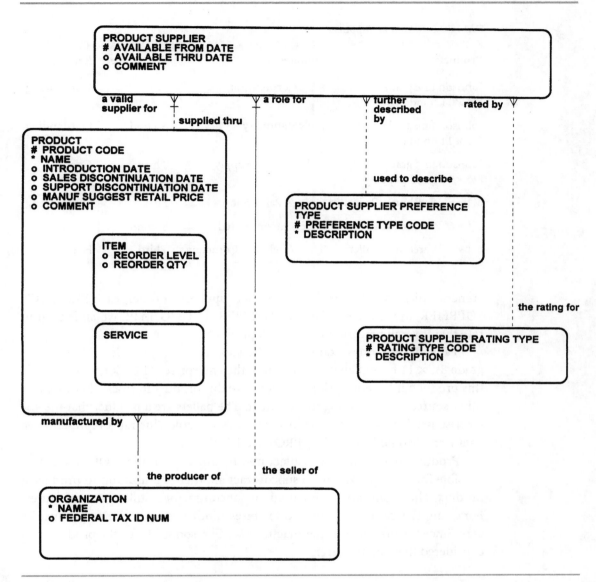

**FIGURE 3.2**

*Product supplier.*

**TABLE 3.3**    *Product Suppliers*

| Product* | Supplier* | Preference | Rating |
|---|---|---|---|
| Johnson fine grade 8½ × 11 bond paper | ABC Corporation | First | Outstanding |
| Johnson fine grade 8½ × 11 bond paper | Joe's Stationary | Second | Outstanding |
| Johnson fine grade 8½ × 11 bond paper | Mike's Office Supply | Third | Good |
| 6' by 6' Warehouse Pallets | Gregg's Pallet Shop | First | Outstanding |
| 6' by 6' Warehouse Pallets | Pallets Incorporated | Second | Good |
| 6' by 6' Warehouse Pallets | The Warehouse Company | Third | Fair |

erences which rank the preferred product suppliers in order, each PRODUCT SUPPLIER also has a PRODUCT SUPPLIER RATING TYPE which is used to rate their overall performance for each product.

Table 3.3 provides examples of the suppliers that provide "Johnson fine grade 8½ × 11 bond paper". Notice that the enterprise, ABC Corporation, sells this product; if the enterprise does not have this product in stock, there are two other sources for obtaining this product. The pallets are a product that the enterprise needs to purchase for its own use. The table illustrates representative data which would be stored by PRODUCT SUPPLIER.

Products may only be manufactured by one organization. Of course, it is possible for an organization to subcontract another organization to produce a product. The organization who hired the subcontractor is still the manufacturer. For example, a car manufacturer often hires another organization to produce its cars. Since the original car manufacturer is still responsible for the product, it is considered the manufacturer.

## INVENTORY ITEM STORAGE

Figure 3.3 shows how inventory items are modeled. While an ITEM represents a catalog item or a standard product that can be purchased, an INVENTORY ITEM represents the physical occurrence of an item at a location. The ITEM may

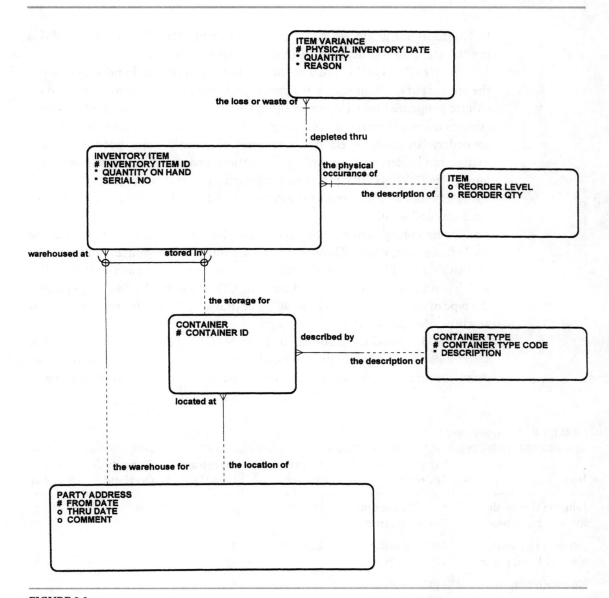

**FIGURE 3.3**

*Inventory item storage.*

be "Johnson fine grade, 8½ × 11, bond paper", while the INVENTORY ITEM is the 100 reams of this item sitting in the central warehouse.

The INVENTORY ITEM has the attribute **quantity on hand** which stores the amount of the item stored at a particular location. The **quantity on hand** attribute is updated based upon incoming and outgoing shipments of this item (shipments will be covered in Chapter 6). The model does not include attributes for **ordered quantity expected in** or **committed quantity going out** as this information can be derived from order information (orders will be covered in Chapter 4). The INVENTORY ITEM may represent several items or it may represent a single item. For some items the attribute **serial number** may be used to identify a physical item.

The inventory item may be either tracked at a warehouse level or it may be tracked at a more detailed level within a warehouse. A warehouse is another type of PARTY ADDRESS. A more detailed location is referred to as a CONTAINER which resides within a party's address. The CONTAINER TYPE entity specifies the type of container such as a "shelf", "file drawer", "bin", "barrel", "room", or any other detailed location.

Table 3.4 provides examples of INVENTORY ITEM. ABC Corporation stores most of its office supplies in bins within each location. The first four rows show how much inventory of each item is located in various bins within a party

TABLE 3.4  *Inventory Item*

| Item* | Party Address* | Container Type * | Inventory Item ID | Quantity On Hand | Serial Number |
|---|---|---|---|---|---|
| Johnson fine grade 8½ × 11 bond paper | ABC Corporation 100 Main Street | Bin 200 | 1 | 156 | |
| Johnson fine grade 8½ × 11 bond paper | ABC Subsidiary 255 Fetch Street | Bin 400 | 2 | 300 | |
| Goldstein Elite Pen | ABC Corporation 100 Main Street | Bin 125 | 1 | 200 | |
| Jerry's box of 3½ inch diskettes | ABC Corporation 100 Main Street | Bin 250 | 1 | 500 | |
| Action 250 Quality Copier | ABC Corporation 100 Main Street | | 1 | 1 | 1094853 |

address. Notice that there are two records for "Johnson fine grade 8½ × 11 bond paper": the inventory of 156 reams (the product record defines the unit of measure in reams) stored at 100 Main Street with ABC Corporation and the inventory of 300 reams stored at 255 Fetch Street with ABC Subsidiary. Large items, such as copiers, as shown in the fifth row, may be stored at a location level (i.e., PARTY ADDRESS) and identified by a serial number. Therefore, the container type is left blank.

The ITEM VARIANCE entity keeps a history of item shrinkage or overages that were noticed during physical inventories or inspections of the item. The **physical inventory date** specifies the date that the item variance was discovered. The **quantity** is the difference between the on-hand amount and the physical inventory at the time of the **physical inventory date**. The **on-hand amount** of the INVENTORY ITEM is reduced if the **quantity** in ITEM VARIANCE is negative and it is increased if the **quantity** is positive. The **reason** attribute provides an explanation of the variance to the inventory item's on-hand amount. For example, if the enterprise discovered that there was a loss of an item due to theft, it can record the date the theft was discovered, the amount of the product that was stolen, and the specific details behind the theft. This serves as an audit trail to account for any changes to the product's **on-hand quantity** resulting from transactions other than incoming and outgoing shipments.

## PRODUCT PRICING

Every organization seems to have different mechanisms for pricing its products. However, there are some common principles behind pricing which are captured in the data model in Figure 3.4.

In most organizations, there are several aspects to pricing a product: The base price for which the organization sells the product, various discounts applied against the base price, freight and handling charges, and perhaps quantity breaks. The PRODUCT PRICE COMPONENT stores these aspects of prices for each supplier's products. This entity is broken down into the sub-types BASE PRODUCT PRICE which has the starting price for the product, DISCOUNT COMPONENT which stores valid reductions to the base price, and SURCHARGE COMPONENT which adds on possible charges. To accommodate other possible types of components, the entity PRODUCT PRICE COMPONENT TYPE is also included.

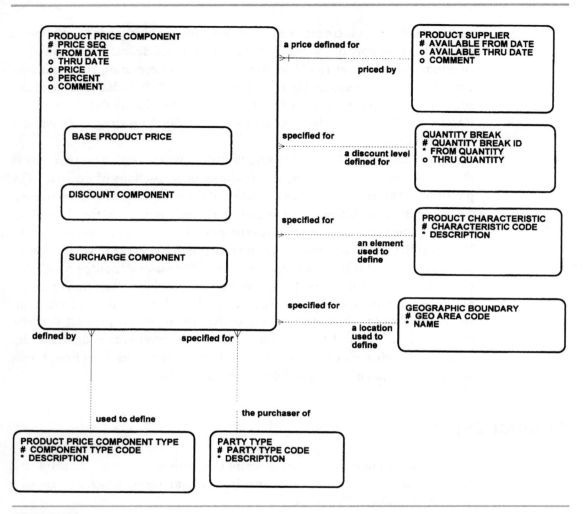

FIGURE 3.4

*Standard product pricing.*

The PRODUCT PRICE COMPONENT stores a **price** attribute filled with a dollar amount and a **percentage** attribute which can be used to record discounts or quantity breaks. Each product price component stores a value in either the **price** attribute or the **percentage** attribute but not both. The **from date** and **thru date** fields indicate the starting and ending dates for which the product price component is valid.

The PRODUCT PRICE COMPONENT entity is related to the PRODUCT SUPPLIER entity, since a product's price will always be determined, at least in part, by the specific product and the organization that is selling the product.

Each sub-type of the PRODUCT PRICE COMPONENT may have values that are based on other variables. The BASE PRODUCT PRICE may be dependent on the type of organization that purchases the product, which is why there is an optional relationship to the PARTY TYPE entity. For example, there may be a lower price for "minority-owned businesses". The base price may be dependent on the geographic area of the delivery, so there is also an optional relationship to the GEOGRAPHIC BOUNDARY entity. For instance, there may be a higher base product price if the item(s) are delivered to an area outside of the enterprise's normal geographic boundaries. The base product price may also be based upon quantities of products ordered. The QUANTITY BREAK entity stores various ranges of quantity breaks in the **from quantity** and **thru quantity** attributes. The enterprise needs to enforce business rules to determine which base price component takes priority over another component. For instance, if there is a base product price for a minority-owned business and a different base product price for customers in the eastern region, and a buyer fits both criteria, then the enterprise needs to build business rules to determine which price takes precedence.

The DISCOUNT COMPONENT may be dependent on the PARTY TYPE, GEOGRAPHIC BOUNDARY, QUANTITY BREAK, or certain PRODUCT CHARACTERISTICs such as the product type or brand names of products. For instance, there may be a 2 percent standard discount for all organizations with a PARTY TYPE of "minority-owned business". The enterprise may specify a discount for any delivery to a customer within the same city or GEOGRAPHIC BOUNDARY as the enterprise, since the delivery charges would be less. Another discount may be based upon the number of products purchased and therefore be dependent on the QUANTITY BREAK. Perhaps if the customer purchases more than 100 reams of a certain type of paper, there could be either an amount or percentage discount per item. There may also be a discount based upon a

PRODUCT CHARACTERISTIC such as 5 percent off for all paper products during the month of September as part of an advertising campaign. Finally, there may be combinations of pricing discounts such as a special on furniture within a certain geographic area. Another example of a pricing combination is when a quantity break applies exclusively to a specific party type, such as a minority-owned business.

A SURCHARGE COMPONENT is a price component which adds to the base price of the product. Examples of surcharges include freight costs and additional mileage costs. Product price surcharges are generally based upon the GEOGRAPHIC BOUNDARY, such as additional freight charges being assessed based upon the distance of the customer from the enterprise's nearest warehouse.

Table 3.5 illustrates an example of product price components for the product "Johnson fine grade 8½ × 11 bond paper". In this example, ABC Corporation has established standard, base prices for certain geographical regions and for certain volumes of quantity ordered. The first four rows show the standard prices for the eastern and western regions and depend on the quantity being ordered. In addition, ABC Corporation has established a 2 percent discount if the purchasing party is a government agency. There is a 5 percent discount on all paper products (i.e., products with a product type of "paper") which is applicable in September of 1997. The dates for this promotion would actually be entered in the PRODUCT PRICE COMPONENT attributes of **from date** and **thru date**. There is a surcharge of $2.00 that is added to the product price for all deliveries to Hawaii.

Since in this model, products can be offered by many suppliers, the same model can be used to store competitors' prices to determine how competitive the enterprise's price is. Notice that the last row of Table 3.5 shows the standard price of the product for its competitor, "Joe's Stationary". This model can also maintain product prices for each product purchased from the enterprise's suppliers. The "price seq" starts again as "1" since this is a PRODUCT PRICE COMPONENT for a different PRODUCT SUPPLIER.

There are many different variations on the way each enterprise prices its products. When it comes to negotiating deals, it is amazing how creative people and organizations can get! Therefore, this pricing model is very flexible and can handle many different pricing scenarios. However, it is important that the enterprise determine its business rules in order to avoid confusion. For example, does the enterprise have a business rule that certain discounts override other discounts? Does the enterprise allow the sales representative to choose which dis-

**TABLE 3.5** *Standard Product Pricing*

| Supplier | Product Type Description* | Price Component Type* | Price Seq | Party Type* | Geographic Boundary* | Quantity Break* | Price | Percentage |
|---|---|---|---|---|---|---|---|---|
| ABC Corporation | Johnson fine grade 8½×11 bond paper | Base | 1 | | Eastern Region | 0–100 | $9.75 | |
| ABC Corporation | Johnson fine grade 8½×11 bond paper | Base | 2 | | Eastern Region | 101– | $9.00 | |
| ABC Corporation | Johnson fine grade 8½×11 bond paper | Base | 3 | | Western Region | 0–100 | $8.75 | |
| ABC Corporation | Johnson fine grade 8½×11 bond paper | Base | 4 | | Western Region | 101– | $8.50 | |
| ABC Corporation | Johnson fine grade 8½×11 bond paper | Discount | 5 | Govt | | | | 2 |
| ABC Corporation | Johnson fine grade 8½×11 bond paper | Discount | 6 | Paper Products (special offer in Sept. 1997) | | | | 5 |
| ABC Corporation | Johnson fine grade 8½×11 bond paper | Surcharge | 7 | | Hawaii | | $2.00 | |
| Joe's Stationary | Johnson fine grade 8½×11 bond paper | Base | 1 | | | | $11.00 | |

count applies if several discounts are applicable? Does the organization include quantity breaks as part of its base price or does it consider quantity breaks a discount to the base price? These types of questions need to be answered in order to use this model effectively and store the right type of information within the attributes.

## PRODUCT COSTING

It is important for organizations to have good information on product costs in order to ensure that the products are priced profitably. Having appropriate product cost information may also help to determine appropriate commissions, if they are based upon profitability.

Some data modelers might have the insight to realize that the actual product costs are in many aspects of a data model and derivable from data in various entities. For instance, purchase orders hold information about the cost of the raw materials. The shipment to the customer will have freight charges which are a cost component of the product. Time sheets and payroll records hold information about the labor costs involved in the manufacturing or delivery of products. For manufactured items, the cost of scheduling equipment in production runs is stored in equipment assignment records. Overhead such as rent, office supplies, and other administrative items can be factored into the product cost as well.

Instead of using actual product costs to figure out the cost of various products, this model uses estimated costs which product analysts will typically enter for each product. The advantage to using estimated costs is that product analysts can predict future trends of how much they think the product will cost instead of simply using historical information. For example, the freight charges might have historically been $1.00 from destination A to destination B. However, there may be available data on current freight charges which may be more appropriate to figure out the real cost of a product. The enterprise can use the actual product costs combined with its understanding of the marketplace and future trends to enter what it believes will be the real costs of selling its products.

Of course, the only product costs that are worthwhile tracking are usually the enterprise's own products. Supplier and competitor cost information is usually not available to track. An exception is that some government organizations need to track the costs of their suppliers' products to ensure that profit margins are not excessive.

Figure 3.5 is a data model for storing product costs. There are many cost components that figure into the overall costs of a product. Therefore, the PRODUCT entity may be priced by many PRODUCT COST COMPONENTs. The ESTIMATED PRODUCT COST COMPONENT entity maintains information on each product and its many costs. The COST COMPONENT TYPE entity specifies what type of cost it is. COST COMPONENT TYPEs include raw material costs, labor costs, manufacturing costs (i.e., the use of machinery and equipment), shrinkage costs (i.e., theft or perishable item losses), shipping costs, costs in selling the product (i.e., commissions or brokerage charges), and administrative costs of running an office. Additionally, product costs may vary by season or over time, so the attributes **from date** and **thru dates** are included to show the time period that the cost is valid.

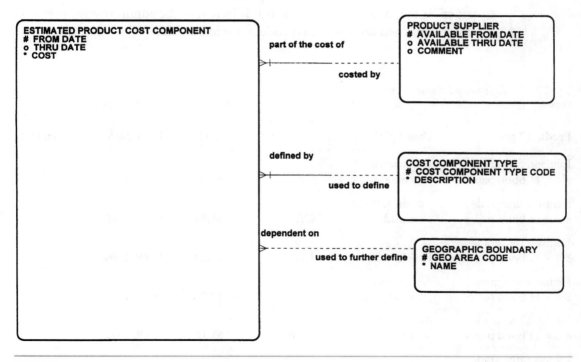

**FIGURE 3.5**

*Estimated product cost.*

The cost component type may vary based upon where the costs are incurred. For instance, manufacturing costs may be less expensive in a plant located in one country versus another country. Delivery costs may be less expensive if the shipment is located in a nearby location versus an overseas shipment. Shrinkage costs due to theft may be higher in certain cities.

Product cost types will vary depending on the type of business. For instance, a distributor may track the cost of buying the goods, shipping and handling charges, selling costs, and administrative overhead. A manufacturer may track the cost of the materials used, labor used to produce the goods, the cost of running manufacturing equipment, selling costs, and administrative overhead. The costs for a service organization generally include the cost of labor, selling costs, and administrative costs.

Table 3.6 shows examples of product cost information that would be stored in ESTIMATED PRODUCT COST COMPONENT. The table shows that while the anticipated purchase cost of the product "Johnson fine grade $8\frac{1}{2} \times 11$ bond paper" is the same for New York as it is in Idaho, the administrative overhead and freight costs are less if this product is sold in Idaho.

**TABLE 3.6**  *Estimated Product Costs*

| Product Type* | Cost Type* | Geographic Boundary* | Cost | From Date | Thru Date |
|---|---|---|---|---|---|
| Johnson fine grade $8\frac{1}{2} \times 11$ bond paper | Anticipated purchase cost | N.Y. | $2.00 | Jan 9, 1996 | |
| Johnson fine grade $8\frac{1}{2} \times 11$ bond paper | Administrative overhead | N.Y. | $1.90 | Jan 9, 1996 | |
| Johnson fine grade $8\frac{1}{2} \times 11$ bond paper | Freight | N.Y. | $1.50 | Jan 9, 1996 | |
| Johnson fine grade $8\frac{1}{2} \times 11$ bond paper | Anticipated purchase cost | Idaho | $2.00 | Jan 9, 1996 | |
| Johnson fine grade $8\frac{1}{2} \times 11$ bond paper | Administrative overhead | Idaho | $1.10 | Jan 9, 1996 | |
| Johnson fine grade $8\frac{1}{2} \times 11$ bond paper | Freight | Idaho | $1.10 | Jan 9, 1996 | |

# PRODUCT COMPONENTS

Most people view the combining of components into a saleable product as a function limited to manufacturing organizations. However, there are other types of organizations that package together components to make a product offering. Some distribution companies assemble kits which include individual items that could also be sold. For instance, a beauty supply distributor may combine combs, scissors, and makeup into a beauty kit that the customer can purchase. Service organizations often bundle together services that are sold as a single product. For instance, there may be a single price for a software application package which consists of the documentation, the software stored on a CD-ROM, introductory training, and a certain number of hours of initial consulting.

Some enterprises need to know the makeup of their products. For instance, some laboratories need to know how their research apparatus is put together. Organizations who repair the equipment they sell need to know how the product is assembled even though they might not have manufactured it themselves.

Figure 3.6 models information regarding the makeup of products. The PRODUCT COMPONENT entity shows which products are made up of other products. A product can be made up of more than one other product and, alternatively, a product may be used in several other products. For example, an office desk set may consist of a pen, pencil, calendar, clock, and wood base. Any one of these components may be used in the assembly of another product. Service organizations may also assemble one or more of their services into a product and, alternatively, use the same service in many product offerings.

The PRODUCT COMPONENT has attributes of **from date** and **thru date** to signify the time periods that certain product components are made of other product components. This implies that the components of a product may change. At one point in time, an office desk set may include a certain type of pen and at a later point it may include a different pen.

Another attribute of PRODUCT COMPONENT is the **quantity used**. This attribute indicates how many of a certain product is used in the assembly of another product. For example, in some office desk sets there may be two pens included in the set. The **instruction** attribute explains how to assemble the products. If a comprehensive set of instructions is needed, then a new entity named INSTRUCTION should be added and related to the PRODUCT COMPONENT. The **comment** attribute is used to describe any other note about

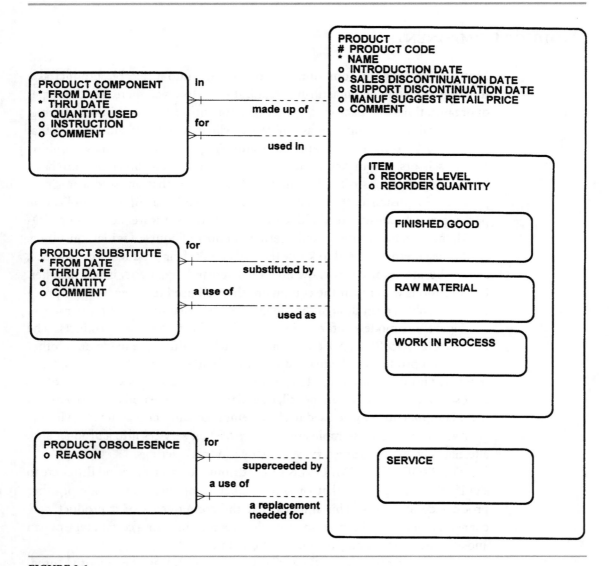

FIGURE 3.6

*Product components.*

**TABLE 3.7** *Product Components*

| Parent Product Type* | Child Product Type* | Quantity | UOM* |
|---|---|---|---|
| Office Supply Kit | Johnson fine grade 8½ × 11 bond paper | 5 | Box |
| Office Supply Kit | Pennie's 8½ × 11 binders | 5 | Each |
| Office Supply Kit | Shwinger black ball point pen | 6 | Box |

the assembly of products. Table 3.7 shows an example of a product that is made up of other products. The UOM (unit of measure) in the table is derived from the PRODUCT DEFINITION for the Child Product Type.

The PRODUCT SUBSTITUTE entity shows which products may be substituted by other products. A PRODUCT may be substituted by many other PRODUCTs. For example, perhaps a certain pen within an office desk set may be substituted by a few other pens of similar quality. Alternatively, a PRODUCT can also be used as a substitute for many PRODUCTs. Perhaps a specific pen is used as a substitute in many circumstances. The **from date** and **thru date** attributes specify the time frames that products may be substituted for each other. The **quantity** attribute allows an item to be substituted for a certain quantity of another product. For example, Table 3.8 provides an example of a small box of pencils being substituted for 12 individual pencils of the same type. The **comment** attribute provides additional information regarding the substitution of a product; for example, "try not to substitute with this product if it can be avoided as the product is of a lower quality than the standard product."

The PRODUCT OBSOLESCENCE entity shows which products are about to be or have already been superseded by other products. There is again a many-to-many recursive relationship from the PRODUCT entity to show that a product can be superseded by numerous new products and a new product may

**TABLE 3.8** *Substitute Products*

| Product* | Substitute Product* | Quantity |
|---|---|---|
| Small Box of Henry #2 Pencils | Henry #2 Pencil | 12 |
| Goldstein Elite Pen | George's Elite Pen | |

supersede many old products. An example is that the next release of a software package may combine several separate pieces of software into a single piece of software or vice versa.

Notice that the ITEM sub-type is broken down into sub-types of FINISHED GOOD, RAW MATERIAL, and WORK IN PROGRESS. A FINISHED GOOD is a product that is ready to be shipped and there has been some type of work performed to get the product to its current state. A RAW MATERIAL is a component used in making a product where there has not been any work performed by the enterprise on the product. A RAW MATERIAL may be sold as an item or used in another item. A WORK IN PROCESS item is a product which is in a state of partial completion such as a sub-assembly and is not generally sold to a customer or purchased from a supplier. If the enterprise purchased the sub-assembly from a supplier, it would be considered a RAW MATERIAL, since the enterprise did not perform any additional work on the product.

## SUMMARY

This chapter has focused on the data model for products which include both items and services. Items are tangible, physical goods whereas services are the selling of professionals' time to accomplish some function. The data models in this chapter incorporate the information needs for the enterprise's own products, suppliers' products, and competitors' products. Product information covered in this chapter includes the definition of products, product suppliers and manufacturers, product storage, product pricing, product costing, and product component information (see Figure 3.7).

Refer to Appendix A for an alphabetical listing of entities and attributes presented in this chapter along with attribute characteristics. To access the SQL scripts to build tables, columns, and constraints derived from this logical model, please refer to the CD-ROM companion product that is sold separately.

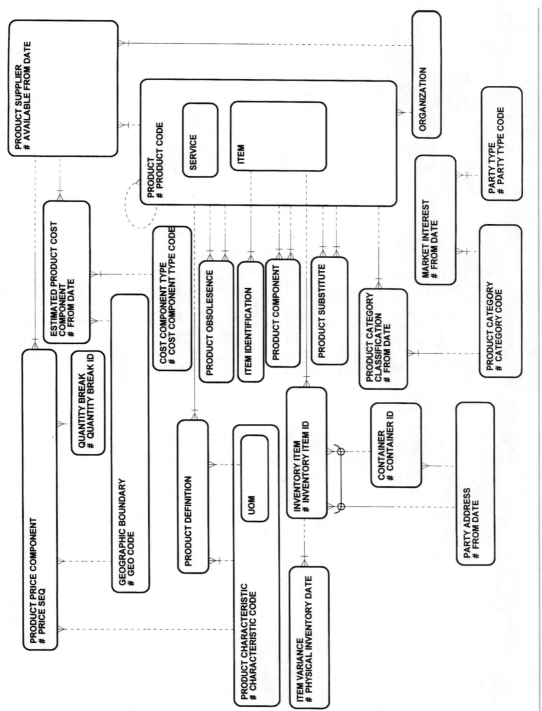

FIGURE 3.7

65

# 4

# ORDERING PRODUCTS

## INTRODUCTION

The previous chapters focused on information about the parties which conduct business and what products they need. This chapter focuses on how parties obtain these products—in other words, the ordering of products.

Businesses need information to answer many questions about orders; they need to know the terms associated with each order. For instance:

When is the expected delivery time and are there consequences for late delivery?

Who is responsible for paying for the order?

What is the negotiated price for each product that is ordered?

What people and organizations are involved in the order?

Who placed the order? To whom is the order being shipped?

Was there an approved requisition for the order?

Were there previous quotes for the order?

Were there requests to many vendors to bid for the order?

Are there general agreements in place which govern the terms of the order such as special pricing arrangements?

This chapter discusses the following models:

- Standard order model
- Order definition
- Order header
- Order line items
- Order relationship to party location
- Person roles for orders
- Requisition definition
- Request definition
- Quote definition
- Person roles for requests and quotes
- Agreement definition
- Relationship of agreement to order
- Agreement pricing

## STANDARD ORDER MODEL

Most organizations model orders using the standard data model which is shown throughout many textbooks on data modeling. Figure 4.1 illustrates this standard data model. A SUPPLIER is related to one or more PURCHASE ORDERs which have PURCHASE ORDER LINE ITEMs that relate to PRODUCT. This model is similar for sales. A CUSTOMER can be related to one or more SALES ORDERs which have SALES ORDER LINE ITEMs that relate to specific PRODUCTs. Table 4.1 shows the example of a typical sales order. A customer, ACME Company, placed a sales order on June 8, 1995, for several items (or line items), each of which is defined in the PRODUCT entity. The sales order stores information such as the date the order was given, the customer placing the order, shipping instructions, and payment terms.

Order line items show the individual products or services which were purchased. Table 4.2 shows examples of LINE ITEMs. In this example, there are three items being ordered: 10 reams of paper, 4 pens, and 6 boxes of diskettes.

When a purchase order is given to a supplier, the same types of relationships exist. A supplier is given many purchase orders, each of which has line items that correspond to a specific product type.

The attributes of sales orders and purchase orders are very similar, if not the

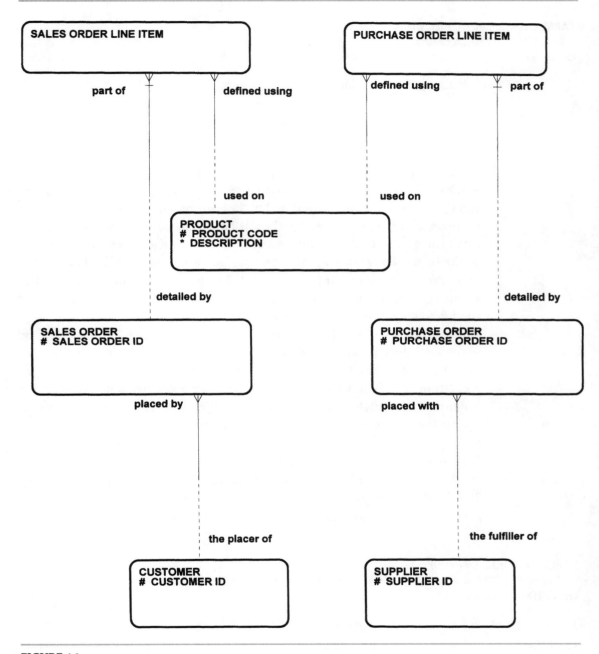

FIGURE 4.1

*Standard order model.*

**TABLE 4.1**  *Standard Order Model*

| Order ID | Customer* | Order Date* | Shipping Instructions | Payment Terms |
|----------|-----------|-------------|-----------------------|---------------|
| 12560 | ACME Company | June 8, 1995 | Via truck | Net 30 |
| 23000 | Jones Corporation | Sept 5, 1995 | UPS | Net 30 |

same. An order is an order; the only real difference between a sales order and a purchase order is a matter of perspective. In other words, the information on the seller's sales order should correspond to the information on the purchaser's purchase order. The only reason that the attributes may be different is that the two parties may require different information depending on whether one is the seller or the buyer. For example, the enterprise taking the sales order may need to know the commissions for the salespeople involved in the order, whereas when a purchase order is given to a vendor, the purchaser is usually not privileged enough to know what the commission is for the salespeople.

As Figure 4.1 shows, the relationships and data structures between sales and purchase orders are very similar. By having two separate models for both of these types of orders, the model is made more complex and developers cannot take advantage of common applications to handle both sales and purchases. For instance, if the structures are the same, developers can create common routines against the same data structures. There could be common routines to look up the terms of an order, to monitor the status of the order against the expected delivery date, or to calculate line-item price extensions.

Another issue with Figure 4.1 is the separate entities for CUSTOMER and SUPPLIER. As discussed in Chapter 2, these are just roles which organizations play. If an organization plays the role of customer in one circumstance and sup-

**TABLE 4.2**  *Order Line Item*

| Order ID | Line Item ID | Product* | Quantity | Unit Price |
|----------|--------------|----------|----------|------------|
| 12560 | 1 | Johnson fine grade 8½ × 11 bond paper | 10 | $8.00 |
| 12560 | 2 | Goldstein Elite Pen | 4 | $12.00 |
| 12560 | 3 | Jerry's box of 3½ inch diskettes | 6 | $7.00 |

plier in another circumstance, then this model would reflect redundant data which will lead to data inconsistencies.

Finally, there is another embedded assumption in this standard order data model: Only one organization can take the order in the sales order model and only one organization can place the order in the purchase order model. Most systems model information from an "I" perspective. This perspective states that the model doesn't have to indicate the party receiving sales orders or placing purchase orders; it's obviously us (meaning the enterprise building the system)! The problem with this perspective is that there may be several internal organizations within the enterprise who may receive the sales order or place the purchase order. Even if an organization is a small business, there may be a broker who takes the sales order or the organization may grow later on to include subsidiaries, divisions, or other related internal organizations.

## ORDER DEFINITION

The data model in Figure 4.2 is more flexible, modular, and maintainable than the data model in the previous section and is the one which will be built upon throughout the remainder of this book. This model portrays a broader perspective than the "I" model of the previous section and has a more stable, object-oriented approach where orders are related to parties that may play several roles depending upon the circumstances.

Figure 4.2 shows that there is a PARTY ADDRESS which is the fulfiller of ORDERs, as in the case of a supplier, and another PARTY ADDRESS which is the placer of ORDERs, as in the case of a customer. The ORDER entity is subtyped into SALES ORDER and PURCHASE ORDER to cover both sales and purchase orders. Orders are composed of ORDER LINE ITEMs which specify the product(s) that are to be ordered, hence the relationship to PRODUCT.

Orders are related to parties at specific addresses. The ORDER is taken by a PARTY ADDRESS (i.e., a supplier at a certain location) and placed by a PARTY ADDRESS (i.e., the party ordering the item at a specific location). The reason an ORDER is not related to a PARTY is that it is important to know not only who placed and took the order, but also from what location the order is taken and placed. For example, the party placing the order may be a particular store within a chain. It would be important to know not only that the order was placed by the chain, but also the particular location of the store. If an order is placed by a small

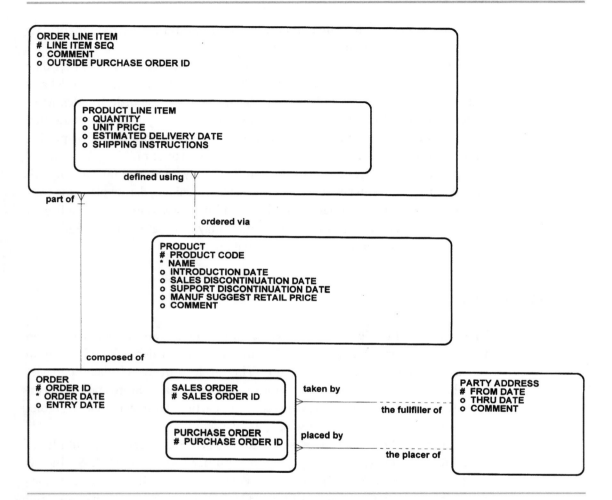

**FIGURE 4.2**

*Order definition.*

organization with only one location, the PARTY ADDRESS still identifies the appropriate party and address responsible for ordering the product(s). This model easily accommodates the different parties associated with an order such as a broker, an internal organization, or a store location.

The attribute on ORDER named **order date** specifies the date upon which the enterprise received or gave the order. The attribute **entry date** is the date upon which the order was entered into the enterprise's system. The ORDER entity is sub-typed into a SALES ORDER and a PURCHASE ORDER entity in order to accommodate specific attributes or relationships related to either a sales or purchase order.

Table 4.3 illustrates the type of information that would be included in sales and purchase orders. The first two rows represent sales orders taken by the enterprise. Notice that the party address of the first sales order shows that the Main Street facility of ABC Subsidiary took the order; in the second order, the Fetch Street facility took the order. Merely stating the party to the order is not enough; the addresses of the parties are necessary. Also, notice that the third row, which represents the purchase order, has the same type of information. The main difference is that in this case, ABC Subsidiary is giving the order to its supplier, Ace Cleaning Service.

The ORDER LINE ITEM entity describes the products which were ordered. The order line item attributes apply whether it is a purchase order or a sales order.

In Chapter 3, the data model shows that the price for each product can be stored as PRODUCT PRICE COMPONENTs and based upon many variables such as geographic location, quantity breaks, the type of party, and outstanding promotions on certain types of products. So why is the **unit price** not a derived field? The **unit price** is important as this attribute allows the user to override the calculated price with the negotiated price for this order. Base, discount, and surcharge product price components can all appear as order line items associated with a particular product.

Table 4.4 illustrates the ORDER LINE ITEM entity. The major difference in this entity from the standard order line item entity in Table 4.2 is that purchase order line items are included in this entity. Notice that the purchase order has

**TABLE 4.3** *Order*

| Order ID | Order Type* | Party Address Placed By* | Party Address Taken By* | Order Date |
|---|---|---|---|---|
| 12560 | Sales Order | ACME Company<br>234 Stretch Street | ABC Subsidiary<br>100 Main Street | June 8, 1995 |
| 23000 | Sales Order | Jones Corporation<br>900 Washington Blvd | ABC Subsidiary<br>255 Fetch Street | Sept 5, 1995 |
| A2395 | Purchase Order | ABC Subsidiary<br>100 Main Street | Ace Cleaning Service<br>3590 Cottage Avenue | July 9, 1995 |

**TABLE 4.4**   *Order Line Items*

| Order ID | Order Type* | Line Item ID | Product* | Quantity | Unit Price |
|----------|-------------|--------------|----------|----------|------------|
| 12560 | Sales order | 1 | Johnson fine grade 8½ × 11 bond paper | 10 | $8.00 |
| 12560 | Sales order | 2 | Goldstein Elite Pen | 4 | $12.00 |
| 12560 | Sales order | 3 | Jerry's box of 3½ inch diskettes | 6 | $7.00 |
| A2395 | Purchase order | 1 | Hourly office cleaning service | 12 | $15.00 |
| A2395 | Purchase order | 2 | Basic cleaning supplies kit | 1 | $10.00 |

two line items; one for a service ("hourly office cleaning service") and one for an item ("basic cleaning supplies kit"). This is the reason that orders are not sub-typed as service and item orders, since one order can include both services and items.

Order line items have a sub-type of PRODUCT LINE ITEM (other sub-types will be discussed later in this chapter). Product line items represent the ordering of specific items or services. Therefore, each PRODUCT LINE ITEM is defined using one and only one PRODUCT. The **quantity** indicates how many of the product was ordered. The **unit price** attribute indicates the agreed price for which the product(s) will be sold on this order. The **estimated delivery date** is the expected date that the customer will receive the shipment of the item or when the service will be completed for the customer. The **shipping instructions** attribute stores directions for transporting products to their destination, for example, "do not leave outside", "fragile—handle with care", or "requires signature by customer when delivering".

## ORDER HEADER

Figure 4.3 illustrates more details about the order header information or, in other words, the key information about the ORDER entity. This figure includes an ORDER STATUS entity to track the progress of orders. The ORDER STATUS TYPE maintains the possible order statuses. The ORDER TERM entity tracks the conditions of business associated with the order. The TERM TYPE entity maintains the possible terms available to use.

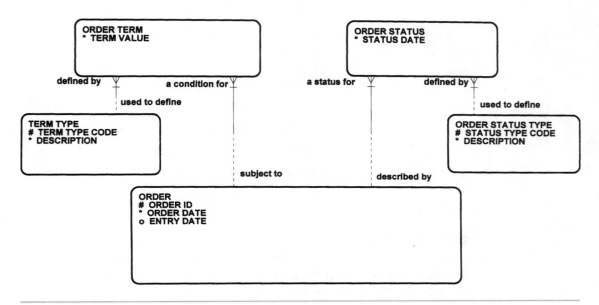

FIGURE 4.3

*Order header.*

## Order Status

Because an order may be in many different states at different points in time, the model in Figure 4.3 shows that the order may have more than one status over a period of time. The **status date** attribute of ORDER STATUS provides for the tracking of when each status of the order occurred. For example, this model will allow the tracking of when the order was received, when it was approved, and when and if it was canceled. The description attribute of the ORDER STATUS TYPE entity stores the possible statuses such as "received", "approved", and "canceled". If it is only necessary to know the current status of the order and not a history of when each status occurred, then there could simply be a many-to-one relationship from ORDER to ORDER STATUS, and ORDER STATUS would just maintain a description attribute.

Why not have "shipped", "completed", "backordered", or "invoiced" as order statuses? As will be discussed in later chapters, since shipments and invoices are tied to orders, "shipped", "completed", and "invoiced" can be derived through the relationships to shipment line items and invoice line items. "Back-

TABLE 4.5   *Order Term*

| Order ID | Value | Term Type* |
|----------|-------|------------|
| 12459 | 25 | Percentage cancellation charge |
| | 10 | Days within which one may cancel order without a penalty |
| | | No exchanges or refunds once delivered |
| 23467 | 5 | Percentage penalty paid by supplier for nonperformance |
| | 30 | Number of days within which delivery must occur |

ordered" can be derived through the ORDER LINE ITEM DEPENDENCY entity discussed later in this chapter. Although these statuses are not present in the logical model, the physical database design may have these statuses available in the ORDER STATUS TYPE table for easy access.

## Order Terms

There may be many arrangements or terms upon which the parties involved may agree. Delivery terms, exchange or refund policies, and penalties for nonperformance are some examples. Each ORDER may have one or more ORDER TERMs, each of which is categorized by a TERM TYPE. The **term value** attribute is applicable only to some of the order terms and its meaning is dependent on the type of term.

Table 4.5 shows examples of order terms. Order 12459 has three terms defined to it. The first two terms document that if the purchaser cancels the order 10 days after placing it, there is a 25 percent cancellation charge. The third term says there are no refunds or exchanges after the items have been delivered. On order 23467, there is a 5 percent nonperformance penalty if the order is delivered more than 30 days past the **estimated delivery date** of any line item.

## ORDER LINE ITEMS

Figure 4.4 illustrates the key structures behind order line items. Each ORDER LINE ITEM is sub-typed into PRODUCT LINE ITEM or ADJUSTMENT.

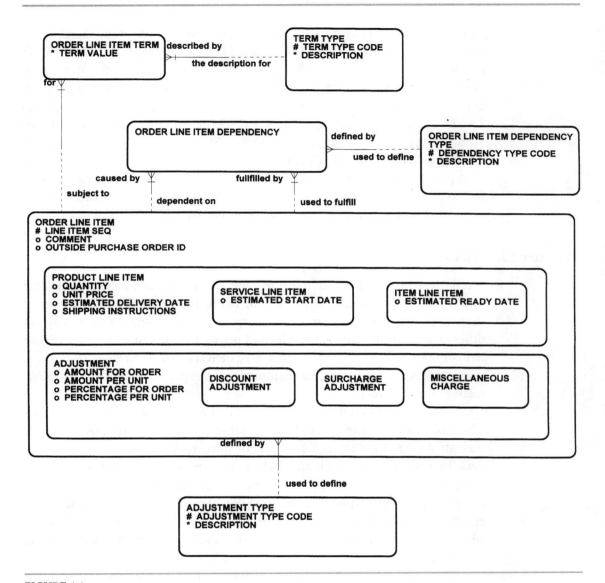

**FIGURE 4.4**

*Order line item.*

PRODUCT LINE ITEMs are orders for specific items or services and therefore are sub-typed into SERVICE LINE ITEM and ITEM LINE ITEM. ADJUSTMENTs are offsets to the price of an ORDER LINE ITEM and have a DISCOUNT sub-type to indicate a reduction and a SURCHARGE sub-type to indicate an upward adjustment. An adjustment may also be an additional charge as in the MISCEL-LANEOUS CHARGE sub-type. The ADJUSTMENT TYPE entity further categorizes the adjustment. The ORDER LINE ITEM DEPENDENCY and ORDER LINE ITEM DEPENDENCY TYPE maintain information on how line items may be dependent on other line items. Finally, each ORDER LINE ITEM may be subject to one or more ORDER LINE ITEM TERMs associated with the individual products being ordered. The terms are described by TERM TYPE.

## Product Line Items

PRODUCT LINE ITEMs include line items for services and items. All product line items have a **quantity** attribute. For items, this represents the number of items that are ordered. For services, this represents the amount of hours, days, or other measurement being billed. The **unit price** attribute stores the charge for an item or the rate for a service. The **estimated delivery date** is the date that the item is expected to be shipped to the customer or the expected date of service fulfillment to the customer.

Within the sub-type ITEM LINE ITEM, **estimated ready date** is the date when the items are estimated to be ready for shipment. The **estimated start date** is an attribute in the SERVICE LINE ITEM since it is mainly used for service orders. This attribute is an estimate of when the party performing the service order is expected to begin the service or work. The actual ready date and actual received date are not attributes of the order line item since they are associated with either the shipment of the products in the case of items or with work efforts which are associated with services. Shipments and work efforts are covered in subsequent chapters.

Many data models show estimated start, ready, and delivery dates on the ORDER entity. The reason that this model shows these attributes on the line item is that each line item may have different estimated start, ready, and delivery dates. In addition, these estimated dates for the ORDER entity are derivable since they can be calculated by the dates from the individual line items. The first three rows in Table 4.6 illustrate examples of product line items.

**TABLE 4.6** *Product Line Items and Adjustments*

| Order ID | Line Item ID | Order Line Item Type | Product* | Quantity | Unit Price | Amount Per Unit | Amount For Order | % Per Unit | % Per Order |
|----------|--------------|----------------------|----------|----------|------------|-----------------|------------------|-----------|-------------|
| 12560 | 1 | Item | Johnson fine grade 8½ × 11 bond paper | 10 | $8.00 | | | | |
| 12560 | 2 | Item | Goldstein Elite Pen | 4 | $12.00 | | | | |
| 12560 | 3 | Item | Jerry's box of 3½ inch diskettes | 5 | $7.00 | | | | |
| 12560 | 4 | Discount | | | | $1.00 | | | |
| 12560 | 5 | Discount | | | | | | | 10 |
| 12560 | 6 | Surcharge—Delivery outside normal geographic area | | | | $10.00 | | | |
| 12560 | 7 | Miscellaneous Charge—order processing fee | | | | $1.50 | | | |

## Adjustments

There are other types of line items which do not reflect the ordering of specific products. DISCOUNT ADJUSTMENT and SURCHARGE ADJUSTMENT are sub-types that store price adjustments to either the complete order or to each unit on a line item. These price adjustments may be either an amount or a percentage. Line items 4, 5, and 6 in Table 4.6 are examples of discounts and a surcharge. Line item 4 shows that there is a $1.00 discount off each unit of a certain line item (the next section will cover how to relate it to the line item it refers to). Line item 5 shows that there is a 10 percent discount off the entire order and line item 6 shows that there is a $10.00 surcharge for delivery outside the normal area.

The MISCELLANEOUS CHARGE sub-type provides a mechanism to store information about other line item charges. Table 4.6 shows an example of a miscellaneous charge for an "order processing fee". Three other examples could be "adjustment error" to correct a prior order, "handling fee" for covering the arrangements of the shipment of an order, or "management fee".

The ADJUSTMENT TYPE entity provides the ability to classify the various types of adjustments into detailed categories. The **description** attribute defines the possible values which may be related to adjustments.

## Order Line Item Dependency

Sometimes there is a relationship from one order line item to another order item. The ORDER LINE ITEM DEPENDENCY entity relates line items to other line items. One example of this is when there are discounts, surcharges, or miscellaneous adjustments that apply to specific order line items. In Table 4.6, there is a "discount" of $1.00 for each unit of a certain line item. The first row of Table 4.7 shows this discount (line item 4) which is applied to line item 3. This means that each box of diskettes has a net price of $6.00 after the discount ($7.00 minus a $1.00 discount).

Another type of order line item dependency is when a sales order line item is dependent upon a purchase order line item. For example, a distributor may receive a sales order but may not have enough inventory in stock to cover one of the items on it. In turn, the distributor may place a purchase order to one of its suppliers (or many purchase orders to many suppliers) to fulfill the item which was short. In other words, the sales order line item was "backordered" and covered by a purchase order line item.

TABLE 4.7   *Order Line Item Dependency*

| Order ID | Order Line Item Seq | Order ID | Order Line Item Seq | Order Line Item Dependency Type* |
|----------|---------------------|----------|---------------------|----------------------------------|
| 12560 | 3 | 12560 | 4 | Discount |
| 13480 | 1 | 23490 | 1 | Purchase order to cover sales order |

A single line item on a purchase order may be used to fulfill several line items on sales orders. Alternatively, a sales order line item may be fulfilled by many purchase orders line items since the additional inventory may be ordered from many different suppliers. The ORDER LINE ITEM DEPENDENCY handles this many-to-many relationship. The second row in Table 4.7 illustrates the data which would occur from a purchase order line item tied to a sales order line item. Order 23490 is a purchase order which has a line item 1 that will provide the items needed for sales order 13480, line item 1.

The ORDER LINE ITEM DEPENDENCY TYPE identifies the type of dependency that exists between the line items. Table 4.7 illustrates the two types of line item dependencies previously discussed: "discount" and "purchase order to cover sales order".

Another situation where sales and purchase orders are linked is when a sales order requires the corresponding purchase order number from the buyer. Since the seller may want to track the buyer's corresponding purchase order ID, the attribute **outside purchase order ID** is on the ORDER LINE ITEM entity. This attribute is defined at the line item level and not the order header since each line item of the sales order may be related to a different purchase order. The reason that the ORDER DEPENDENCY entity is not used to relate the purchase order to a sales order in this case is that the seller is generally not interested in recording the full details behind the purchase order—the seller usually only needs the purchase order number.

In this latter case, one sales order line item is generally not related to multiple purchase orders. If an item on a sales order is placed due to two or more purchase order line items, the sales order line item should be split into separate sales order line items in order to be able to trace the exact amount of the item that corresponded to each purchase order.

## Order Line Item Term

In some cases, not only do orders have terms associated with them, but the individual line items also have terms associated with them. Figure 4.4 shows that each ORDER LINE ITEM may be subject to one or more ORDER LINE ITEM TERMs, each of which is described by a TERM TYPE. An example of a term associated with an order line item is that a certain item ordered may not be exchanged or refunded.

## ORDER RELATIONSHIP TO PARTY LOCATION

Figure 4.5 illustrates the relationships of ORDER to PARTY ADDRESS and PARTY CONTACT MECHANISM. In many of these relationships both PARTY ADDRESS and PARTY CONTACT MECHANISM are related to ORDER since a party address is a physical location and a party contact mechanism is a virtual location. Therefore, they are both ways to identify the locations of the parties involved in the order.

The key parties involved in an order are:

- The party placing the order and the party taking the order
- The parties that will receive the delivery of the order
- The party that will pay for the order
- The people who were involved in various roles regarding the order

The data model in Figure 4.5 addresses the first three points; the last point will be covered in a later section and illustrated in Figure 4.6.

Note that there is not a relationship defining the **customer of** an order. This is because the customer of an order may have several different meanings depending on what type of information the enterprise is interested in. Is the customer the party that is responsible for paying for the order, the consumer of the order (where it is being shipped), or the party placing the order? This model provides the flexibility to maintain all these relationships.

## Party Placing Order

Orders may be placed by an individual or an organization depending on the business requirements of the organization for whom the system is built. In mail-order catalog businesses, the order is usually placed by a person. In manufacturing firms, the order is usually placed by an organization. The order may also be placed by an agent or broker of a party. The PARTY RELATIONSHIP entity can identify if this type of relationship exists.

Relating the order directly to a party alone is insufficient. In addition to the party, enterprises generally need to know the address or contact mechanism (in the case of orders placed electronically such as through Internet electronic mail) of the party placing the order. This location may be used to confirm the order or it may be used to designate which location of an organization is placing the order.

Figure 4.5 shows that orders are placed by either a PARTY CONTACT MECHANISM or a PARTY ADDRESS which, in turn, will relate to the party that is placing the order. For example, ACME Company may have many retail stores; therefore, it may be important to track that the order came from a particular store. If the order comes from a corporation that does not give a specific address, the corporate headquarters address for that organization can be recorded.

## Party Taking Order

The order is always taken by a party at a particular address or contact mechanism. Figure 4.5 shows that an ORDER must be taken by either a PARTY CONTACT MECHANISM or PARTY ADDRESS. The order may be taken by a particular location of the organization or by a corporate location. For example, a particular store may take an order or the corporate headquarters may be the location. The order may also be taken through the World Wide Web; therefore, the order would be associated with a party contact mechanism which, in turn, is related to a party.

## Ship to Party

In certain circumstances, orders are placed by one party and delivered to other parties. It is possible for someone to order a gift which is to be shipped to another party. It is also possible for an authorized agent of an organization to place an order that may be delivered to their client's address or addresses.

Figure 4.5 shows that each ORDER LINE ITEM may be designated to be

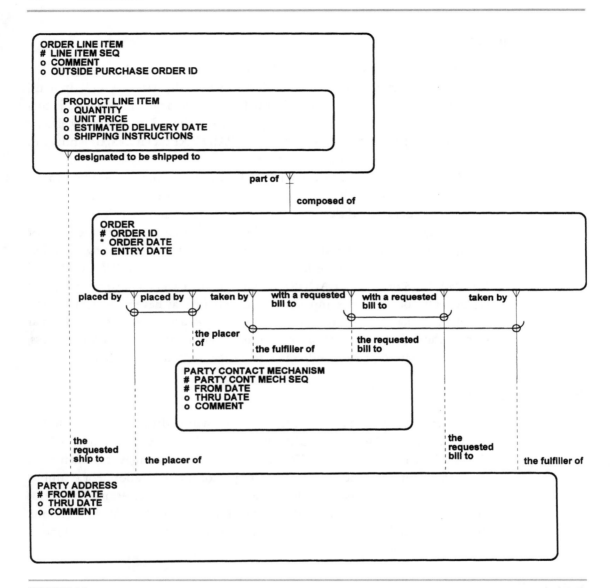

FIGURE 4.5

*Order relationships to party location.*

shipped to one and only one PARTY ADDRESS. Physical items will always require a destination where the items need to be shipped. Orders for service are also generally delivered to a specific location. This relationship is at the line item level because one order could have many destinations. For example, a large department store chain may order 5,000 cases of cola with instructions to deliver 1,000 cases to each of its five regional stores. With this model it is possible to then record five line items of 1,000 cases each, then specify a different delivery address for each line item. If this relationship was to the ORDER entity, it would be necessary to record five different orders which would result in storing redundant information and increase the margin for error during data entry.

It may seem as though this information should be specified as part of the SHIPMENT model, but there is a reason it is not. As will be seen in the next chapter, a SHIPMENT can be made up of line items from many orders. That is, if several line items from *different* orders (for the same party) are to be sent to the same location, these can be consolidated into one delivery. Therefore, if the order line item destination information was entered as shipment information, this could result in the creation of many redundant shipment records, all of which would be going to the same destination. In other words, the information on **requested ship to** parties cannot be specified by a SHIPMENT because it has not yet been determined which orders will be combined together on which shipments.

Note that this relationship is optional since there are cases where the location of the delivery is immaterial. For example, an order to provide cleaning services for a corporation may be provided across the entire enterprise, so there may not be a need for a **requested ship to** since there is not a single delivery address for the work.

The **ship from** party relationship is not specified in this chapter since this will most likely be determined after the order is created, when the SHIPMENT is determined. This relationship is included in the data model in Chapter 5 which covers shipments.

## Bill to Party

The order needs to specify who the invoice is sent to, which could either be a PARTY CONTACT MECHANISM or a PARTY ADDRESS. This identifies not only the party responsible for paying for the invoice, but also the address or contact mechanism of where to send the bill and where to follow up. Table 4.8 gives examples of orders and the associated party addresses or contact mechanisms.

TABLE 4.8    *Order Parties*

| Order ID | Party Location Placing Order* | Party Location Taking Order* | Party Location Designating The Ship To* | Party Location Billed To* |
|---|---|---|---|---|
| 12560 | ACME Company 234 Stretch Street | ABC Subsidiary 100 Main Street | ACME Company 2300 Drident Avenue | ACME Company 234 Stretch Street |
| 23000 | Jones Corporation 900 Washington Blvd | ABC Subsidiary supplies@ABC.com | Jones Corporation 2300 Drident Avenue | Jones Corporation 900 Washington Blvd |
| 24830 | bford@person.com | supplies@ABC.com | Bob Ford 2930 Briarwood Avenue | Bob Ford 2930 Briarwood Avenue |
| A2395 | ABC Subsidiary 100 Main Street | Ace Cleaning Service 3590 Cottage Avenue | ABC Retail Store 2345 Johnson Blvd | ABC Corporation 100 Main Street |

## PERSON ROLES FOR ORDERS

Many people could be involved in taking orders. Examples include the person giving the order, the person processing the order, the person approving the order, and the person responsible for fulfilling the order. Therefore, people have various roles which they play in an order. Figure 4.6 shows a data model which maintains the roles that people play in orders.

Table 4.9 gives examples of the various roles that people could play in an order. In order 23000, John Jones and Nancy Barker were the salespeople involved in closing the sale. Since they are both equally involved, the **percent contribution** attribute stores the fact that they were both given 50 percent of the credit for the sale. This information could possibly be used in a commissions system. Frank Parks is responsible for processing the order or, in other words, entering the data into the system. Joe Williams is the party responsible for reviewing the information in the order. The order needs to be authorized or approved as a valid commitment by John Smith. Notice that the person roles dictate the party responsible for accomplishing these functions so even if the function has not been performed yet, a party can still be slotted to play a role.

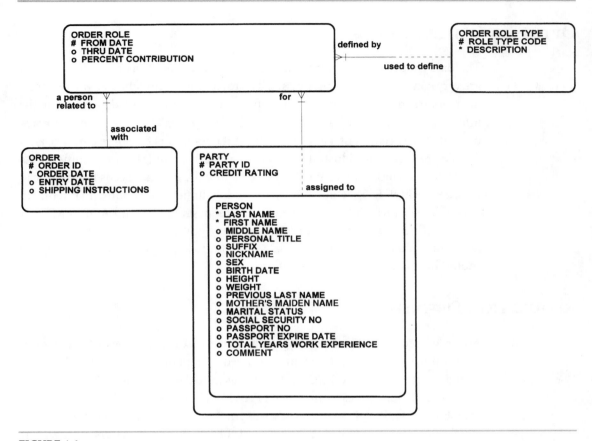

**FIGURE 4.6**

*Person roles for orders.*

**TABLE 4.9**    *Person Order Roles*

| Order ID | Person* | Role* | Percent Contribution |
|----------|---------|-------|----------------------|
| 23000 | John Jones | Salesperson | 50 |
| 23000 | Nancy Barker | Salesperson | 50 |
| 23000 | Frank Parks | Processor | |
| 23000 | Joe Williams | Reviewer | |
| 23000 | John Smith | Authorizer | |

## OPTIONAL ORDER MODELS

The data models and information about orders covered thus far in this chapter are very common to most enterprises. The remainder of this chapter will illustrate data models that may or may not be applicable to an enterprise, depending on the information requirements of each specific enterprise. The data models already presented may represent a complete ORDER data model for some enterprises.

The next sections illustrate additional aspects around the order subject data area. These include: REQUISITIONs to identify the internal needs that may lead to orders, REQUESTs which represent the solicitations of vendors to bid on orders, QUOTEs which are the responses to requests to bid, and AGREEMENTs which define terms and conditions that may govern orders. Each enterprise needs to evaluate which of these data models are applicable to its business and should be incorporated into its design.

## REQUISITION DEFINITION

An order occurs because a party has a need for something. Many enterprises track information about their internal needs. The enterprise's internal need is stored in an entity called REQUISITION, as modeled in Figure 4.7.

A requisition comes from either a PARTY ADDRESS or PARTY CONTACT MECHANISM. People may play various roles in the requisition as shown in the REQUISITION ROLE, REQUISITION ROLE TYPE, and PERSON entities. The requisition may have many statuses over time, so it is related to a REQUISITION STATUS which has possible values from the REQUISITION STATUS TYPE entity. Requisitions have REQUISITION LINE ITEMs, each of which is related to PRODUCTs. Finally, REQUISITION LINE ITEM has a many-to-many relationship to ORDER LINE ITEM in order to identify which requisition line items are fulfilled via which order line items.

### Requisitions and Party Locations

Requisitions have a **requisition date** specifying when the requisition was first created. The **description** attribute defines the need required in the requisition and the **reason** attribute explains why there is a need for the requisition.

Just as orders are tied to party addresses and party contact mechanisms, each REQUISITION may be from either a PARTY ADDRESS or a PARTY CONTACT MECHANISM. This relationship specifies which organization at which location created the requisition.

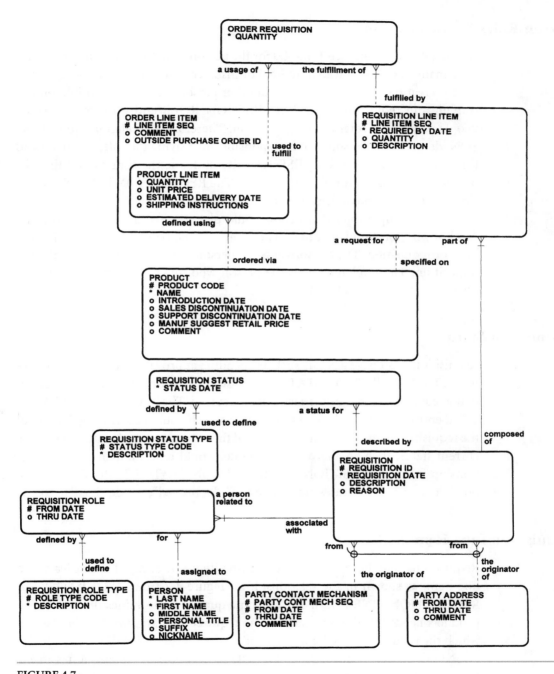

FIGURE 4.7

*Requisition definition.*

## Person Roles for Requisition

Also similar to orders (see Table 4.9 for the person order roles), requisitions may have many people involved in them. For instance, one person may be responsible for creating the requisition and another person may be responsible for approving the requisition. The REQUISITION ROLE entity maintains which people play which roles in the requisition. Therefore, the relationship to PERSON identifies the person who is responsible for playing the role. The from and thru date attributes on REQUISITION ROLE define the time period that the person is responsible for playing the role. The REQUISITION ROLE TYPE entity maintains the possible values for these role types.

Some example roles that people could play in a requisition are "creator", "authorizer", or "implementor". The creator is the person who identified the need or requisition. The authorizer is the person(s) who approves or denies the requisition. The implementor is the person who makes sure that once authorized, the requisition is fulfilled.

## Requisition Status

Requisitions also have a status such as "pending approval", "approved", or "denied". The REQUISITION STATUS entity stores a history of the various statuses of the requisition and the date each status occurred. The REQUISITION STATUS TYPE entity maintains the types of statuses which could occur. If the history of the requisition statuses is unimportant and the enterprise is only interested in the current status, then an alternate data model would reflect a many-to-one relationship from REQUISITION to REQUISITION STATUS TYPE. Examples of possible requisition statuses are "requested", "approved", or "declined".

## Requisition Line Items

Requisitions may have more than one line item but always have at least one line item, as shown in the relationship in Figure 4.7 from REQUISITION to REQUISITION LINE ITEM. The attribute **quantity** determines the number of products needed in the requisition. The **required by date** specifies the date by which the requisition line item is needed.

Notice that the relationship to PRODUCT is optional. A requisition is an enterprise's internal need for *anything*. Some requisitions are for products while others may be for internal work that needs to be done (see Chapter 6 on work efforts for the relationship from requisition to work orders). The **description** attribute allows nonproduct needs to be described.

Table 4.10 shows some examples of requisitions. Requisition 24905 is a requisition to have PCs repaired. The line item specifies a request to fix 14 PCs. The "PC repair" data in the line item refers to a **service** type product which is obtained through the relationship to PRODUCT.

Requisition 30003 shows that the 255 Fetch Street facility of ABC Subsidiary is in need of office supplies to run its own office. These items will most likely be taken out of the existing stock of its own inventory items or they will need to be ordered. Requisition 43005 shows that there was a need for pencils for the 100 Main Street facility of ABC Subsidiary.

Notice that in requisitions 30003 and 43005, the items are specified at a higher level of product since there is not a need to be that specific in these cases. For example, there may be many products that satisfy the first line item in the requisition (i.e., Johnson's #2 pencils, William's #2 pencils, etc.). The recursive relationship on the PRODUCT entity, discussed in Chapter 3, accommodates the ability to specify product needs at various levels of detail, depending on the requirement.

## Order Requisition

A requisition or a need to obtain products can naturally result in orders. One requisition line item may lead to many orders. The need for 150 #2 pencils in Table 4.10 may be fulfilled by several purchase orders. Alternatively, there may be several outstanding requisitions for #2 pencils which may all be ordered in a single order line item. Figure 4.7 therefore shows a many-to-many relationship between REQUISITION LINE ITEM and ORDER LINE ITEM.

The ORDER REQUISITION determines how many items are allocated from an order line item to a requisition line item. For instance, suppose there are two requisitions, each with line items for 150 #2 pencils (300 total pencils needed), and one order line item for 200 of these items which partially fulfills the requisitions. Then it is necessary to specify how many of the order line items were used to fulfill each requisition. The **quantity** attribute in ORDER REQUISITION serves this purpose.

TABLE 4.10  *Requisition and Requisition Line Items*

| Requisition ID | Requisition Date | Requisition Party Location | Description | Reason | Line Item Seq | Qty | Product* | Required By Date |
|---|---|---|---|---|---|---|---|---|
| 24905 | Apr. 13, 1995 | ABC Corporation 100 Main Street | Repair PCs | PCs are inoperable | 1 | 14 | PC Repair | Apr 20, 1995 |
| 30003 | May 15, 1995 | ABC Subsidiary 255 Fetch Street | Requirement for office supplies | Need office supplies for this location's own use | 1 | 150 | #2 Pencils | May 20, 1995 |
|  |  |  |  |  | 2 | 100 | Black Pens | May 20, 1995 |
|  |  |  |  |  | 3 | 200 | Reams of $8\frac{1}{2} \times 11$ white copier paper | May 20, 1995 |
|  |  |  |  |  | 4 | 20 | Boxes of paper clips | May 30, 1995 |
| 43005 | May 16 1996 | ABC Subsidiary 100 Main Street | Requirement for office supplies | Need to increase the stock of pencils | 1 | 200 | #2 Pencils | June 1, 1995 |

# REQUEST DEFINITION

Instead of immediately ordering the products on a requisition, sometimes there is a process of requesting and receiving quotes. A request is a means of asking vendors for bids, quotes, or responses to the requisition.

Figure 4.8 shows the key entities associated with requests. The PARTY ADDRESS and PARTY CONTACT MECHANISM are the creators of a REQUEST. They are also the location of the RESPONDING PARTYs which are the parties that receive the requests. Requests have REQUEST LINE ITEMs specifying the details behind each product required, therefore creating the need for the relationship to PRODUCT. Finally, REQUEST LINE ITEMs are mapped to REQUISITION LINE ITEMs through the REQUISITION REQUEST entity to determine which needs or requisitions of the organization are being requested from other organizations.

## Request

There are several types of requests. The REQUEST entity has three sub-types which are the most common forms of requests. The **RFP** sub-type stands for "request for proposal" and asks vendors to propose a solution to the needs which are specified in the details of the request. The **RFQ** sub-type stands for "request for quote" and asks for bids from vendors on specific products. The **RFI** sub-type stands for "request for information" and is generally sent out before an RFP or RFQ in order to determine preliminary information about the qualification of vendors. This is often used as a mechanism to screen the vendors that will be allowed to respond to an RFP or RFQ.

The REQUEST entity maintains the **request date** which is when the request was created, a **request required date** which is the deadline when vendors need to respond to the request, and a **description** which describes the nature of the request.

Table 4.11 illustrates the information contained in a REQUEST. The first row is a request for information to determine which vendors are qualified enough to bid on repairing PCs. The second row is a request for proposal which follows the RFI and is asking vendors to bid on solutions to the PC repair maintenance needs. The third row illustrates an RFQ which asks vendors to quote their prices and terms for specific office supply products.

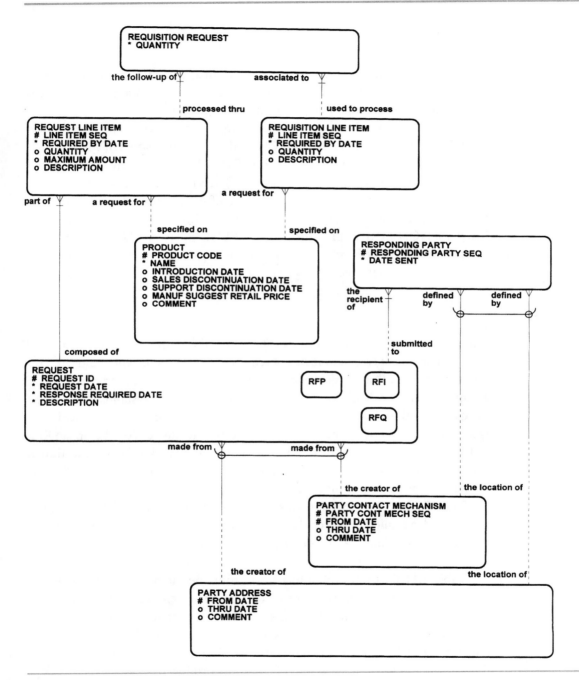

FIGURE 4.8

*Request definition.*

TABLE 4.11   *Requests*

| Request ID | Request Type* | Request Date | Response Required Date | Description |
|---|---|---|---|---|
| 23498 | RFI | Jan 12, 1996 | Feb 10, 1996 | To request information concerning PC repair vendors |
| 38967 | RFP | Mar 13, 1996 | Apr 23, 1996 | To request a quote from vendors on repairing PCs |
| 38948 | RFQ | Mar 13, 1996 | Mar 21, 1996 | To request a quote on office supplies |

Requests are sent by a certain party and sent to certain parties. The data model shows relationships from a REQUEST to either a PARTY ADDRESS or a PARTY CONTACT MECHANISM in order to determine not only the party but the location of the party sending the requests. The request can, of course, be sent to many parties; in the data model this is represented as the relationship to RESPONDING PARTY. A RESPONDING PARTY is one that is asked to respond to a request with either information or a bid, quote, or proposal to the request. Again the RESPONDING PARTY is identified not only by party but also by location in order to track exactly where the request was sent. The **date sent** attribute indicates when the enterprise sent the request to the responding party.

## Request Line Items

Requests have line items describing the various things they need in the request. The REQUEST LINE ITEM has an attribute of **quantity** stating how many of the line items are needed. The **required by date** indicates when the line items need to be delivered to the requesting organization. The **maximum amount** attribute describes an upper limit price for the line item, beyond which the enterprise will not even consider.

The request may be for a specific product, as in an RFQ, or it may be a request asking vendors to provide solutions to a specific problem. If the request is for a product, then the relationship to PRODUCT accommodates these types of request line items. If the request is for a proposal to specific problems as in an RFP, then the **description** attribute maintains a description of the problem.

TABLE 4.12    *Request Line Items*

| Request ID | Request Type* | Description | Request Line Item | Quantity | Product* | Requisition* |
|---|---|---|---|---|---|---|
| 23498 | RFI | To request information concerning PC repair vendors | 1 | | Repair PCs | 24905 |
| 38967 | RFQ | To request a quote from vendors on repairing PCs | 1 | 14 | Repair PCs | 24905 |
| 38948 | RFQ | To request a quote on office supplies | 1 | 350 | #2 Pencils | 30003 |
| | | | 2 | 100 | Black Pens | 43005 |

Requisition line items are related to request line items. One REQUISITION LINE ITEM may be related to more than one REQUEST LINE ITEM. For example, the first two rows of Table 4.12 show that requisition 24905 had two requests associated with it. A request for information was sent out first, then a request for quote followed.

One REQUEST LINE ITEM may be associated with more than one REQUISITION. Table 4.12 also shows that the request for quote 38948 combined the need from requisitions 30003 and 43005. Since there is a many-to-many relationship between requisition line items and request line items, the intersection entity REQUISITION REQUEST is shown on Figure 4.8.

## QUOTE DEFINITION

A *quote* is a response to a request; it is synonymous with a bid or proposal. The quote provides the pricing and terms associated with products which fill the need for the request.

Figure 4.9 shows the data model associated with quotes. Quotes are issued by a party location which is either a PARTY ADDRESS or a PARTY CONTACT MECHANISM. The entity QUOTE stores the basic information related to the quote and is composed of QUOTE LINE ITEMs which describe the specific products being quoted. Therefore, each QUOTE LINE ITEM is a price quote for

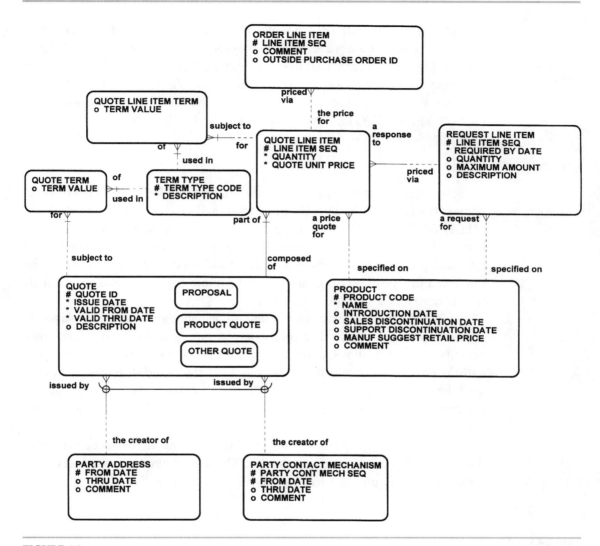

FIGURE 4.9

*Quote definition.*

one and only one PRODUCT. Quotes must be related to a single REQUEST LINE ITEM since quotes are defined as responses to requests. Each QUOTE LINE ITEM may, in turn, lead to one or more ORDER LINE ITEMs, since the quote may be ordered more than once. Each QUOTE or QUOTE LINE ITEM may have terms associated with it which create the need for the relationships to QUOTE TERM, QUOTE LINE ITEM TERM, and TERM TYPE.

## Quote

A quote originates from a party at a location, whether the location is a physical address (i.e., PARTY ADDRESS) or a virtual address (i.e., PARTY CONTACT MECHANISM). The QUOTE entity stores header information about the quote. For example, the **issue date** maintains when the quote was communicated to the intended party. The **valid from date** and **valid thru date** maintain when the quote can first be acted upon and when the quote expires. The **description** attribute describes the nature of the quote.

A QUOTE has a sub-type of PROPOSAL which is generally more elaborate and includes many sections, such as statements of need, proposal descriptions, benefits, cost justifications, resources required, and so forth. Another sub-type is a PRODUCT QUOTE which is simpler and just tracks the terms and prices behind the products being quoted. There may be other types of quotes, such as bids or offers, depending on the enterprise and its terminology. Table 4.13 gives some examples of quotes.

The first quote is a proposal, since within the quote there may be a description of the approach to repairing the PCs. The second quote is a product quote, since it is simply quoting prices for specific pens and pencils.

TABLE 4.13    *Quotes*

| Quote ID | Quote Type | Issue Date | Description | Valid From | Valid Thru |
|----------|------------|------------|-------------|------------|------------|
| 35678 | Proposal | Feb 19, 1996 | Proposal to support the repair of PCs | Feb 19, 1996 | Mar 19, 1996 |
| 36908 | Product Quote | Mar 12, 1995 | Bid on pens and pencils | Mar 12, 1996 | Mar 30, 1996 |

## Quote Line Items

The QUOTE LINE ITEM entity contains information for specific products and is therefore related to PRODUCT. The QUOTE LINE ITEM is also associated with a REQUEST LINE ITEM. One may conclude from looking at this model that the relationship to PRODUCT is unnecessary since it is possible to derive the product that a quote line item references. This may be done by traversing the model from QUOTE LINE ITEM to REQUEST ITEM to PRODUCT. However, the product from the quote may be different from the product requested. For instance, the product requested may be a "#2 pencil". The product quoted may be more specific, such as a "Johnson Red Striped #2 Pencil".

QUOTE LINE ITEM has a many-to-one relationship with REQUEST LINE ITEM. When a request is sent out, the quote, bid, or proposal should correspond to a specific request from an organization, whether it is verbal or written. However, a request, such as an RFP, may have many quotes associated to it since many suppliers may respond.

Table 4.14 shows examples of quotes which correspond to the requests of Table 4.12. Each quote line item corresponds to a request line item. The original request ("38967") called for a quote to fix 14 PCs. The corresponding quote in the first row of Table 4.14 ("35678") was for 70 hours of service which is the estimate for fixing the PCs. Also, notice that in rows 2 and 3, the quote shows more specific products than were asked for in the corresponding requests from Table 4.12.

The QUOTE LINE ITEM may also be associated with an ORDER if the quote is accepted. An ORDER LINE ITEM will generally not have more than one

TABLE 4.14    *Quote Line Item*

| Quote ID | Line Item Seq | Quantity | Product* | Quote Unit Price | Request ID* | Request Line Item Seq* |
|---|---|---|---|---|---|---|
| 35678 | 1 | 70 | PC Repair | $75 | 38967 | 1 |
| 36908 | 1 | 350 | Johnson Red Striped #2 Pencil | $.75 | 38948 | 1 |
| | 2 | 100 | Johnson Black Pens | $1.25 | 38948 | 2 |

QUOTE LINE ITEM associated with it. However, the quote line item may be the basis for the pricing on several orders; therefore, there may be several ORDER LINE ITEMs associated with one QUOTE LINE ITEM.

## Quote Terms

Both quotes and quote line items may have terms associated with them. A quote to fix PCs may have a term stating that someone within the organization needing the repair must act as a central point of contact. The term may specify that if this doesn't exist, the quoted price may be raised. A term of a particular quote line item on furniture items may be that the receiving party needs to pay the actual freight costs incurred.

The relationship from QUOTE to QUOTE TERM allows many terms to be associated with the quote. The QUOTE LINE ITEM may also have many terms associated with it via the relationship to QUOTE LINE ITEM TERM. The TERM TYPE identifies the possible terms that can be applied.

## PERSON ROLES FOR REQUESTS AND QUOTES

Just as orders and requisitions have people associated with them in various roles, requests and quotes also have people playing various roles. Figure 4.10 shows the data model for request and quote roles. This model is very similar to Figure 4.6, except the roles are for requests and quotes instead of for orders. Examples of roles for a request might be "entered by", "written by", "reviewed by", and "sent by". Examples of roles for a quote might be "quoted by", "reviewed by", and "approved by".

## AGREEMENT DEFINITION

An *agreement* is a set of terms and conditions which govern the relationship between two parties—for example, a customer and a supplier. A key difference between an order and an agreement is that an order is a one-time commitment to buy products while an agreement specifies how the two parties will conduct business over time.

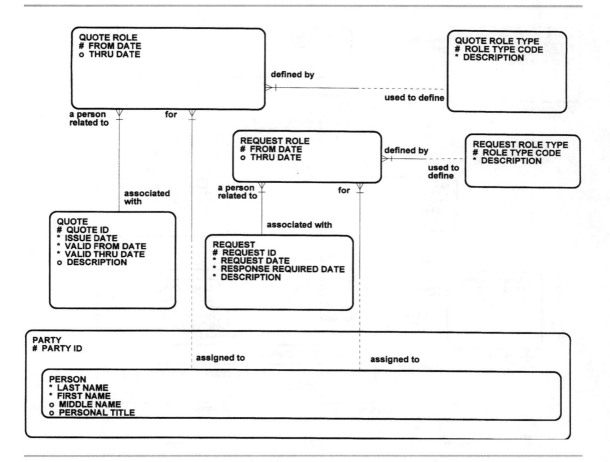

FIGURE 4.10

*Person roles for requests and quotes.*

Figure 4.11 shows the data model associated with agreements. An AGREE-MENT is associated with one and only one PARTY RELATIONSHIP. Agreements are classified into AGREEMENT TYPEs. EXHIBITs to further describe the agreement and ADDENDUMs to modify the agreement may be attached. Each AGREEMENT may be composed of one or more AGREEMENT LINE ITEMs which, in turn, may be related to a specific PRODUCT. Both AGREE-MENT and AGREEMENT LINE ITEM may have terms associated with them

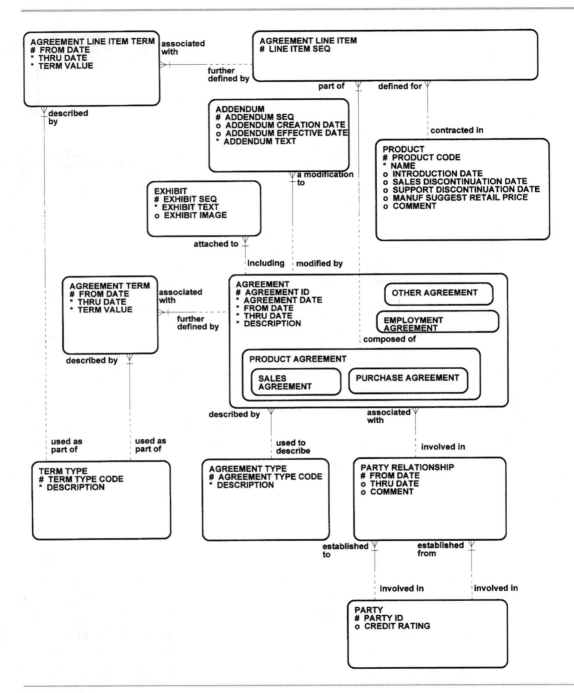

FIGURE 4.11

*Agreement definition.*

and are thus further defined by one or more AGREEMENT TERMs or AGREE-MENT LINE ITEM TERMs.

## Agreement

The party relationship defines the parties involved in the agreement and the roles of the parties. Therefore, each PARTY RELATIONSHIP may be involved in one or more AGREEMENTs. For example, there may exist an informal customer and supplier party relationship which, when formalized, is done so through an agreement.

There are many different types of agreements. PRODUCT AGREEMENTs define the terms and conditions of the buying and selling of products. A PRODUCT AGREEMENT may be sub-typed as either a SALES AGREEMENT or a PURCHASE AGREEMENT. Agreement 10002 in Table 4.15 is a SALES AGREE-MENT. The EMPLOYMENT AGREEMENT sub-type defines the arrangement behind an employee and employer relationship. Agreement 86749 in Table 4.15 is an employment agreement. There may be other types of agreements depending on the enterprise involved. For example, there may be ownership agreements, real estate agreements, franchising agreements, licensing agreements, and so on. The AGREEMENT TYPE maintains the various types of agreements that are valid for the enterprise.

TABLE 4.15 *Agreement*

| Agreement ID | Type | Description | From Party | To Party | Starting Date | Ending Date |
|---|---|---|---|---|---|---|
| 10002 | Customer-vendor relationship agreement | Agreement regarding the pricing and terms of buying inventory items | ACME Company | ABC Corporation | Jan 1, 1996 | Dec 30, 1996 |
| 86749 | Employment agreement | Hired William as an entry-level information systems programmer | William Jones | ABC Corporation | May 7, 1990 | |

## Agreement Exhibits and Addendums

Agreements may have exhibits and addendums. Exhibits illustrate details behind the agreement, such as a schedule of payments or a full description of the products being agreed upon. Addendums are modifications to an agreement.

Each AGREEMENT may include one or more EXHIBITs. The EXHIBIT entity includes an attribute for text which describes the exhibit. The attribute **exhibit image** may maintain a scanned image or other information representation of the exhibit, or it may just maintain the file location of an image or document.

Each AGREEMENT may be modified by one or more ADDENDUMs. The ADDENDUM entity maintains the **addendum creation date** which is when the addendum was created and an **addendum effective date** which is when the addendum goes into effect. The **addendum text** describes the addendum. An example of an addendum is a time extension to the thru date of a customer-vendor agreement. In this case the **thru date** would be updated in the AGREEMENT entity and an ADDENDUM would be added to show the history of changes to the agreement.

## Agreement Line Item

Each PRODUCT AGREEMENT is composed of one or more AGREEMENT LINE ITEMs which must be defined for one and only one PRODUCT. The purpose of the AGREEMENT LINE ITEM is to specify parts of the agreement which relate to a specific product. The key information for each AGREEMENT LINE ITEM is maintained via its relationships to the PRODUCT it refers to, the terms associated with the agreement line item (discussed in the next section), and the pricing of the agreement line item (discussed later in this chapter).

Table 4.16 shows a simple example that agreement 10002 is an agreement that has two line items and therefore it is an agreement that governs the terms for the buying of two products: "Johnson fine grade 8½ × 11 blue bond paper" and "Jerry's box of 3½-inch diskettes".

## Agreement and Agreement Line Item Terms

An agreement and its line items each have terms associated with them. The AGREEMENT TERM entity stores the valid terms of the agreement as well as the

**TABLE 4.16**  *Agreement Line Items*

| Agreement ID | Agreement Line Item Seq | Product* |
|---|---|---|
| 10002 | 1 | Johnson fine grade $8\frac{1}{2} \times 11$ blue bond paper |
| | 2 | Jerry's box of $3\frac{1}{2}$ inch diskettes |

effective dates of the terms. There are different types of terms which can be referenced from the TERM TYPE entity. Terms and conditions can include clauses for renewals, agreement termination, indemnification, noncompetition, and provisions for exclusive relationships.

For example, a product agreement between a supplier and its customer may call for an exclusive arrangement preventing the supplier from selling its products to the customer's competitors. An example of this exclusive arrangement is found when a consulting firm performs services for its client that involves sensitive inside information which would need to be safeguarded from the competition. Therefore, the customer may request that the supplier not do business with the customer's competitors for a specified time in order to protect its confidentiality. In Table 4.17, the first row of data gives an example of an AGREEMENT TERM that is subject to agreement 23884. The term is that the agreement calls for an exclusive arrangement prohibiting the supplier from supplying similar services to the customer's competitors for up to 60 days.

Each agreement line item may have terms associated with it. The AGREEMENT LINE ITEM TERM entity stores the valid terms of the agreement line item. These terms can be independent of product pricing. The second, third, and fourth rows of Table 4.17 show examples of agreement line items and the terms associated with them. The second and third rows (agreement ID #10002, line item #1) represent the same AGREEMENT LINE ITEM for the product "Johnson fine grade $8\frac{1}{2} \times 11$ blue bond paper". There is more than one term associated with this agreement line item. The two terms specify that the agreement line item  is only valid for up to 1,000 of these items between January 1, 1996 and December 31, 1996. The agreement also has a term that the dollars expended cannot exceed $10,000 from January 1, 1996 through June 30, 1996. The fourth row (agreement ID #10002, line item #2) specifies that the customer is agreeing to buy these types of products  exclusively from the supplier.

TABLE 4.17    *Agreement and Agreement Line Item Terms*

| Agreement ID | Agreement Line Item Seq | Product* | Term Type* | Term Value | From Date | Thru Date |
|---|---|---|---|---|---|---|
| 23884 | | | Exclusive arrangement prohibiting supplier from supplying similar services to customer's competitors for specified number of days | 60 | | |
| 10002 | 1 | Johnson fine grade 8½ × 11 blue bond paper | Quantity not to exceed | 1000 | Jan 1, 1996 | Dec 31, 1996 |
| | | | Dollars not to exceed | $10,000 | Jan 1, 1996 | June 30, 1996 |
| | 2 | Jerry's box of 3½ inch diskettes | Customer will exclusively buy from supplier | | Jan 1, 1996 | Dec 30, 1996 |

## Relationship of Agreement to Order

As illustrated in Figure 4.12, each ORDER may be governed by one and only one AGREEMENT. Each AGREEMENT and ORDER have line items which are related to PRODUCT.

The fact that orders are governed by agreements means that the order is subject to the pricing and terms of the agreement. Of course, it is possible for an order to override the pricing and terms of an agreement in some circumstances. For example, perhaps there is an agreement between a customer and a supplier that a certain type of pen will cost $2.00 each. All orders generally follow the terms of this agreement; however, the supplier might make an exception and discount the price of pens by $.50 for a specific order due to a complaint on a late delivery of a previous order. This may be a gesture on the part of the supplier, even though there are no terms or conditions to give this discount.

Instead of directly relating the order to the agreement, why not realize that

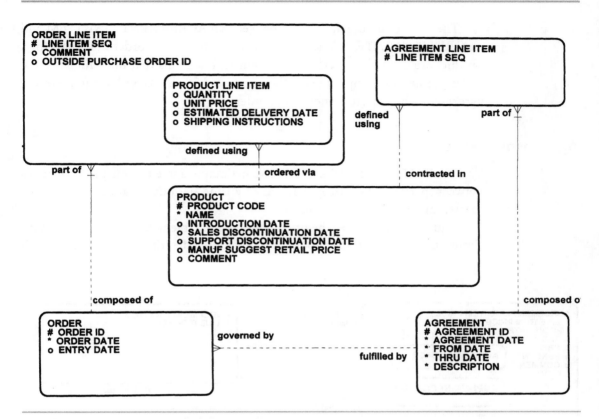

**FIGURE 4.12**

*Relationship of agreement to order.*

orders are affected by agreements if they both have the same parties involved? This would eliminate the need for the relationship between the ORDER and the AGREEMENT since this relationship could be derived by selecting the orders and agreements with the same parties. The problem with this is that the same two parties may have several different agreements in place.

For example, ABC Corporation and ACME Company may have an agreement in place to purchase certain items at specified prices, but they may also have a separate agreement in place for any repairs required to products. In this case, it is important to apply the terms of the appropriate agreement to the order. Therefore, it is necessary to specify the direct relationship from the order to the agreement which it references.

There is no direct relationship between an AGREEMENT LINE ITEM and an ORDER LINE ITEM. The reason for this is that when order line items for a product are created, any effective agreement line items that may influence the order can be looked up by using the same product key as well as the ID of the agreement which corresponds to the order.

## Agreement Pricing

The entity AGREEMENT LINE ITEM maintains agreed-upon product prices between parties. The prices may vary by time periods, quantities, party addresses, and geographic regions.

Figure 4.13 illustrates the pricing model for agreements. This model is very similar in structure to the product pricing model described in Chapter 3. Each

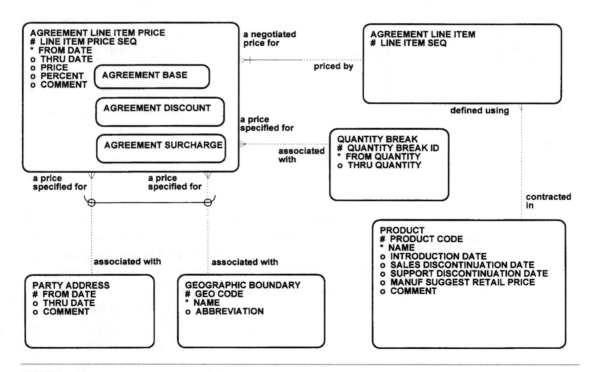

FIGURE 4.13

*Agreement pricing.*

AGREEMENT LINE ITEM may have many AGREEMENT LINE ITEM PRICEs. These AGREEMENT LINE ITEM PRICEs may be either a base price (AGREEMENT BASE), discount (AGREEMENT DISCOUNT), or a surcharge (AGREEMENT SURCHARGE) similar to the sub-types of PRODUCT PRICE COMPONENT in Figure 3.4. The attribute **price** is used to record base prices, flat discounts, or flat surcharges. The term flat implies that the attribute contains only dollar amounts. The attribute **percent** is used to record percentages for discounts or surcharges to certain agreement line items. The relationships to QUANTITY BREAK allow prices to be dependent on the number of products agreed to be purchased. The relationship to either PARTY ADDRESS or GEOGRAPHIC BOUNDARY allows agreements to be based upon the customer's specific address or the customer's geographic area.

Table 4.18 gives some examples of product agreement pricing. The three rows are the pricing arrangement for agreement 10002 line item 1 which refers to the product "Johnson fine grade 8½ × 11 blue bond paper". The agreement says that the price in the eastern region for this product is $7.00 and in the western region the price is $7.50. If more than 1,000 reams are ordered in the same order, then there is a 2 percent discount on this product.

With the addition of this agreement pricing model, product pricing may be determined by three different means: through the standard price associated with a product, through an agreement made in advance, or through a specific negotiation of an order. It is important to specify the business rules that govern when to use which price. Most enterprises have business rules in place that an agree-

**TABLE 4.18**  *Agreement Line Item Price*

| Agreement ID | Agreement Line Item Seq | Product* | Agreement Line Item Price Type* | Geographic Boundary* | Qty Break From | Qty Break Thru | Price | Percent |
|---|---|---|---|---|---|---|---|---|
| 10002 | 1 | Johnson fine grade 8½ × 11 blue bond paper | Base Region | Eastern | | | $7.00 | |
| | | | Base | Western Region | | | $7.50 | |
| | | | Discount | | 1000 | | | 2 |

ment will override the standard product price and specific negotiation on an order will overrule standard product prices or agreements.

## SUMMARY

The data model from this chapter provides a way to maintain information about orders, requisitions, requests, quotes, and agreements (see Figure 4.14). These models incorporate both sales and purchase order perspectives as well as service and item perspectives.

Orders go through a process, beginning with a requisition or a need for a product(s). The requisition may be directly fulfilled by an order or it may lead to a request to suppliers, a quote, then an order. Agreements may be established in advance which govern relationships between parties and influence terms and pricing. This chapter models most of the information that many enterprises need to establish commitments between parties. Models for delivering these commitments are covered in Chapters 5 and 6.

Please refer to Appendix A for more detailed attribute characteristics or the CD-ROM product, that must be purchased separately, for SQL scripts used to implement this data model. The CD-ROM includes scripts to build tables, columns, and constraints.

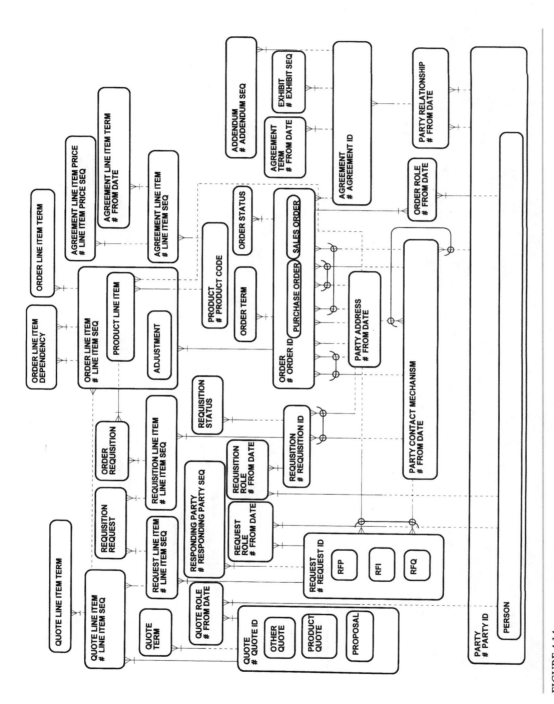

FIGURE 4.14

*Complete order model.*

111

# 5

# ORDER DELIVERY AND INVOICING

## INTRODUCTION

Now that orders have been taken, how do they get to their destinations and, once there, how are they paid for? Other questions to answer are:

What is being shipped?

When will it ship?

To and from where is it shipped?

What is the current status of the shipment?

Was the entire order shipped or only part of it?

Has anyone been billed for it?

Who was billed and what was it for?

How were they billed?

When was the bill sent?

This chapter will deal with the shipment of items and the billing or invoicing for products which have been delivered. As will be shown, the information to support these functions does not, at first glance, seem very complex; however, the data interrelationships in a real-world environment can be complicated.

Models discussed in this chapter are:

- Shipment definition
- Shipment methods
- Shipping lots
- Shipment and order association
- Invoice definition
- Shipment and invoice association
- Invoice billing

## SHIPMENT DEFINITION

The basic data model for shipments is fairly straightforward (see Figure 5.1). There is the SHIPMENT entity, which can have many types. The relationships from SHIPMENT to PARTY ADDRESS track where the shipment began and where the shipment was delivered to. Each SHIPMENT may be detailed by many SHIPMENT LINE ITEMS. The INVENTORY ITEM entity provides a mechanism to track what was shipped or received via the line items. Since shipments may change state during their life cycle (i.e., from "in transit" to "delivered"), the SHIPMENT STATUS HISTORY entity is needed to describe the state of the shipment at various points in time.

There are many things that an enterprise may need to know about a shipment. Some are critical; some are not so critical. The first thing to record in the SHIPMENT entity is the **estimated ship date**, which indicates when the shipment is expected to begin its journey to the client. This will be critical to customer service personnel when an irate client calls to see what happened to his or her order. The **estimated ready date** documents when the item is expected to be ready for shipment (perhaps there is packaging or other preparation needed for the item). Other bits of information to know include **estimated arrival date, estimated shipping cost, actual shipping cost** (may be important for billing), and any special **handling instructions** (i.e., "fragile", "requires signature upon delivery", etc.). In the case of a cancellation, there is a need to know the latest date the shipment could be canceled. The **last updated** attribute provides a way to determine when this information was last changed, since the estimated dates may

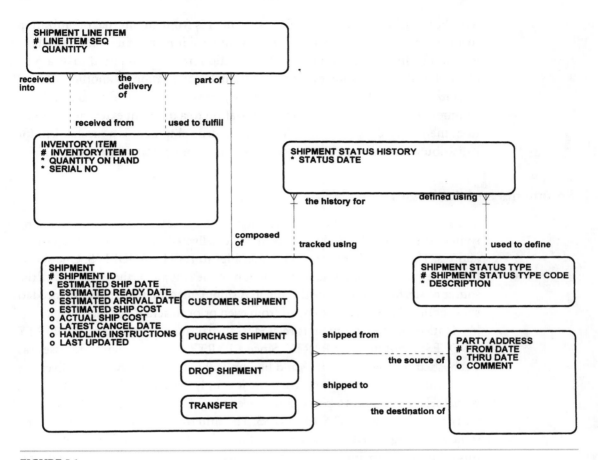

FIGURE 5.1

*Shipment definition.*

change frequently, although the enterprise would hope not. The actual dates of all these events are recorded in SHIPMENT STATUS HISTORY, which is discussed in a later section.

## Shipment Types

As can be seen in Figure 5.1, several sub-types on the SHIPMENT entity are included in the model to distinguish between some basic types of shipments. These types could be inferred based on the organizations involved in the shipment, but have been included for clarity. If the shipment is from an internal organization to an external organization, then it is a customer shipment. If it is an external organization shipping to an internal organization, then it is referred to as a purchase shipment. A shipment from an internal organization to another internal organization (e.g., from department A to department B) is called a transfer. If the shipment moves from an external organization to a different external organization, then it is a drop shipment. Typically, a drop shipment is a mechanism for a distributor to ship products directly from its supplier to its customer.

## Shipments and Addresses

The shipment would not be a shipment if the enterprise wasn't sending something somewhere—but where? Shipments must be delivered to and from a location or address. Therefore, there are two relationships to PARTY ADDRESS. One shows the address that is the ultimate destination of the shipment; the other shows the source or starting point of the shipment. A shipment, once scheduled, will need to show both **shipped to** and **shipped from** even prior to actual shipment.

Notice that the shipment is related to a party at an address (i.e., the PARTY ADDRESS), not just to a PARTY. Since a PARTY can have many addresses (as established in Chapter 2), it would be impossible to know where to deliver the shipment if the shipment information was only related to the PARTY entity. Nonetheless, the **ship to party** is still needed and can be determined from the party related to the PARTY ADDRESS. The **ship to party** will most likely be the same as the **requested ship to party** of the order. Therefore, it is possible to use this information to limit the number of possible addresses when creating the relationship from the SHIPMENT to the PARTY ADDRESS. (Actually this would need to be enforced with a business rule—the party ID on a shipment must be the same as the party ID of the requested ship to on the order.)

This may appear to be a duplication of data (party address information tied to both shipment and order data), but the information needs to appear in both places since the shipment record may not be created until much later than the order. If the shipment record was created during order entry, then the information could be stored only in the shipment record. This, of course, could also be controlled through business rules and processes.

The **ship from party** also needs to be determined. The shipment might be from a physical warehouse within an enterprise or it may be drop-shipped from the supplier. In either case, the party and its address (i.e., the PARTY ADDRESS)

TABLE 5.1 *Shipment Data with Addresses*

| Shipment ID | Estimated Ship Date | Estimated Arrival Date | Ship to Party Address* | Ship from Party Address* |
|---|---|---|---|---|
| 1235 | Mar 6, 1996 | Mar 8, 1996 | ACME Company 234 Stretch Street | ABC Subsidiary 100 Main Street |
| 1294 | Apr 9, 1996 | Apr 12, 1996 | General Goods Corporation | ABC Corporation 100 Main Street |

needs to be specified. Table 5.1 shows some sample data regarding SHIPMENT and related PARTY ADDRESS information.

## Shipment Line Items

Now that one can tell where a shipment is going to and coming from, and when it is being shipped, it is necessary to know what is being shipped and how many items are being shipped. The SHIPMENT LINE ITEM entity will provide information on how many items will be shipped or are scheduled to be shipped. Details about what was shipped are found in the INVENTORY ITEM entity, including the item ID. Table 5.2 highlights possible data for SHIPMENT LINE ITEM.

There are two relationships from SHIPMENT LINE ITEM to INVENTORY ITEM that not only track what is sent, but also what has been received. The optional relationships allow for all the possible types of shipments described earlier. With this model, it is possible to record not only outgoing shipments but incoming shipments as well. The tracking of incoming shipments could be very useful for an automated inventory tracking system. Once the arrival of a shipment has been recorded, a process could then automatically update the **quantity on hand** attribute of the INVENTORY ITEM entity.

TABLE 5.2 *Shipment Line Items*

| Shipment ID | Line Item Seq | Quantity | Inventory Item* |
|---|---|---|---|
| 1223 | 1 | 20 | Goldstein Elite Pens |
| | 2 | 300 | Jones #2 Pencils |
| | 3 | 500 | Standard Erasers |

Note that in the Order model (see Chapter 4), ORDER LINE ITEMs are related to the type of product or ITEM; however, SHIPMENT LINE ITEMs are related to the actual physical item shipped or INVENTORY ITEM. Not only is this an important distinction for inventory tracking, but it could also be important for such things as warranty support or part replacement and repair.

## Shipment Status History

The entity SHIPMENT STATUS HISTORY in Figure 5.1 allows for the accurate tracking of the status of the shipment over its life. The status (from SHIPMENT STATUS TYPE) identifies the state of the shipment at a point in time. Possible statuses include: "scheduled", "shipped", "enroute", "delivered", "canceled". This model will allow the storage of any and all statuses of interest to the enterprise. Table 5.3 shows sample data that could be stored with this entity.

# SHIPMENT METHODS

Figure 5.2 covers information about the method of shipment in order to track shipments and the vehicle used in shipments. The SHIPMENT METHOD entity contains information about the way the item(s) was shipped. The various types of shipment methods described in SHIPMENT METHOD TYPE include "truck", "UPS", "air", "U.S. Postal Service", "ship", "train", or any other method a company chooses. Each SHIPMENT may be shipped via one or more SHIPMENT METHODS. For example, a shipment may require transportation by train, then by truck.

**TABLE 5.3**   *Shipment Status History Data*

| Shipment ID | Shipment Status* | Status Date |
|---|---|---|
| 1235 | scheduled | Mar 6, 1996 |
| | shipped | Mar 7, 1996 |
| | delivered | Mar 9, 1996 |
| 1294 | scheduled | Apr 9, 1997 |
| | canceled | Apr 10, 1997 |

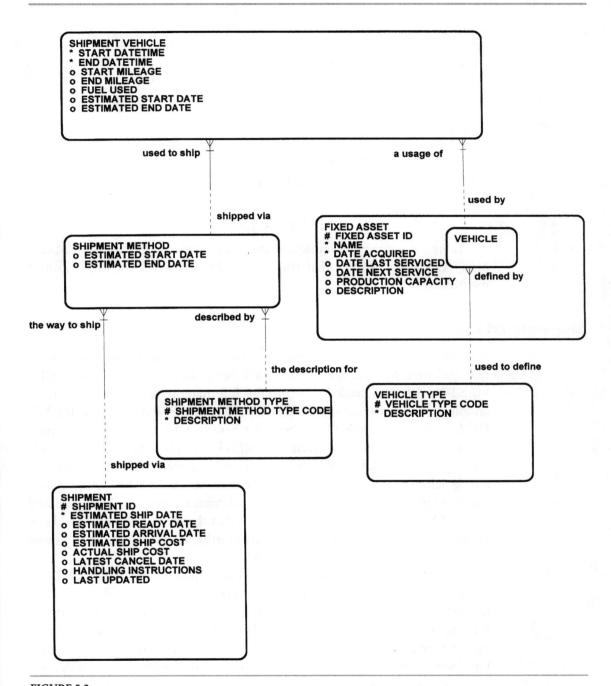

FIGURE 5.2

*Shipment method and shipment vehicle.*

**TABLE 5.4**  *Shipment Method*

| Shipment ID | Shipment Method* |
|-------------|-------------------|
| 1235        | Train             |
|             | Truck             |
| 1498        | Cargo ship        |
| 2390        | United Parcel Service |
| 2396        | United States Postal Service |

Table 5.4 contains examples of what might be stored in the SHIPMENT METHOD entity. Notice that shipment 1235 is shipped via two shipment methods.

## Shipment Vehicle

If an enterprise does its own shipping and owns the method of shipment, then it may also need to track the actual vehicle being used. Thus, the entity SHIP-MENT VEHICLE is needed to record this information (see Figure 5.2). This is an intersection entity between SHIPMENT METHOD and the sub-entity VE-HICLE which is part of FIXED ASSET (further explained in Chapter 7). There is a one-to-many relationship from SHIPMENT METHOD to SHIPMENT VE-HICLE because a package may be transferred from one vehicle to another over a long delivery route. Conversely, one truck could certainly be used to deliver many shipments, thus the one-to-many relationship between VEHICLE and SHIPMENT VEHICLE. Notice in Table 5.5 that shipment 1235, which had two methods of shipment, is now broken down further into the actual trucks being used in the "*truck*" portion of the shipment.

Information that enterprises may want to keep about the SHIPMENT VE-HICLE would be the statistics behind the usage of the vehicle, such as the start-ing and ending mileage (if appropriate), and amount of fuel used. For detailed tracking one may also want to track the date and time a particular vehicle picked up a shipment and when it unloaded it. With this information it can easily be de-termined in what order multiple vehicles were used to deliver a single shipment and how long it took, including transfers. See Table 5.5 for examples.

**TABLE 5.5** *Shipment Vehicle Data*

| Shipment ID | Shipment Method | Vehicle Name* | Actual Start Time | Actual End Time | Start Mileage | End Mileage | Fuel Used |
|---|---|---|---|---|---|---|---|
| 1235 | Truck | Truck #1 | Mar 7, 1996, 10:00 A.M. | Mar 7, 1996 11:35 A.M. | 52,000 | 52,061 | 2 gallons |
| | | Truck #25 | Mar 7, 1996 12:05 P.M. | Mar 7, 1996 8:16 P.M. | 73,525 | 74,006 | 25 gallons |
| 1333 | | Truck #1 | Mar 7, 1996 10:00 A.M. | Mar 7, 1996 2:12 P.M. | 52,000 | 52,190 | 6.5 gallons |

In the example given, one shipment (#1235) is delivered using two vehicles (Truck #1 and Truck #25). Looking at the appropriate start and end times, it is possible to determine that there was a 30-minute delay in the delivery of shipment #1235 while it was being transferred from the first vehicle to the second. Also, notice in the data that the vehicle "Truck #1" was used to deliver a second shipment (#1333). The reason the start time is the same as the previous shipment is that the truck contained two shipments which were loaded at the same time.

The data shown also provides information for calculating the real cost of the delivery. It shows the mileage and amount of fuel used. Knowing the cost of fuel, it would be possible to determine this part of the cost of delivery for each shipment. Additionally, mileage could be used to determine wear and tear on the vehicles used.

An enterprise may also need to track estimated dates for each shipment method and for each vehicle in order to determine if the shipment is running behind schedule. The **estimated start date** and **estimated end date** attributes on SHIPMENT METHOD and SHIPMENT VEHICLE provide this additional functionality, if it is needed.

## SHIPPING LOTS

A concept found in some production-oriented industries is that of the LOT. A lot is simply a grouping of items of the same type generally used to track inventory items back to their source; it is often the result of a production run. This information is very important in the event a recall of items is required.

Inventory items can be separately identified by lots because an INVEN-TORY ITEM may be made up of one and only one LOT (see Figure 5.3). This implies that there may be more than one inventory item of the same item type at a specific location, if there is more than one lot involved.

Shipment line items, by definition, belong to one and only one inventory item that may be identified by one and only one lot. If a shipment line item could be associated with more than one inventory item, then there would be no way to identify which items came from which lots. For example, a supplier wants to ship two tons of a specific metal compound. The lot sizes for this supplier are one ton each. Because of this, it is necessary for the shipment to contain two line items—one for each ton of metal sent. While each ton shipped may be for the same type of item, the lot ID and inventory item ID would be different, allowing items to be traced back to their originating lot. In this manner, the customer will be able to tell which lot the metal received belonged to.

A SHIPMENT LINE ITEM may be received into one and only one INVEN-TORY ITEM. When this occurs, the inventory item's **quantity on hand** increases. If the enterprise has a need to subdivide the inventory item into separate lots, then the inventory item may be subdivided after it is has been received. Out-

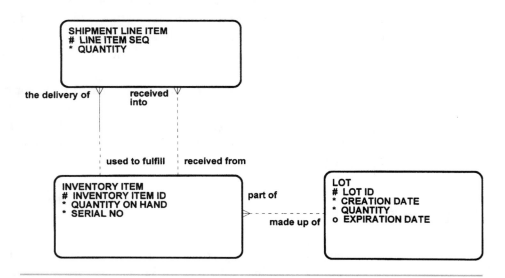

FIGURE 5.3

*Shipping lots.*

**TABLE 5.6**  *Inventory Item Lot Information*

| Shipment Type* | Shipment ID* | Line Item Seq* | Quantity | Inventory Item* | Lot ID |
|---|---|---|---|---|---|
| Purchase Shipment | 2909 | 1 | 100 | Williams Invisible Ink Pens | A1245 |
| Customer Shipment | 3590 | 1 | 50 | Office Desk Set | 13893 |

going shipments of inventory items require the reducing of the **quantity on hand** attribute from the INVENTORY ITEM identified by the appropriate lot.

Table 5.6 gives sample data regarding items identified by lots. Shipment 2909 shows an incoming shipment line item where the enterprise wishes to track the supplier's lot ID. If an INVENTORY ITEM record and LOT record already exist for ID #A1245, then the **quantity** from the SHIPMENT LINE ITEM will be added to the **quantity on hand** on the INVENTORY ITEM. In this way, the lot identification is maintained. If this lot ID does not exist in the LOT entity, then a new LOT record and INVENTORY ITEM record will be created using the information from the SHIPMENT LINE ITEM. The second row shows that on a customer shipment (#3590), for the office desk sets that are shipped, the lot identification number is tracked so that if there is a customer complaint at a later time, it will be possible to identify where the items came from.

## SHIPMENTS AND ORDER ASSOCIATION

For the data model to be truly integrated and functional, there is a need to link orders taken to the shipments made. This will be handled through the entity ORDER SHIPMENT (see Figure 5.4). This entity is the resolution of a many-to-many relationship between SHIPMENT LINE ITEM and ORDER LINE ITEM. The many-to-many is required in order to handle partial shipments and combined shipments. Tables 5.7, 5.8, and 5.9 give some sample data to demonstrate this relationship. The data in these tables may seem complex, but there is a very good explanation behind this: In the real world, the relationship between orders and shipments is a complex one.

Table 5.9 illustrates how one order line item could be distributed across multiple shipments. The first two lines of Table 5.9 show the relationship of one

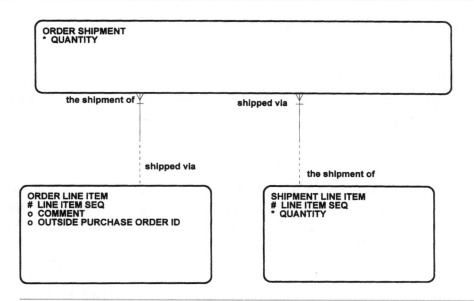

FIGURE 5.4

*Shipment and order association.*

order line item to two shipment line items. Order ID #100, line item #1 (from Table 5.7) was partially delivered by shipment #9000, item #1, then completed in a later delivery of shipment #9400, item #1, with a quantity of 1,000 to the first and 500 to the second. In this way, the entire order of 1,500 Jones #2 Pencils was delivered.

Conversely, one shipment line item could be used to deliver items from more than one order. The third and fifth rows of Table 5.9 illustrate this point. Shipment ID #9000, line item #2, combines a partial shipment of order #100, item #2 (700 out of 2,500 Elite Pens ordered), with order #200, item #1 (300 Elite Pens). The partial shipment could be due to a lack of inventory at the time the shipment was made. This scenario assumes that business rules and processes are in place to ensure that both orders (i.e., #100 and #200) are intended to go to the same location and are for the same product. Note that the relationship is not between ORDER (as opposed to ORDER LINE ITEM) and SHIPMENT be-cause it is usually necessary to track the actual line items being ordered and shipped.

**TABLE 5.7**    *Order Line Item Data*

| Order ID | Line Item Seq ID | Quantity | Product* |
|----------|------------------|----------|----------|
| 100      | 1                | 1500     | Jones #2 Pencils |
|          | 2                | 2500     | Goldstein Elite Pens |
|          | 3                | 350      | Standard Erasers |
| 200      | 1                | 300      | Goldstein Elite Pens |
|          | 2                | 200      | Boxes of HD Diskettes |

**TABLE 5.8**    *Shipment Line Item Data*

| Shipment ID | Line Item Seq | Quantity | Product* |
|-------------|---------------|----------|----------|
| 9000        | 1             | 1000     | Jones #2 Pencils |
|             | 2             | 1000     | Goldstein Elite Pens |
|             | 3             | 100      | Boxes of HD Diskettes |
| 9200        | 1             | 350      | Standard Erasers |
|             | 2             | 100      | Boxes of HD Diskettes |
|             | 3             | 1500     | Jones #2 Pencils |
| 9400        | 1             | 500      | Jones #2 Pencils |

**TABLE 5.9**    *Order Shipment Cross-reference Data*

| Order ID | Order Line Item Seq | Shipment Id | Shipment Line Item Seq | Quantity (Shipped) |
|----------|---------------------|-------------|------------------------|--------------------|
| 100      | 1                   | 9000        | 1                      | 1000               |
|          | 1                   | 9400        | 1                      | 500                |
|          | 2                   | 9000        | 2                      | 700                |
|          | 3                   | 9200        | 1                      | 350                |
| 200      | 1                   | 9000        | 2                      | 300                |
|          | 2                   | 9000        | 3                      | 100                |
|          | 2                   | 9200        | 2                      | 100                |

## INVOICE DEFINITION

Now that items have been shipped, it is critical for the enterprise to make sure that correct invoices are sent out which correspond to the appropriate shipments. As many data modelers will agree, like shipments, invoices also have headers and detail line items (see Figure 5.5). First there is the INVOICE entity which can have multiple INVOICE STATUSes and INVOICE TERMs. In addition, invoices are composed of one or more INVOICE LINE ITEMs.

As with shipments, there are many things needed in order to send a correct bill to customers. The first thing to record about the invoice (besides a unique identifier) is the invoice creation date or **invoice date**. This will be an important piece of information used in tracking the progress of the invoice when a client calls to discuss his or her bill. Some systems may want to include a specific note or message to the customer on the invoice, so the model includes the attribute **message**. Table 5.10 shows sample data for the INVOICE entity.

### Invoice Status

Similar to orders, the state of an invoice changes over time. To track this, the entity INVOICE STATUS is used. It is an intersection entity between INVOICE and INVOICE STATUS TYPE. Examples of statuses include: "sent", "void", and "approved". "Paid" is not a valid status because it can be determined via payment transactions which will be discussed later in Chapter 7. Additionally, the need to know when this status took effect is provided by the attribute **status date**. Table 5.11 shows how this data might look.

To find the current status, look for the most recent date. Note that if the number of statuses is somewhat limited, these items would be good candidates

TABLE 5.10    *Invoice Data*

| Invoice ID | Invoice Date | Message | Description |
|---|---|---|---|
| 30002 | May 25, 1996 | | Fulfillment of office supply order |
| 30005 | June 5, 1996 | Thanks for the business! | |

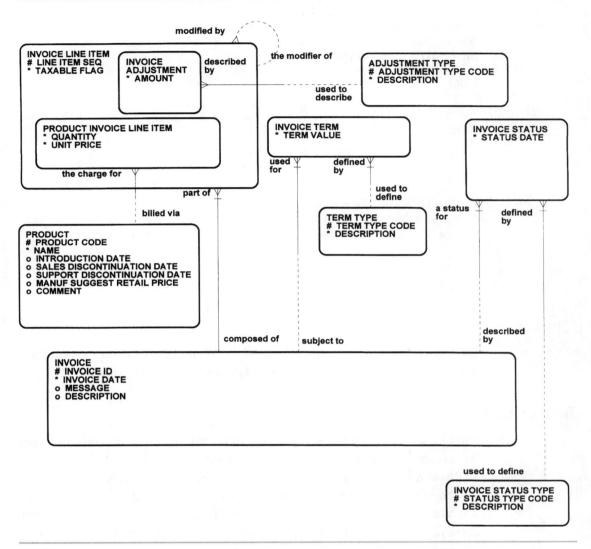

FIGURE 5.5

*Invoice definition.*

**TABLE 5.11**  *Invoice Status Data*

| Invoice ID | Status Type* | Status Date |
|---|---|---|
| 30002 | Approved | May 25, 1996 |
| | Sent | June 30, 1996 |
| 30005 | Sent | June 5, 1996 |
| | Void | June 6, 1996 |

**TABLE 5.12**  *Invoice Term Data*

| Invoice ID | Term Type Description* | Term Value |
|---|---|---|
| 30002 | Payment—net days | 30 |
| | Late Fee—percent | 2 |
| | Penalty for collection agency—percent | 5 |

for denormalization in a physical model. If the model was denormalized, there may be **approved date**, **sent date**, **paid date**, and **void date** attributes.

## Invoice Terms

Some systems or enterprises might need to record various terms and conditions on invoices, such as payment terms. The model handles this with the INVOICE TERM and INVOICE TERM TYPE entities. Table 5.12 shows some sample data.

This data indicates that for invoice #30002, the payment is due in 30 days. If it is late, there is a 2 percent late fee added. If the invoice is sent to a collection agency, then there is an additional 5 percent added to the amount due. Discounts for early payment may also be tracked through this entity.

## Invoice Line Items

Invoices, like shipments and orders, have many line items showing the detailed information about the items or services sold. This data is represented by the entity INVOICE LINE ITEM. Within this entity the majority of the information will be associated with the sub-entity PRODUCT INVOICE LINE ITEM. This sub-entity has the relationship to PRODUCT. Examples of product line item data are shown in Table 5.13.

In addition to the invoice ID and product code, the details include: the quantity of items being billed, the unit price, and whether this is a taxable transaction. Note that product-specific information, such as unit of measure for the quantity, can be derived through the relationship to PRODUCT, then to PRODUCT CHARACTERISTIC (see Chapter 3 for more on product definition). Also, notice that the extended price for the line item is not an attribute since this is derivable information.

A **taxable flag** is stored on the invoice line item to signify if the item is to be taxed. This cannot always be determined by the item being invoiced, since the taxability of a line item could vary depending on many circumstances, such as the source and destination of the shipment or the tax status of the purchasing organization. The information needed to calculate taxes is not included in this model since it is highly dependent on the rules and regulations of each geographic boundary.

Other information that enterprises may want to know about an invoice include the total tax (after it is calculated) on the invoice, freight charges, and handling charges. The second sub-entity INVOICE ADJUSTMENT provides the mechanism for storing this data. The relationship to ADJUSTMENT TYPE specifies the type of adjustment, while the attribute **amount** will hold the actual dollar amount of the adjustment. Table 5.14 contains examples of this type of data for an invoice.

Using this structure, an enterprise can include any number or type of adjustments to an invoice as line items. This is much more flexible than including attributes such as **tax amount** or **freight charge** on the INVOICE entity, since new attributes would have to be added to the entity if the enterprise discovered

**TABLE 5.13**    *Invoice Line Item Data*

| Invoice ID | Line Item Seq | Product Name* | Quantity | Unit Price | Taxable? |
|---|---|---|---|---|---|
| 30002 | 1 | Jones #2 Pencils | 1000 | $0.40 | Y |
| | 2 | Goldstein Elite Pens | 1000 | $5.00 | Y |
| | 3 | HD 3½″ Diskettes | 100 | $12.00 | Y |

**TABLE 5.14**   *Invoice Adjustment Data*

| Invoice ID | Line Item Seq | Adjustment Type* | Amount | Taxable? |
|---|---|---|---|---|
| 30002 | 4 | Freight | $16.00 | Y |
| | 5 | Handling | $5.00 | N |
| | 6 | Tax | $25.65 | N |

other adjustments that needed to be tracked. With this model, the enterprise simply defines new adjustment types, then adds a line item to the invoice.

Just as order line items may be related to other order line items, invoice line items may be related to other invoice line items. For example, various INVOICE ADJUSTMENTs may be related to a specific PRODUCT INVOICE LINE ITEM. For instance, freight charges or tax charges may be related to specific invoice line items. Additionally, a PRODUCT INVOICE LINE ITEM may need to be related to an invoice line item which appeared on a past invoice. For example, suppose there was a mistake where the quantity of items invoiced was 10 instead of 8. A future invoice line item showing a credit of 2 items could be used to correct the invoice. This correction would be implemented using a PRODUCT INVOICE LINE ITEM with a **quantity** of "–2" that related back to the original PRODUCT INVOICE LINE ITEM which had a **quantity** of "10". Many enterprises will show corrections using this approach as opposed to modifying the invoice which could lead to control and audit issues. The recursive relationship around the IN-VOICE LINE ITEM provides the information necessary for relating invoice line items together.

## SHIPMENT INVOICE ASSOCIATION

So how does one assure that everything shipped actually gets billed? The SHIPMENT INVOICE entity allows enterprises to track this information (see Figure 5.6). This entity provides a means to store intersection information between INVOICE LINE ITEM and SHIPMENT LINE ITEM. Each of the invoice line items should represent the bill for one or more shipment line items. One shipment line item could also be related to many invoice line items in the case where adjustments to the original invoice line item were needed. For example, if

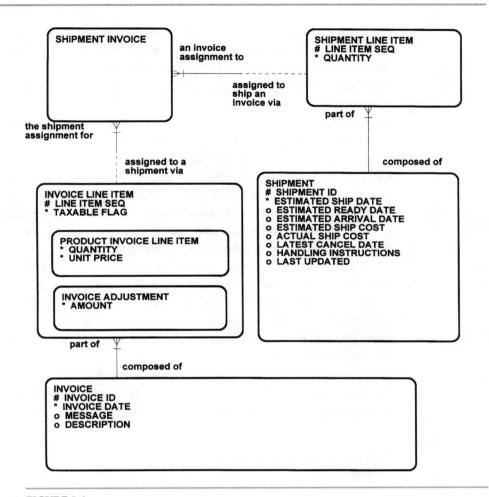

FIGURE 5.6

*Shipment and invoice association.*

some of the goods for the original shipment were damaged, a credit for these items would be needed. The credit would take the form of an invoice line item on a second invoice. Thus, the one shipment line item would actually have a relationship to two different invoice line items. It is unlikely that one shipment line item would be related to two invoice line items on the same invoice (though this would need to be enforced with a business rule).

Table 5.15 gives some examples of the data held by this entity. The table shows an example of a single shipment which resulted in two invoice line items. Observe that the same shipment line item (shipment ID #1235, line item #1 ) is related to two invoice line items. The first invoice line item was a bill for the shipment of 1,000 items. Upon receipt, the customer found 10 items damaged; therefore, on a subsequent invoice an adjustment was made to the customer's invoice for the 10 damaged items. This adjustment was then linked to the original shipment line item to allow for proper tracking.

The example of shipment ID #1330 shows the opposite situation. In this case, three shipment line items are mapped to only one invoice line item. This can occur when the shipment line items show component parts for an item, but the invoice only shows the price for the entire assembly. This situation could also occur when three shipments on different dates were grouped together into one invoice (perhaps due to a prearranged billing agreement).

Notice that there is not a **quantity** attribute on the SHIPMENT INVOICE and that the quantity shown in Table 5.15 comes from the INVOICE LINE ITEM. The reason for this is that an enterprise will usually not partially invoice for items that have been shipped. If this case can exist and it is necessary to map quantities of invoice line items to shipment line items, then the **quantity** attribute could be added.

Keep in mind that there will not always be a SHIPMENT INVOICE record. Some shipments, such as transfers, will not show up on an invoice, unless the enterprise wants to keep track of internal transactions.

TABLE 5.15  *Shipment Invoice Data*

| Shipment Id | Shipment Line Item Seq | Invoice Id | Invoice Line Item Seq | Quantity (from invoice line item) |
|---|---|---|---|---|
| 1235 | 1 | 30002 | 1 | 1000 |
|  | 2 | 30002 | 2 | 1000 |
|  | 3 | 30002 | 3 | 100 |
| 1235 | 1 | 30045 | 1 | −10 |
| 1330 | 1 | 30005 | 1 |  |
|  | 2 | 30005 | 1 |  |
|  | 3 | 30005 | 1 |  |

## INVOICE BILLING

Of course, enterprises also need to know where to send the invoice and where it came from. Standard models often record only the customer address, and the supplier address is assumed to be the enterprise doing the billing (the 'I' model). This model accommodates a more centralized system for a multilocation or multicompany organization. Invoices can be **billed to** or **billed from** any PARTY ADDRESS or PARTY CONTACT MECHANISM (see Figure 5.7).

An invoice will not be sent directly to a PARTY for the same reasons a SHIP-MENT isn't. A location is needed to send the invoice information to and from, even if it's a virtual location such as an Internet address or some other electronic mail site. Table 5.16 shows representative data resulting from the resolution of these relationships.

Notice that invoice #30002 has standard **bill to** and **bill from** locations, but #30005 has a **bill to** that is an Internet address. So, in this situation, the invoice is being sent via E-mail (however, the data only shows the physical address of the sender). For invoice #30010, the data indicates that the invoice is being sent from one electronic mail address to another.

As more and more enterprises and people get online, this type of transaction will become more prevalent; thus, the need for a more flexible data model will become apparent. Current invoicing systems that require a physical address to mail an invoice to may become unusable in the future.

PARTY ADDRESS ROLES could be used for additional validation if an enterprise wanted to implement additional business rules. A possible example would be a rule that states that an invoice may only be sent to a PARTY ADDRESS with a role of "location for receiving invoices".

**TABLE 5.16**  *Invoice and Address Data*

| Invoice Id | Invoice date | Bill to Party* | Bill to Party Location* | Bill from Party* | Bill from Party Location* |
|---|---|---|---|---|---|
| 30002 | May 25, 1996 | ACME Corporation | 123 Main Street | ABC Subsidiary | 100 Bridge Street |
| 30005 | June 5, 1996 | John Smith | jsmith@us.com | ABC Subsidiary | 100 Bridge Street |
| 30010 | June 5, 1996 | Tom Jones | 1235,678@cis.com | ACME Corporation | acorp@acme.com |

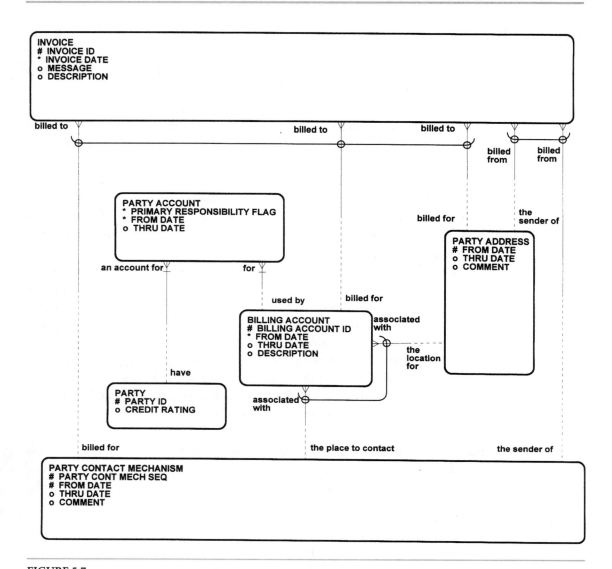

FIGURE 5.7

*Invoice billing.*

## Billing Account

As shown in Figure 5.7, there is a third way to bill an invoice to a customer in addition to sending a bill to a physical address or a PARTY CONTACT MECHANISM—through the use of a BILLING ACCOUNT. This method of billing is only used in certain circumstances for specific types of businesses. Therefore, the BILLING ACCOUNT, PARTY ACCOUNT, and PARTY entities and their associated relationships in Figure 5.7 are optional and are only included if the enterprise uses billing accounts.

A BILLING ACCOUNT provides a mechanism for showing different types of items on different invoices. A client might want a separate account for his or her office supplies and another account for furniture purchases. A billing account allows customers to receive separate invoices to track different types of items separately. Banks and credit card companies use this concept frequently to allow separation of various charges for their customers. Table 5.17 provides the example of ACME Corporation setting up an account for its office supplies and a separate account for using consulting services.

The BILLING ACCOUNT needs a **start date** (when it became active), an **end date,** and some description information. In order to determine where to send the invoice, the account in question must, in turn, be related to either a PARTY CONTACT MECHANISM or a PARTY ADDRESS. Eventually, all invoices must end up at a location of some sort. Also, note that if the enterprise uses billing accounts the order model in Chapter 4 (Figure 4.5) should include a **with a requested bill to** relationship to the BILLING ACCOUNT entity.

TABLE 5.17  *Billing Account Data*

| Billing Account Id | From Date | Thru Date | Party* | Party Location* | Description |
|---|---|---|---|---|---|
| 1295 | Apr 15, 1995 | | ACME Corporation | 123 Main Street | All charges for office supplies |
| 1296 | Apr 15, 1995 | | ACME Corporation | 123 Main Street | All charges for consulting services |

TABLE 5.18   *Party Account Data*

| Party* | Billing Account ID | From Date | Thru Date | Primary Flag |
|--------|--------------------|-----------|-----------|--------------|
| John Smith | 1459 | Apr 15, 1995 | | N |
| Jane Smith | 1459 | Apr 30, 1995 | | Y |
| Joe Smith | 1459 | Apr 15, 1995 | Apr 15, 1996 | N |

## Party Account

Some enterprises may have a need to track more than one party who is responsible for paying an invoice that is sent to a BILLING ACCOUNT. Therefore, the model shows an intersection entity between PARTY and BILLING ACCOUNT so that the invoice is sent to an account, not to a PARTY. This entity is called PARTY ACCOUNT. Other important attributes needed include the date the party became active on the account (the **from date**) and a flag to indicate which party has the primary responsibility for the account. Sample data is shown in Table 5.18.

The sample data shows a typical situation that could occur for a credit card account, possibly with many individual cards. Initially the account was opened with both John and Joe Smith assigned to the account on April 15, 1995. Each received a personal card. Then, on April 30, 1995, Jane Smith was added to the account when she received a card. She was given the primary responsibility. Later, in 1996, Joe Smith turned in his card and was removed from the account, leaving the other two active. Since the **thru date** is blank, it can be inferred that both John and Jane are still active on the account.

Another example of this type of situation could occur in the telecommunication industry. In some cases, all phone services for several phone numbers might appear on one billing account, while all charges for other phone numbers for the same location might appear on a different account. This could allow the charges for standard telephone service to be included on one account while other services, such as dedicated line and network services, might appear on another account.

## SUMMARY

In this chapter there has been discussion of the details of shipment and invoicing and how they relate to orders and to each other. The main relationships (shown in Figure 5.8) are straightforward to most data modelers. It is the inter-

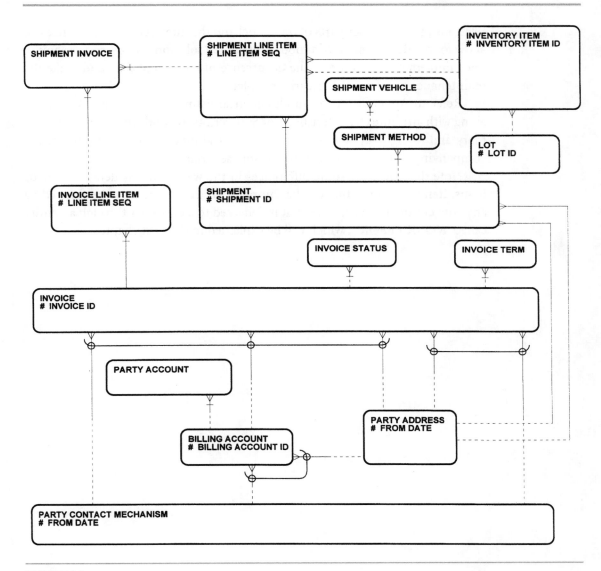

FIGURE 5.8

*Delivery model.*

relationships with other parts of the model and the intersection entities that will allow for the development of a robust, integrated solution. These models should, once implemented, minimize the occurrence of redundant data and make the maintenance of referential integrity simpler.

Refer to Appendix A for an alphabetical listing of entities and attributes along with attribute characteristics. For SQL scripts to build tables, columns, primary and foreign keys derived from this logical model, please refer to the accompanying CD-ROM product that is sold separately.

Note that there are some differences in the way service is delivered versus items. Items are things that can be shipped. Service cannot really be shipped by any conventional means; instead, it is delivered to a customer through an entity called WORK EFFORT, which will be explained in the next chapter.

# 6

# WORK EFFORT

## INTRODUCTION

A key component of conducting business is the act of providing various types of service to various parties. As previously noted, businesses generally provide two types of product offerings: They either sell inventory items or provide services. When businesses sell services, they have a responsibility to perform those services and then they need to bill for them. This often involves the completion of some type of work effort. Businesses also perform work efforts within their internal organizations to accomplish tasks, such as completing a project, producing inventory for sale, or maintaining some corporate asset.

Some questions that enterprises need to answer in the course of doing business include:

What type of work effort is required?

What items need to be produced, or what services need to be delivered?

Who will be involved and what are their roles?

Where will the work take place?

How long will it take?

What is the current status of the effort?

Are the appropriate resources (people, inventory, equipment) available? If not, when will they be?

This chapter will illustrate the following models which help answer those questions:

- Work order definition
- Work order roles
- Work effort generation
- Work task definition
- Work effort and party allocations
- Work task assignments
- Inventory assignments
- Fixed asset assignments
- Party asset assignments
- Work task type requirements
- Work effort invoicing

## WORK ORDERS AND WORK EFFORTS

A WORK ORDER and a WORK EFFORT are two different but related entities. A work order is the *requirement* to perform some type of work. This could be a requirement stemming from a decision to manufacture inventory items, deliver services, conduct a project, or repair an asset of the enterprise such as a piece of equipment or a piece of software.

A work effort is the *fulfillment* of the work requirement. This includes setting up and planning for the actual work which will be performed, as well as recording the status and information related to the efforts and tasks that are taking place.

## WORK ORDER DEFINITION

*Where does a work order come from?* A work order is created when there is a need to perform some type of work by the enterprise, for the enterprise. This means that the enterprise decided to perform the work itself, as opposed to using an external organization. Think of a work order as a special type of ORDER since it involves a commitment to complete some type of work. WORK ORDER has *not* been modeled as a sub-type of ORDER since the transaction is internal to the enterprise and as such has major differences in structure and attributes from a standard order. For instance, there is generally no need to track the terms of a work order, relate it to agreements, or include pricing structures. Examples of work orders include:

- The need to manufacture a particular item because market research indicates an increased demand for that item beyond previous projections.
- The need for a piece of equipment within the enterprise to be repaired.
- The need for an internal project such as an analysis of existing operations, development of a plan, creation of a new product or service.

Figure 6.1 shows the key entities used to define a work order. First, the WORK ORDER is created as the result of a REQUISITION LINE ITEM. The WORK ORDER entity is created and tied to the REQUISITION LINE ITEM once a decision is made for an internal organization to complete this work. The WORK ORDER TYPE defines the possible categories for work orders. The WORK ORDER is associated with either a DELIVERABLE, FIXED ASSET, or a PRODUCT.

## Requisition Line Item

As indicated in Chapter 4, a REQUISITION LINE ITEM can specify an enterprise's internal need for anything. The REQUISITION LINE ITEM may be fulfilled via a purchase order line item if the decision is made to go outside the organization to meet the need (see Chapter 4). If, however, the enterprise makes a decision to complete the work itself, then it must be filled by a WORK ORDER. A REQUISITION LINE ITEM is then the factor which initiates a WORK ORDER within an enterprise.

One WORK ORDER may fulfill the requirements specified in many REQUISITION LINE ITEMs. For example, there could be many requisitions for the enterprise to produce a particular item. Since all these requisitions may be filled with one production run, only one WORK ORDER is really needed.

On the other hand, there could be many internal requisitions from various departments requesting the repair of their personal computers (PCs). Each of these requisitions will have requisition line items for the *specific* PCs that need work. In this case, each line item may need its own WORK ORDER so that the **asset ID** of each computer can be properly recorded (see the section on Work Order Types).

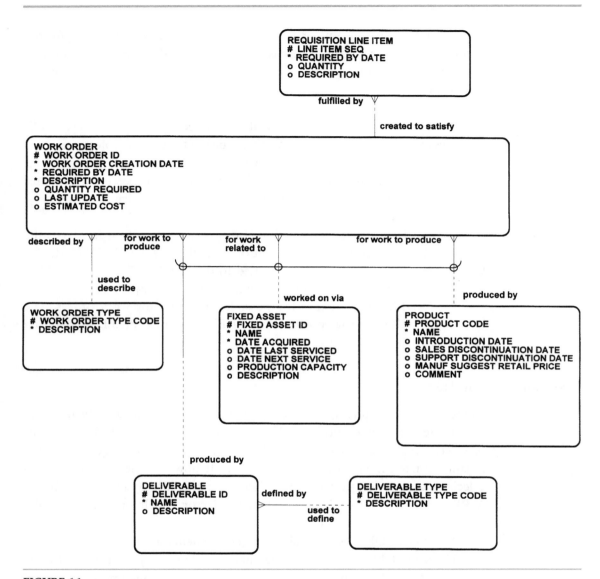

FIGURE 6.1

*Work order definition.*

## Work Order

There are several key pieces of information that need to be kept in the WORK ORDER entity. These include the **work order creation date,** a date when the work is required by, the type of work order being created, the **estimated cost,** and a **description** of the work requested. Possible values for WORK ORDER TYPE include "project", "maintenance", and "production run". Table 6.1 shows some data that could appear in the WORK ORDER entity.

## Work Order Types

In addition, there is other information needed depending on the WORK ORDER TYPE. If the type is "production run", then information about what is to be produced and how many is of critical importance. This is why the model includes an optional attribute for **quantity** and a possible relationship to PRODUCT.

If the type is "maintenance" or "repair", then there is a definite need to know what piece of equipment needs to be worked on. To accommodate this need, the model also includes an optional relationship to FIXED ASSET.

Finally, if the type is "internal project", then WORK ORDER may be associated with a DELIVERABLE. This would include such things as a management report, analysis document, or the creation of a particular business method or tool. The DELIVERABLE TYPE entity would contain a list of the possible types of deliverables an enterprise may produce for itself, such as "management report", "project plan", "presentation", or "market analysis".

**TABLE 6.1**   *Work Order Data*

| Work Order ID | Work Order Type* | Work Order Creation Date | Required by Date | Description |
|---|---|---|---|---|
| 50985 | Production Run | Jul 5, 1996 | Aug 5, 1996 | Anticipated demand of 2000 custom-engraved black pens with gold trim |
| 60102 | Internal Project | Oct 15, 1996 | Dec 15, 1996 | Develop sales and marketing plan for 1997 |
| 70485 | Maintenance | June 16, 1996 | June 18, 1996 | Fix engraving machine |

Note that there is an exclusive arc across DELIVERABLE, FIXED ASSET, and PRODUCT because a single WORK ORDER can be related to either one PRODUCT, one DELIVERABLE, or for work on one FIXED ASSET, but not all three. Table 6.2 shows examples of various types of work orders.

The data shown indicates that work order #50985 is a "production run". Because of this, the product to be produced ,"engraved black pen with gold trim", and the required quantity to produce, 2000 of these items, is also included. Order #60102 is an "internal project", related to the deliverable "1997 Sales/Marketing Plan". Work order #70485 is a "maintenance" task that requires a particular piece of equipment to be repaired, so the asset ID for this machine is also included. As discussed with previous examples, appropriate business rules need to be in place to ensure that work orders of certain types are appropriately related to the entities describing what the work order produces.

This data model does not include work orders or work efforts to manage the delivering of inventory items. Usually, the sales order and shipping entities covered in Chapters 4 and 5 provide enough information to help the enterprise manage the delivery of items. The enterprise generally doesn't need to track the tasks involved in delivering a product, since they are usually quite simple and consist of loading, shipping, and unloading of the items. However, this model can be easily modified to provide for tracking work orders and work efforts as-

TABLE 6.2  *Work Order Types*

| Work Order ID | Work Order Type* | Description | Product* | Quantity Required | Deliverable | Fixed Asset ID |
|---|---|---|---|---|---|---|
| 50985 | Production Run | Anticipated demand of 2000 custom-engraved black pens with gold trim | Engraved black pen with gold trim | 2000 | | |
| 60102 | Internal Project | Develop sales and marketing plan for 1997 | | | 1997 Sales/ Marketing Plan | |
| 70485 | Maintenance | Fix engraving machine | | | | 5025 |

sociated with delivery of items by creating a relationship from a WORK EFFORT to a SHIPMENT (work efforts will be discussed in the Work Effort Generation section).

## Anticipated Demand

**Anticipated Demand** is a type of WORK ORDER that warrants special consideration. Not only do actual orders generate the need to schedule a production run, but so can anticipated or forecasted demand (as shown in Tables 6.1 and 6.2). Anticipated demand from a corporate forecaster can result in an internal work order to produce certain inventory item types. For example, a forecast based upon the trend analysis in a sales data warehouse could show that there should be a spike in future sales of a particular item. Rather than wait for the actual sales orders to start coming in, a work order to produce the expected increase is entered so that when orders do come in the enterprise will have an ample supply on hand to meet the demand.

Anticipated demand only applies to inventory items, not services, since it is not really possible to prefabricate a service. It is not possible to fix something or provide accounting, legal, or professional services to a client before a contract or order for this is in place. It is, however, possible to prepare for anticipated service orders by preparing standard work products to be used as templates, but those would be treated as internal projects. For instance, an enterprise may initiate a work order for an infrastructure project to prepare an outline project plan in anticipation of an accounting audit review or other consulting-type engagement.

## WORK ORDER ROLES

Just as there are many roles which parties play in a purchase or sales order (refer to Chapter 4), there are many roles that organizations and people play in the work order. Among these roles, several could be important to an enterprise including: the internal organization for whom the work order is created, the person requesting the work, people involved in the authorization of the work order, and the person responsible for ensuring the work order is completed. Figure 6.2 depicts the entities needed to maintain this information.

The WORK ORDER ROLE TYPE entity is used to store all the valid roles defined by an enterprise that could be related to a WORK ORDER. The PARTY

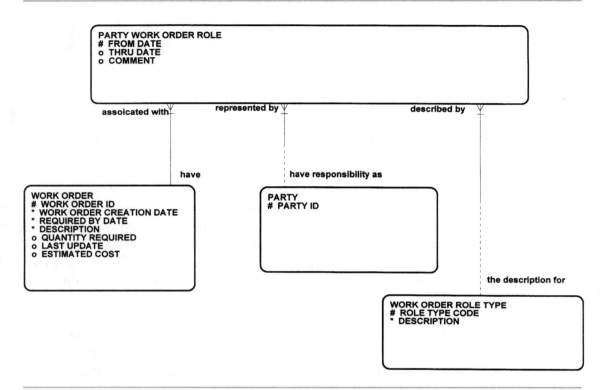

FIGURE 6.2

*Work order roles.*

WORK ORDER ROLE entity contains the intersection of PARTY, WORK ORDER, and WORK ORDER ROLE TYPE. In this case, the primary key will be a combination of the **work order ID**, **party ID**, and **role type code**. This, however, is not enough since it is possible (though not likely) that one party may be assigned the same role at different times over the life of a work order. Because of this, the model includes a date as part of the primary key in order to ensure uniqueness. Table 6.3 contains sample data to demonstrate some of these possibilities.

As the example data shows for work order ID #50985, John Smith has two roles. He created the work order and he is responsible for the fulfillment of the work order. At one point he is replaced by Dick Jones, but later is reassigned his original role. Notice, too, that Dick Jones has the role "responsible for" on two work orders during overlapping time periods. As with the model for role assignments in orders, this model is flexible enough to allow for a variety of options.

**TABLE 6.3**   *Party Work Order Role Data*

| Work Order ID | Party* | Work Order Role Type* | From Date | Thru Date |
|---|---|---|---|---|
| 50985 | ABC Manufacturing, Inc. | Created for | Jul 5, 1996 | |
| | John Smith | Created by | Jul 5, 1996 | |
| | John Smith | Responsible for | Jul 5, 1996 | Dec 15, 1996 |
| | Sam Bossman | Authorized by | Jul 8, 1996 | |
| | Dick Jones | Responsible for | Dec 16, 1996 | Feb 20, 1997 |
| | John Smith | Responsible for | Feb 21, 1997 | |
| 60102 | Sam Bossman | Created for | Jun 10, 1996 | |
| | Dick Jones | Responsible for | Jun 15, 1996 | Jan 1, 1997 |

## WORK EFFORT GENERATION

The WORK EFFORT entity tracks the performance of work that results from a WORK ORDER or an external requirement such as a PRODUCT LINE ITEM from a sales order (see Figure 6.3). So, the work effort may result from one of these scenarios:

- A work order (as defined in the previous section)
- A customer orders an item which needs to be manufactured
- A service which was sold now needs to be performed
- A customer places an order to repair or service an item which was previously sold to him or her

In addition to defining the basic information for a WORK EFFORT, the model also keeps track of WORK EFFORT TYPE, whether the effort is the result of a WORK ORDER or a PRODUCT LINE ITEM, and the location where the work takes place (through a relationship to PARTY ADDRESS).

Keep in mind that not all product line items will result in work efforts. If the order is for items that are readily available, then a shipment can be scheduled instead of creating a work effort. For a review of the specific attributes in the PRODUCT LINE ITEM please refer to Chapter 4.

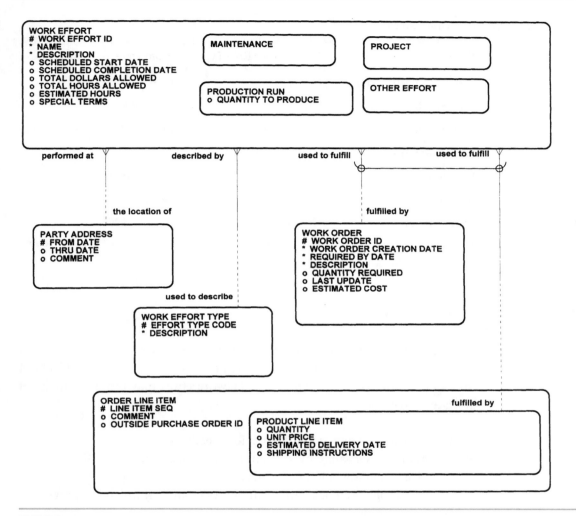

FIGURE 6.3

*Work effort generation.*

## Work Effort and Type

In order to fulfill the requirement of either a work order or an order line item, the WORK EFFORT entity is used. A WORK EFFORT tracks the work to fix or produce something for manufacturing and involves the allocation of resources: people (labor), parts (inventory), and fixed assets (equipment). The work effort may be a MAINTENANCE effort such as performing preventative maintenance on various pieces of equipment. It could be a PRODUCTION RUN to fulfill an immediate or anticipated request. Another type of work effort is a PROJECT which may be the development of a computer system application. The OTHER EFFORT sub-type allows for any enterprise-specific categories of work efforts not already defined. More detailed breakdowns of work efforts within each of these main categories may be stored in the WORK EFFORT TYPE entity (see Figure 6.3).

Other information that an enterprise may want to record about the WORK EFFORT could include a name for the overall effort (such as a project name) and a detailed description of the effort. To facilitate project tracking, the enterprise may also want to list a scheduled start date, scheduled completion date, and total estimated man hours for the effort. The actual start date, actual completion date, and actual man hours are not stored here because that data can be derived based on task-level information (this will be discussed later in the chapter). If there is a need for any **special terms** the team needs to know about the effort, those can be recorded as well.

Some institutions have other considerations that need to be accounted for. There may be funding or time limits imposed under certain circumstances by various agencies, so the model includes attributes to store **total dollars allowed** and **total hours allowed**. An example of this would be IRS regulations restricting the amount of time a contractor can work for an enterprise without being considered an employee. Also, many government-funded organizations have spending limits set by budget appropriations or even by law. Table 6.4 contains data samples for a few of these attributes.

**TABLE 6.4**   *Work Effort Data*

| Work Effort ID | Name | Description | Source Type* | Source ID | Scheduled Start Date |
|---|---|---|---|---|---|
| 28045 | PRUN #1 | Production run of 400 pencils | Work Order | 50985 | Nov 30, 1995 |
| 29034 | Database Conversion | Convert internal system from old db to new db | Work Order | 60102 | Feb 23, 1996 |
| 29405 | PRUN #2 | Production run of 700 pencils | Product Line Item (from a sales order) | 25, Line #6 | Mar 1, 1996 |

Note that the current status (or a history of statuses) of the work effort is not tied to the WORK EFFORT entity because the status can be derived based on the combination of statuses from the related work task assignments (this will be covered later). In the same manner, there is no need for work order status because it can be determined from the statuses of the various work efforts related to the work order.

## Work Effort Sources

As indicated by the data in Table 6.4, the source of a work effort could be either a PRODUCT LINE ITEM or an internal WORK ORDER. **The product line item** will typically be from a sales order and not a purchase order, since only sales orders may create a need to track a work effort. The enterprise usually will not track work efforts for items that they have purchased.

The model shows an exclusive arc to indicate that a WORK EFFORT can be used to fulfill either a WORK ORDER or PRODUCT LINE ITEM, but not both of these. It is possible, though, for a WORK ORDER or PRODUCT LINE ITEM to lead to several work efforts. There may be a sales order which has a product line item for 1,000 items. The management may decide to manage this as three separate work efforts and perhaps create three production runs in separate plants in order to generate the inventory needed to fulfill this one order. (For this reason, the **quantity to produce** must also be stored at the WORK EFFORT level for the PRODUCTION RUN sub-type.) Likewise, an internal work order to revamp an enterprise's computer systems could be divided into multiple projects in order to phase the development effort.

In this model one work effort will *not* be used to satisfy multiple work orders or multiple order line items. For orders, this model assumes that the work effort to fill those orders will be managed separately. If there are multiple internal needs, this can be handled by updating a single work order. For example, if there are several anticipated needs to manufacture a certain type of pen, only one work order should be created. As the requirement changes, the existing work order will be updated until such time as the work effort to fulfill it has begun. In this way , these several requirements would be maintained as a single work order. To enforce this process, the enterprise would need to put appropriate business rules in place.

If the enterprise needs to manage multiple work orders or order line items by a single work effort, then the model would simply be changed to include a many-to-many relationship from WORK EFFORT to both WORK ORDER and PRODUCT LINE ITEM.

## Work Effort and Party Address

A final question to ask is: Where is the WORK EFFORT going to take place? As shown in Figure 6.3, the WORK EFFORT must be performed at or associated with one and only one PARTY ADDRESS. This would represent the main office or location responsible for an effort. It is, of course, conceivable that certain tasks within the effort may need to occur at a different location (i.e., a corporate PC upgrade at different sites across the country). This is also handled in the model and will be discussed later in this chapter under the Work Task and Party Address section.

# WORK TASK DEFINITION

Work tasks are the activities or steps that need to occur to accomplish a work effort. For any WORK EFFORT there may be one or more work tasks (see Figure 6.4). Each of these tasks is assigned a WORK TASK TYPE, and may be associated with a PARTY ADDRESS. In addition, for some tasks there may also be a WORK TASK DEPENDENCY.

## Work Task and Type

Table 6.5 shows the work tasks for a work effort of producing pencils on a particular production run. Included in the data are the attributes for scheduled start and end dates, and estimated man hours. These tasks will be useful for planning staff and equipment assignments (discussed in a later section). Also included is data from the resolution of the relationship to WORK TASK TYPE, which contains a list of standard work tasks carried out by the enterprise along with the **standard work hours** usually spent on this type of task. Notice that the **estimated hours** of the WORK TASK may be different from the **standard work hours** for the WORK TASK TYPE since there are particular circumstances involved in the execution of the task (perhaps the project manager knows that very efficient workers will be assigned and will therefore lower the estimate).

To allow for detailed task tracking, there is also a recursive relationship on

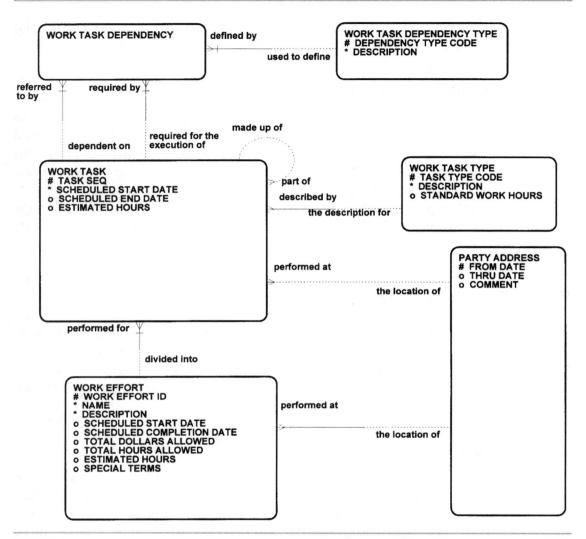

FIGURE 6.4

*Work task definition.*

WORK TASK. This allows for the situation where some tasks may be made up of other, more detailed, tasks. Table 6.6 shows an example of the work break down of the first task, "set up production line".

As this data shows, tasks #5, #6, and #7, are all sub-tasks of #1 from Table 6.5. In this case, the estimated work hours for the sub-task add up to the esti-

**TABLE 6.5** *Work Task Data*

| Work Effort ID | Work Task Seq | Work Task Type* | Standard Hours | Scheduled Start Date | Scheduled End Date | Estimated Hours |
|---|---|---|---|---|---|---|
| 28045 | 1 | Set up production line | 24 | Jun 1, 1996 | Jun 2, 1996 | 20 |
|  | 2 | Operate machinery | 10 | Jun 3, 1996 | Jun 3, 1996 | 10 |
|  | 3 | Clean up machinery | 5 | Jun 4, 1996 | Jun 4, 1996 | 5 |
|  | 4 | Quality assure goods produced | 10 | Jun 3, 1996 | Jun 4, 1996 | 10 |

mated hours for the original task. Additional business rules are needed to enforce this condition in an actual online system.

The actual hours worked are not stored at the task level in this model because that information can be summarized based on time spent by parties assigned to the task. This will be discussed more in the next section, Work Effort and Party Allocations. The same holds true for task status; this, too, can be determined based on the status of the individual task assignments.

## Work Task and Party Address

As stated in the discussion of WORK EFFORT, there may be some tasks in a work effort that do not happen at the main site. Take, for example, an internal

**TABLE 6.6** *Work Task Hierarchy*

| Work Effort ID | Parent Work Task* | Work Task Seq | Work Task Type* | Estimated Work Hours |
|---|---|---|---|---|
| 28045 | Set up production line | 5 | Move pencil manufacturing machinery in place | 5 |
|  | Set up production line | 6 | Move raw materials in place for production run | 8 |
|  | Set up production line | 7 | Set up assembly line rollers | 7 |

project to produce a book on standard data models. The effort is associated with a main office with which the publisher corresponds. However, various tasks associated with this effort, such as writing certain chapters, may happen at a branch office, while others, such as developing the actual entity relationship diagrams, happen at the main office. For the tasks that do not occur in the main office, there may be a desire to record that secondary work location. For this reason, the model includes an optional relationship to PARTY ADDRESS from WORK TASK (refer to Figure 6.4). For those tasks which have no address association, it is assumed that they occur at the main address associated with the parent WORK EFFORT (or that location is immaterial in this case).

## Work Task Dependency

The WORK TASK DEPENDENCY entity allows the enterprise to track the fact that some tasks may not be a *breakdown* of other tasks, but may actually be *dependent* on other tasks. For example, the task "operate machinery" cannot be executed until the task "set up production line" is completed. The WORK TASK DEPENDENCY TYPE provides a method for identifying the different ways in which tasks may be dependent on each other. In the example regarding "operate machinery" and "set up production line", the second task is dependent on the "scheduled end date" of the first task. The dependency type would then be "scheduled start date >= scheduled end date". Other situations may occur where two tasks need to be executed in parallel. In that case, the dependency type is based on the "scheduled start date" of the two tasks and would be represented as a dependency type of "scheduled start date = scheduled start date".

# WORK EFFORT AND PARTY ALLOCATIONS

In order for the WORK EFFORT to be completed, certain resources need to be made available. In some cases, people, inventory, and equipment may need assignment to both WORK EFFORTs as well as WORK TASKs. This section discusses the assignment of parties to WORK EFFORTs (the following section discusses assignments of parties to WORK TASKs). It includes the entities PARTY ALLOCATION, PARTY SKILL, and SKILL TYPE (see Figure 6.5).

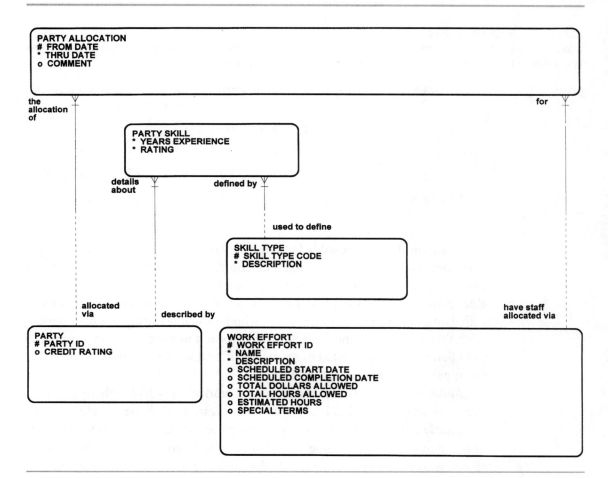

**FIGURE 6.5**

*Work effort and party allocation.*

## Party Allocation

For planning and scheduling purposes, the model includes a means by which people, or groups of people, can be preassigned or allocated to a WORK EFFORT. This is accomplished through the PARTY ALLOCATION entity (refer to Figure 6.5). With this it is possible to maintain a list of parties that are available as resources for a particular work effort and when they are and are not available. Table 6.7 gives examples of the data available when the relationships are resolved.

TABLE 6.7    *Party Allocation Data*

| Work Effort ID | Party* | From Date | Thru Date | Comment |
|---|---|---|---|---|
| 28045 | John Smith | Jul 5, 1996 | Jul 6, 1997 | Leaving for 2-month vacation on Aug 1, 1996 |
| | John Smith | Oct 1, 1997 | Jan 2, 1999 | |
| | Dick Jones | Jan 2, 1997 | Jan 2, 1999 | |
| | Jane Smith | Jan 1, 1996 | Aug 1, 1997 | Very excited about assignment |
| 29001 | USA Consulting | Jul 1, 1996 | Jul 1, 1997 | Contracted outside |

With this data it is possible for a manager to then make assignments to specific work tasks necessary to complete an effort. Looking at the data, the manager can see that there will be a two-month period when John Smith will not be available (even though he is allocated) and that there will be an employee, Jane Smith, with a lot of interest in this work effort who is available during this time period. With this information the manager will know not to assign John to any critical tasks that must be completed in August (or if he does, he will need to schedule a fill-in person for that time, possibly Jane).

Additionally, the data indicates that for work effort #29001, there is an outside contracting firm allocated for an entire year. This allows for efforts to be completely outsourced with no internal employee actually assigned to the work, only a particular organization. In this case, the internal manager is not concerned with who does the work, only that it can be sent to this outside firm.

## Party Skill and Skill Type

When doing these allocations, managers need to know what the assigned parties are qualified to do. This can be handled using the PARTY SKILL and SKILL TYPE entities. PARTY SKILL contains a list of parties, skill types, years of experience, and a skill rating. Table 6.8 contains sample data.

As indicated by the data, skills are associated not only with people but with companies as well (this is why the entity is PARTY SKILL not PERSON SKILL). This information could be vital to project managers who are staffing new efforts. If no people within the enterprise are available for use, the manager can evaluate outside agencies for their ability to support the effort in question. Addition-

**TABLE 6.8**  *Party Skill Data*

| Party * | Skill Type* | Years Experience | Rating |
|---|---|---|---|
| John Smith | Project Management | 20 | 10 |
| | Machine Operator | 5 | 6 |
| Dick Jones | Fork Lift Operator | 12 | 8 |
| USA Consulting | Database Design | 25 | 10 |
| | Information Engineering | 15 | 7 |
| | Data Warehouse | 5 | 5 |

ally, for people that have not already been allocated, this information can be used to determine appropriate task assignments.

## WORK TASK ASSIGNMENTS

In order to get tasks completed, there is generally a need to have people (or parties) assigned to specific tasks to do the work. It is possible to do this by using the intersection entity WORK TASK ASSIGNMENT (see Figure 6.6). Other information that needs to be tracked regarding the work includes the TASK ASSIGNMENT STATUS TYPE, the WORK TASK ROLE TYPE, and of course the enterprise needs the TIME ENTRY entity in order to pay its workers.

### Work Task Assignment

This entity allows a WORK TASK to be mapped to a PARTY. If desired, an enterprise could put in place business rules that require parties used on assignments to first exist in PARTY ALLOCATION for the related work effort. Due to personnel changes, illness, vacations, and so on, there may be multiple parties assigned to a single task over time. For this reason, a start and end date are included as attributes on this entity. The end date is optional to handle such things as ongoing service contracts. Since an enterprise may also wish to track such things as assignment extensions, the **start date** is also included in the primary key.

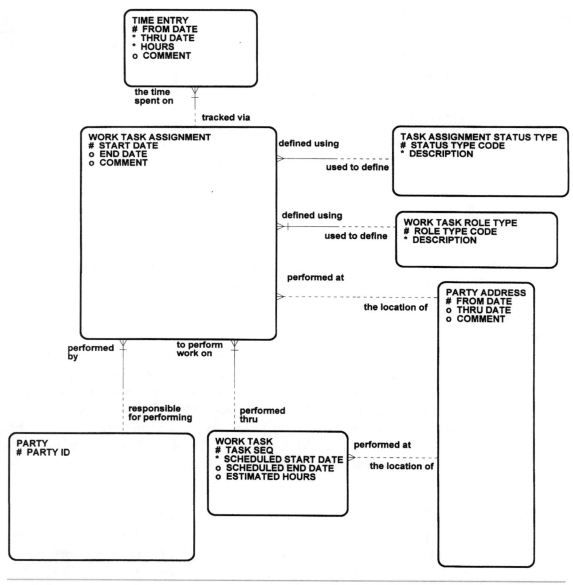

FIGURE 6.6

*Work task assignments.*

## Work Task Role Type

Since many parties could be assigned to a single task, some other information that may be important to track would be the role a particular party plays in a work task. This is tracked by selecting the appropriate role from the entity WORK TASK ROLE TYPE. This information is especially useful when one party fills multiple roles, as is often the case, or for identifying who does what on a task that requires a team of people. Possible roles could be "supervisor", "analyst", "laborer", or "contractor".

## Task Assignment Status

Another required piece of information is the status of the assignment. It is through the association to TASK ASSIGNMENT STATUS TYPE that the status for WORK TASK, WORK EFFORT, and ultimately WORK ORDER, is determined. For example, if a task has assignments that are still "in progress", then the status of the task will also be "in progress", as will the status of the effort and the original work order. Only when all the assignments for all the tasks are "complete", will the effort be "complete". In the same manner, once all the efforts are "complete", then the work order will finally be "complete". Since this is such a long chain of relationships to check, this is another place where denormalization may be called for in a physical model. In fact, this type of reporting would be an excellent candidate for inclusion in a project status data warehouse that is refreshed at the end of each work day.

Some example data for task assignments with roles and statuses is provided in Table 6.9.

Based on this data, a manager could see that the first two task assignments are not complete yet, the third assignment is complete, and the last task assignment is in progress. From this, the manager can deduce that the work effort is still "in progress", then report back to whomever placed the original work order that it has not yet been finished.

## Task Assignment and Party Address

Once again in Figure 6.6, PARTY ADDRESS appears. Why is that? This optional relationship is there to handle tasks that must be completed in what is now a very mobile society. With the increased rise in telecommuting, there is no longer any

**TABLE 6.9**   *Work Task Assignment Data*

| Task Seq | Work Task* | Party* | Role* | Start Date | End Date | Status* |
|---|---|---|---|---|---|---|
| 5 | Move pencil manufacturing machinery in place | John Smith | Laborer | Mar 15, 1995 | Mar 16, 1995 | In progress |
| 5 | Move pencil manufacturing machinery in place | Jerry Johnson | Supervisor | Mar 10, 1995 | Mar 20, 1995 | In progress |
| 6 | Move raw materials in place for production run | John Smith | Laborer | Mar 17, 1995 | Mar 19, 1995 | Completed |
| 7 | Set up assembly line rollers | Dick Jones | Machinist | Mar 10, 1995 | Mar 20, 1995 | In progress |

assurance, or requirement, that a particular task must always be in a particular location. Take, for example, the task of building a complex data warehouse model for a large corporation. This task could involve many data modelers as well as business analysts. It is entirely conceivable that they could all work remotely from home offices, communicating with each other and the client via fax, e-mail, and voice mail. In this case, the location is associated with the individuals assigned to the task.

Why can't a party address for that individual be used? It may very well be that, in fact, the location is an address for that party, but since a party can have many addresses, there is no way to be certain which address the party will use for any given task. So, if this information is important for task tracking, the PARTY ADDRESS related to the actual WORK TASK ASSIGNMENT should be recorded.

Some business rules may be useful in these cases; such as, only a valid PARTY ADDRESS with a PARTY ADDRESS ROLE (see Chapter 2) of "office" for the PARTY involved in the WORK TASK ASSIGNMENT can be referenced as the location for the WORK TASK ASSIGNMENT.

As in the case of WORK TASK, for those work task assignments which have no address association, it is assumed that they occur at the address associated with the parent WORK TASK (or again that location is immaterial).

## Time Entry

Some other very useful information is also shown in this model (Figure 6.6): That is the idea of TIME ENTRY. Of course, it is very important for payroll, but it is also important for task tracking, cost determination, and perhaps client billing. This entity quite simply holds information about how much time was spent during a given period on a particular WORK TASK ASSIGNMENT. Included in this information are the party ID and work task data (inherited from WORK TASK ASSIGNMENT), and the hours worked. Table 6.10 contains some sample data.

It is through this data that accurate calculations for total work hours on a task or an effort are calculated. An analyst needs to summarize all the hours from the time entries for all the task assignments for all the tasks that make up one WORK EFFORT. If a WORK ORDER happens to consist of several efforts, then the totals for the efforts are summarized to get a total for the order. In order to simplify reporting for executives and supervisors, consider including the data, in a presummarized form, in a project data warehouse. In a similar way, this data is also used to determine the actual start and end dates of the various activities discussed.

## INVENTORY ASSIGNMENTS

In order to complete certain work tasks, raw materials or other items may be required. Figure 6.7 shows the intersection entity INVENTORY ASSIGNMENT

**TABLE 6.10**  *Time Entry Data*

| Work Effort ID | Work Task Seq | Party* | From Date | Thru Date | Hours |
|---|---|---|---|---|---|
| 19876 | 2 | John Smith | Jan 1, 1996 | Jan 14, 1996 | 80 |
|  |  |  | Jan 15, 1996 | Jan 31, 1996 | 88 |
| 30425 | 5 | Dick Jones | Mar 1, 1996 | Mar 31, 1996 | 180 |

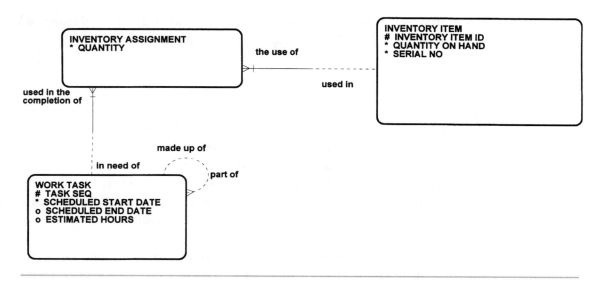

**FIGURE 6.7**

*Inventory assignments.*

between WORK TASK and INVENTORY ITEM. This tracks the actual use of inventory during the execution of an internal operation. Table 6.11 shows the data that might be associated with assembling pencil components, which is a task in the work effort to produce 100 pencils.

As indicated by the data shown, this one task (Assemble pencil components) requires the use of three different items from inventory to be completed. For each item used, a quantity of 100 is required. When this assignment is made, business processes need to be in place to ensure that the inventory information is updated to reflect the depletion from inventory.

**TABLE 6.11**    *Inventory Assignment*

| Work Task* | Inventory Item* | Quantity |
|---|---|---|
| Assemble pencil components | Pencil cartridges | 100 |
| Assemble pencil components | Erasers | 100 |
| Assemble pencil components | Labels | 100 |

# Fixed Asset Assignments

As with inventory, some work tasks will require various pieces of equipment, machinery, vehicles, or property in order to be completed. These are called FIXED ASSETS in this model (see Figure 6.8). This entity shows several sub-types of interest: EQUIPMENT, VEHICLE, and PROPERTY. In addition, other asset types are listed in the entity FIXED ASSET TYPE. In order to track when and for what an asset is being used, the model includes the entity FIXED ASSET ASSIGNMENT. To further establish the state of the assignment, a reference to FIXED ASSET ASSIGNMENT STATUS TYPE is used.

## Fixed Asset

Other information stored in FIXED ASSET that may be of interest to an enterprise includes the **asset ID**, a **name** for identification, when the asset was acquired (important for depreciation, which will be discussed in Chapter 7), the last time the asset was serviced (if applicable), and when the next scheduled service is. Also included is the **production capacity** value for the asset and a relationship to UNIT OF MEASURE which is used to modify the production capacity information. Examples of data that could be found in FIXED ASSET are shown in Table 6.12.

## Fixed Asset Type

Of course, there are many kinds of assets that may be important to an enterprise for various reasons. These can be listed using the FIXED ASSET TYPE entity. No-

TABLE 6.12  *Fixed Asset Data*

| Fixed Asset ID | Asset Type | Name | Date Acquired | Date last Serviced | Date Next Service | Production Capacity | UOM* |
|---|---|---|---|---|---|---|---|
| 1000 | PENCIL | Pencil Labeler #1 | Jun 12, 1955 | Jun 12, 1996 | Jun 12, 1997 | 1,000,000 Pens/day | |
| 2000 | CAR | Car Pool #1 | Mar 1, 1994 | Mar 15, 1996 | Aug 1, 1996 | 5 | People |

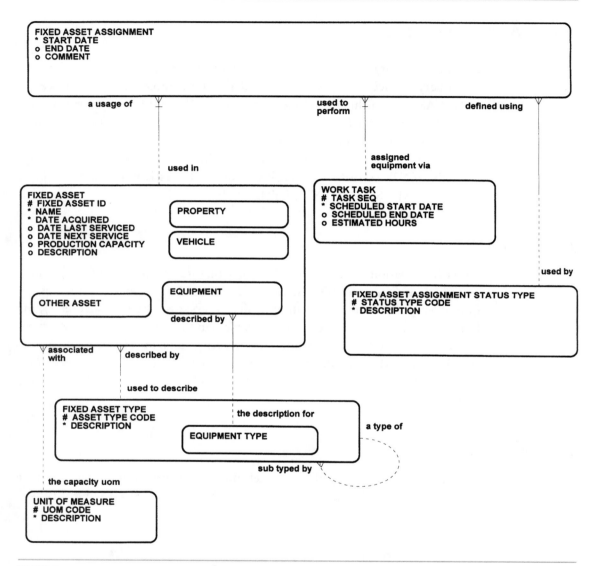

FIGURE 6.8

*Fixed asset assignments.*

tice that there is a recursive relationship on this entity. This relationship allows for the detailed breakdown of the various asset types. As an example, take the fixed asset type of EQUIPMENT TYPE. The information that a given asset is a piece of equipment is probably not enough in some cases. It would be nice to know what kind of equipment it is, should it be needed for a work task. In the same manner, it might be good to know that a "vehicle" is a "minivan" and that the "minivan" is actually a "Ford Aerostar". Table 6.13 shows sample data for this entity.

In the examples, there are three asset types ("pencil", "pen", "paper") that roll up to a type of "equip". In addition, there are two types, "truck" and "jet", which roll up to "vehicle". Then there is the type "mac18" which is a type of "truck" which is a type of "vehicle". All of these are asset types. This model is flexible enough to allow as much detail as needed.

## Fixed Asset Assignment and Status

Since a machine or piece of equipment can usually be used only for one task at a time, it is necessary to tell what is being used and when it is in use. Figure 6.8 shows the model for tracking this information. In it there is the FIXED ASSET ASSIGNMENT entity which is at the intersection of WORK TASK and FIXED ASSET. In this entity are attributes for storing the start and end date for the assignment. These will be very important for task scheduling purposes. In addi-

TABLE 6.13    *Fixed Asset Type Data*

| Fixed Asset Type Code | Description | Parent Asset Type |
|---|---|---|
| EQUIP | Equipment | |
| PENCIL | Pencil-making machine | EQUIP |
| PEN | Pen-making machine | EQUIP |
| PAPER | Paper-making machine | EQUIP |
| VEHICLE | Automotive vehicle | |
| TRUCK | Truck | VEHICLE |
| MAC18 | Mac truck—18 wheels | TRUCK |
| JET | Jet airplane | VEHICLE |

**TABLE 6.14**   *Fixed Asset Assignment Data*

| Work Task* | Fixed Asset* | Start Date | End Date | Comment |
|---|---|---|---|---|
| Label pencils | Pencil Labeler #1 | Jun 12, 1996 | Jun 15, 1996 | |
| Move raw materials in place for production run | Fork Lift #25 | Apr 15, 1996 | May 15, 1996 | May need for longer time |
| Test database tool | Office Laptop #2 | Jul 1, 1995 | | Ongoing task |

tion, there is a relationship to FIXED ASSET ASSIGNMENT STATUS TYPE. The status type will indicate such things as whether the assignment is requested, assigned, or perhaps under repair. Table 6.14 gives some examples.

Note that the start and end date for the assignment may not be the same as the scheduled start and end date on the WORK TASK. A certain machine may only be needed for part of the task. However, business rules (or database constraints) need to be in place to ensure that the equipment assignment is at least within the scheduled date range for the associated task.

## PARTY ASSET ASSIGNMENTS

Besides being assigned to tasks, it also possible for assets to be assigned or *checked out* to a PARTY. During this time, it is not uncommon to hold the party responsible for the safe keeping or use of the asset in question. This association is depicted in Figure 6.9. Again, there is an intersection called PARTY ASSET ASSIGNMENT, which joins information from PARTY and FIXED ASSET. Also related to this entity is PARTY ASSET ASSIGNMENT STATUS TYPE which provides additional information about the assignment. Sample data is provided in Table 6.15.

Assignment data like this provides the enterprise with vital information for tracking the condition and whereabouts of its assets. In this case, the enterprise knows that John Smith has the car known as "Car Pool #1" until the first of 1997, so if they need to give someone else a car, it is known that this car is not available. The data also shows that Dick Jones was assigned a particular tool set and that he lost it. It also shows that a factory was assigned to ABC Corporation

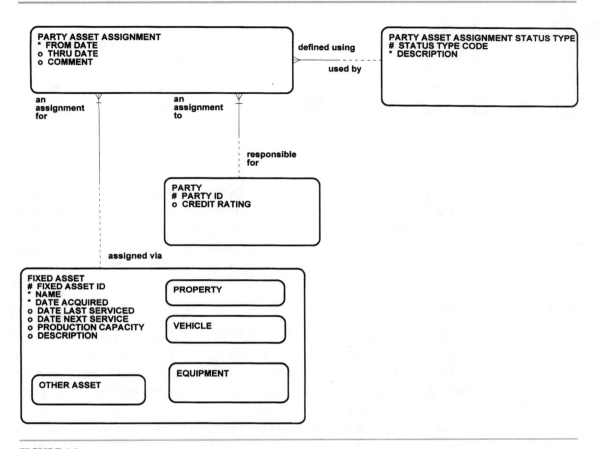

**FIGURE 6.9**

*Party asset assignments.*

(an internal organization) and that the factory is currently under repair and not available for use.

## WORK TASK TYPE REQUIREMENTS

In order to facilitate planning, this model includes additional entities to map various requirements for the different *types* of work tasks that exist (see Figure 6.10). In previous sections, models were discussed that showed how WORK EFFORTS

TABLE 6.15    *Party Asset Assignment Data*

| Party* | Fixed Asset* | Start Date | End Date | Status* |
|--------|--------------|------------|----------|---------|
| John Smith | Car Pool #1 | Jan 1, 1996 | Jan 1, 1997 | Active |
| Dick Jones | Toolset #5 | Mar 15, 1995 | Mar 15, 1996 | Lost |
| ABC Corp | Factory #6 | Jun 1, 1990 | | Under repair |

could be broken down into 'WORK TASKS'. In fact, there can be WORK EFFORT TYPES which can have standard WORK TASK TYPES associated with them. Each WORK TASK TYPE may have requirements for inventory, fixed assets, and skills that have been predetermined and can be used for scheduling resources and estimating time and costs for a task, and therefore for an effort.

## Inventory Requirement

The WORK TASK INVENTORY REQUIREMENT entity connects WORK TASK TYPE to ITEM. As additional information, the entity also includes an attribute for the **estimated quantity** required. This information can be used for assuring that enough items exist in inventory to execute a particular task. Table 6.16 contains sample data for this entity.

Note that the relationship is to ITEM not INVENTORY ITEM. Because this information is for planning, it is only necessary to know the *type* of item needed. There is no need to locate an actual item in stock. If, in examining this information, it is determined that for a planned WORK EFFORT, the WORK TASK TYPE will require more of an ITEM than is currently in inventory, then the enterprise will know that it needs to reorder that item in order to complete the planned effort.

Another point to note is that not all WORK TASK TYPES will have inventory requirements. For example, a task type of *prepare project plan*, which is a type of service task, would not have any inventory requirements.

## Fixed Asset Requirement

In a similar manner, WORK TASK FIXED ASSET REQUIREMENT will provide information for the scheduling and assignment of types of fixed assets. Other in-

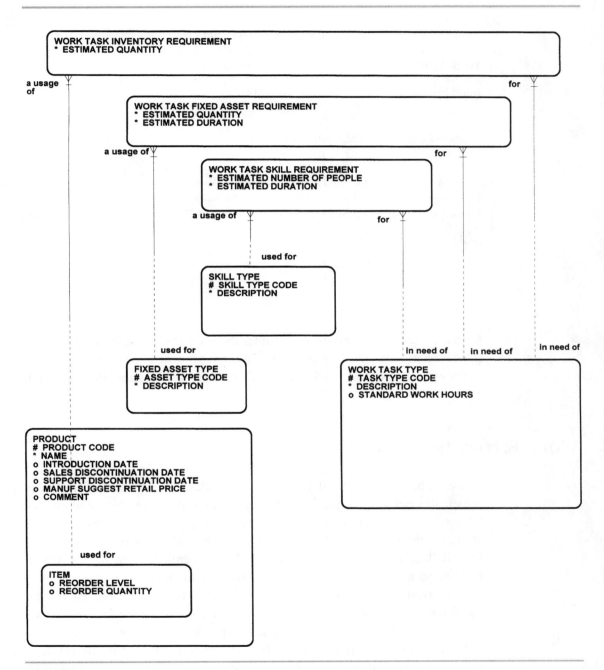

FIGURE 6.10

*Work task type requirements.*

TABLE 6.16   *Work Task Inventory Requirement Data*

| Work Task Type* | Item* | Estimated Quantity |
|---|---|---|
| Build pencils | Erasers | 1000 |
|  | Labels | 1000 |
| Produce Pens | Ink Cartridges | 2000 |

TABLE 6.17   *Work Task Fixed Asset Requirement Data*

| Work Task Type* | Fixed Asset Type* | Estimated Quantity | Estimated Duration |
|---|---|---|---|
| Build Pencils | Pencil Labeler | 1 | 10 days |
|  | Fork Lift | 2 | 5 days |

formation carried by this entity includes the **estimated quantity** of the type of fixed asset needed and the estimated amount of time the fixed assets will be used in the execution of this WORK TASK TYPE. Examples of this data are given in Table 6.17.

## WORK EFFORT INVOICING

There are basically three different methods by which services are billed to a customer: flat rate for a project or service, flat rate by deliverable or phase, and billing by time using hourly rates. Of course, any given enterprise may have variations on these, but these three are the most common. The relationships from INVOICE LINE ITEM to the various work-related entities allow an enterprise to tie invoices to the actual work performed (see Figure 6.11).

The relationship from INVOICE LINE ITEM to WORK EFFORT handles the flat-rate type billing. An example of this would be a systems development project. In this case, the customer is going to pay for a full-blown system and will only pay when the project is completed. The customer does not care about intermediate phases or specific deliverables and has no intention of paying by the hour. So a fixed fee is set for the project (and recorded in the appropriate

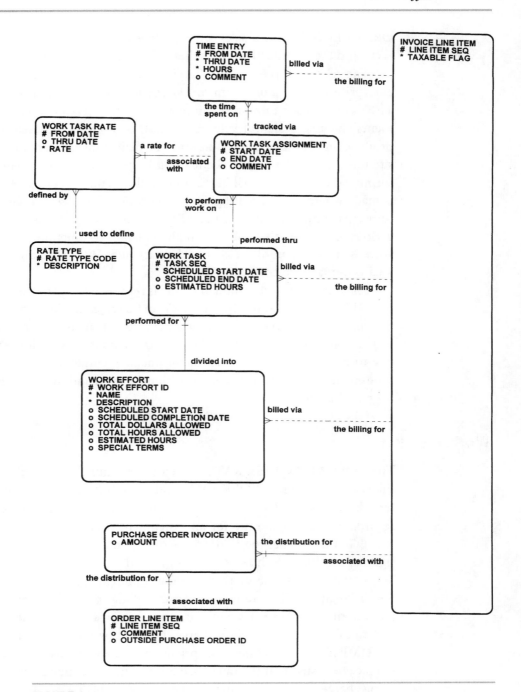

FIGURE 6.11

*Work effort invoicing.*

ORDER LINE ITEM for sales orders). Once the project is complete, an invoice is cut and the WORK EFFORT is then related to that invoice.

The relationship to WORK TASK from INVOICE LINE ITEM allows the enterprise to trace a line item to a particular phase of an effort. The WORK TASK can be used to represent a phase in the project life cycle (i.e., requirements analysis, design, development, etc.) or it could represent the effort to produce one of many deliverables (as in a deliverables-based project). For this situation, imagine that the client has a large project and the enterprise performing the work is not willing to wait until the end to get paid. A compromise is made whereby the client agrees to pay some of the fee as each phase of the project is completed. Again, a SALES ORDER is prepared which outlines the various phases and the cost of each phase. Upon completion of a phase, an invoice is cut and sent to the client. The particular WORK TASK is then associated with that invoice line item.

The third approach, billing by time, is represented by the relationship from INVOICE LINE ITEM to TIME ENTRY. In this case, the time worked represents the *shipment* of a service to the customer; when the invoice is cut, the line items will indicate the hours spent by the various parties involved. Notice that this is a one-to-many relationship; it allows for one line item to be the billing for many time entries. This is required because billing period and time recording periods may not match.

## Work Task Rate

The entity WORK TASK RATE is used to determine how much to charge for time entered against a WORK TASK, and possibly how much to pay the PARTY that did the work. The entity has a **from date** and **thru date** to allow for the recording of multiple rates for an assignment over time. The relationship to RATE TYPE provides the ability to record various kinds of rates against an assignment. Table 6.18 shows examples of this data.

As the example shows, there are four different rate types recorded for Mr. Smith: "regular billing" rate, an "overtime billing" rate, a "regular pay" rate, and an "overtime pay" rate. Using the information for the billing rates, it would be easy to calculate how much to charge the client by multiplying the hours from the TIME ENTRY times the appropriate rate. Note that business rules need to be in place to ensure that the rates used are for the same time period as the hours being charged for. In the same manner, it is possible to calculate how much to

**TABLE 6.18**   *Work Task Rate Data*

| Work Task* | Party* | Rate Type* | From Date | Thru Date | Rate |
|---|---|---|---|---|---|
| Develop accounting program | Gary Smith | Regular billing | May 15, 1996 | May 14, 1997 | $65.00 |
| | | Overtime billing | May 15, 1996 | May 14, 1997 | $70.00 |
| | | Regular pay | May 15, 1996 | May 14, 1997 | $40.00 |
| | | Overtime pay | May 15, 1996 | May 14, 1997 | $43.00 |
| | | Regular pay | May 15, 1997 | | $45.00 |
| | | Overtime pay | May 15, 1997 | | $45.00 |

pay Mr. Smith. Also there is a need to put business rules in place to determine what constitutes overtime work.

Notice also in the table that Mr. Smith has an increase in pay rate recorded to be effective on May 15, 1997. There is no **end date**. This indicates that the rate will be good until the end of the assignment. Also, note that the "overtime pay" is the same as the "regular pay" after the increase occurs. This would indicate that the enterprise may have automated rules on when to pay overtime, but in this case Mr. Smith no longer gets a higher rate. By recording the second rate, the payroll process that calculates his check does not need to be changed; it will simply calculate his overtime pay as always, but it effectively is at the same rate.

## Purchase Order Invoice Xref

The only hole left in the model now is a way to link an enterprise's purchase orders to invoices for services rendered by external parties. Again, since there is no real shipment information that can be recorded, the model from Chapter 5 will not help in this area. To fill this information gap, the entity PURCHASE ORDER INVOICE XREF is used (see Figure 6.11). It is a cross-reference entity used to resolve the many-to-many relationships that could occur between an ORDER LINE ITEM (on purchase orders) and an INVOICE LINE ITEM. The **amount** attribute is provided to allow distribution of the **amount** from a purchase order to multiple invoices or vice versa.

Take as an example, a purchase order line item for a year's worth of accounting services at a cost of $120,000. The accounting firm invoices on a monthly basis. So an invoice arrives with a line item for $10,000. This is then linked to the appropriate line item on the purchase order (using PURCHASE ORDER INVOICE XREF) and the amount of $10,000 is entered to show that $10,000 of the original $120,000 has been billed. This allows the enterprise to easily track over time how much of the original commitment has actually been billed to date (and also to notice if it has been billed beyond the amount of the purchase order).

On the other side, consider an enterprise in need of hardware support for its internal computer systems. Over the course of time, it executes three separate purchase orders to the same external company to provide this support. Each order has a line item for 40 hours of on-site support for a total of 120 hours. Again, over time, the services are delivered, but due to the billing cycles at the vendor company, the first invoice has one line item for 100 hours. The final 20 hours are billed on the next invoice. Table 6.19 shows the details for these transactions.

Using this construct, it is possible to handle almost any combination of order and invoicing. Why go to such lengths to provide this flexibility in the data model? This is because an enterprise has no real way of controlling service vendors and how they invoice. With this model it does not matter. How the vendor chooses to do business regarding customer purchase orders will make no difference to the enterprise because this model is flexible enough to handle a variety of situations.

TABLE 6.19   *Purchase Order Invoice Cross-reference Data*

| PO ID | Line Item Seq | Original Amount* | Invoice ID | Invoice Line Item Seq | Invoice Amount* | Allocated Amount |
|-------|---------------|------------------|------------|-----------------------|-----------------|------------------|
| 10001 | 1 | 40 | 99999 | 1 | 100 | 40 |
| 10002 | 1 | 40 | | | | 40 |
| 10003 | 1 | 40 | | | | 20 |
| 10003 | 1 | 40 | 90001 | 1 | 20 | 20 |

## Summary

The details of the data model that involves the scheduling, completion, and invoicing of work (see Figure 6.12) were discussed in this chapter. Included are the complete breakdown of efforts to tasks and the tracking of assignments of people, fixed assets, and inventory necessary for the completion of the tasks. Incorporated into the model as well are the entities needed to record the generic requirements for various types of tasks.

With this data model, enterprises should be able to effectively maintain lists of on-going efforts and the various resources that are available or already assigned to the completion of these efforts. The availability of this information could be critical to the continued success and development of the enterprise and is therefore of importance and needs to be included in the overall corporate model.

Refer to Appendix A for an alphabetical listing of entities and attributes presented above along with attribute characteristics. For SQL scripts to build tables, columns, and constraints derived from this logical model, please refer to the CD-ROM product that accompanies this text and is sold separately.

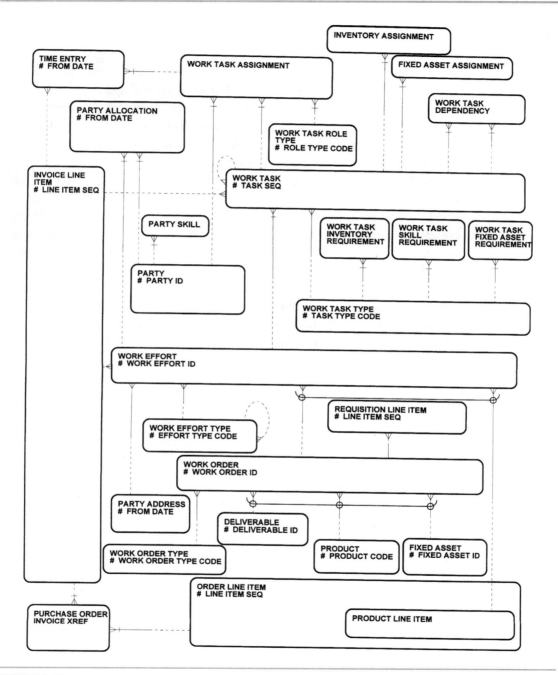

**FIGURE 6.12**

*Work order and work effort model.*

# 7

# ACCOUNTING AND BUDGETING

## INTRODUCTION

Many accounting functions are very similar across enterprises. Enterprises need to record transactions, post these transactions to each internal organization's chart of accounts, set up budgets, track variances to their budgets, and report on the results of their business operations.

An accounting and budgeting data model needs to maintain financial information to answer many important questions that affect an enterprise's existence:

What is the financial position of the enterprise and how did this change from previous periods?

What type of transactions occurred in each period and how much of each transaction occurred? For instance, what payments were made to which invoices and what invoices are still outstanding?

What expenses were incurred during various periods?

What effect did transactions such as depreciation, capitalization, and amortization have on the enterprise?

What budgets were set up and how did the enterprise perform compared to these budgets?

This chapter illustrates data models with the following types of information:

- Chart of accounts for internal organizations
- Accounting transaction definition
- Asset depreciation
- Budget definition
- Use of budgeted money
- Budget relationship to general ledger

## CHART OF ACCOUNTS FOR INTERNAL ORGANIZATIONS

Generally, the first step in setting up an accounting system is determining a chart of accounts for each organization. A chart of accounts is simply a list of the buckets or categories of transactions which the enterprise will use to track its business activity for accounting purposes.

Figure 7.1 shows a data model that can establish and maintain a chart of accounts for each organization within the enterprise. The GENERAL LEDGER ACCOUNT represents a financial reporting *bucket* to which transactions are posted. Each GENERAL LEDGER ACCOUNT may be categorized by one and only one GL (GENERAL LEDGER) ACCOUNT TYPE to specify the type of account (for instance, asset or liability). Each INTERNAL ORGANIZATION may have many GENERAL LEDGER ACCOUNTs and each GENERAL LEDGER ACCOUNT may be associated with more than one INTERNAL ORGANIZATION. The ORGANIZATION GL ACCOUNT resolves this many-to-many relationship. Each internal organization needs to establish the ACCOUNTING PERIOD for which it reports its business activities.

### General Ledger Accounts and Types

General ledger accounts are mechanisms to categorize similar types of transactions together for the purpose of financial reporting. The field name shown in the GENERAL LEDGER entity identifies the **name** of the account which will be used for reporting purposes in financial statements. Examples of general ledger account names include "cash", "accounts receivable", "notes payable", or "advertising expense". The **description** attribute provides a definition behind the account to ensure that it is understood properly.

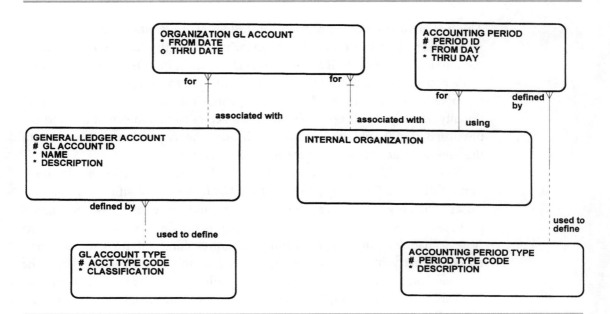

FIGURE 7.1

*Chart of accounts for internal organizations.*

The key to a GENERAL LEDGER ACCOUNT entity in this model is the **GL** (general ledger) **account ID** and is filled with a *nonmeaningful* unique number. Many other accounting systems assign a meaningful pneumonic to the GL account ID so that accounts are easily identified. The key may start with an organization component, then have a sub-organization portion, then have the type of account, and then have a number representing the account. An example of this ID structure is ABC100-200-A-101, where "ABC100" represents the organization, "200" represents a specific division, "A" stands for asset, and "101" represents the account "cash." The problem with having a meaningful key is that if things change within the enterprise such as a re-organization of the enterprise, then it creates a major problem for the system since key values and foreign key values need to be changed and there is a high chance of data inconsistencies. This is not what is desired especially in an accounting system which needs to be precise.

In most accounting systems there is an account balance associated with each general ledger account. Why is the amount balance not shown as an attribute?

This information is not appropriate for the logical model since the amount is derived information from the transactions which affect the account. However, in the physical implementation of this logical model, it may be a good idea to include account balances for various time periods. Even though this information is derived, the information doesn't change much after the period ends. Additionally, managers will no doubt need fast access to this information, and the physical design should not have to scan through the transactions associated with the general ledger account to determine the account balance.

The GENERAL LEDGER ACCOUNT TYPE entity identifies the classification of the GENERAL LEDGER ACCOUNT. Valid classifications include "asset", "liability", "owners equity", "revenue", and "expense". This information provides a mechanism to group information on financial statements. The "asset", "liability", and "owners equity" categories along with the associated general ledger accounts are generally used for the organization's balance sheet. The "revenue" and "expense" categories are generally used for the income statement.

Table 7.1 shows examples of general ledger accounts along with the type associated with each account.

**TABLE 7.1**    *General Ledger Account*

| GL Account ID | Name | Description | GL Account Type* |
|---|---|---|---|
| 110 | Cash | Liquid amounts of money available | Asset |
| 120 | Accounts Receivable | Total amount of moneys due from all sources | Asset |
| 240 | Notes Payable | Amounts due in the form of written contractual promissory notes | Liability |
| 300 | Retained Earnings | Identifies the difference between assets and liabilities which the owners have earned | Owners Equity |
| 420 | Interest Income | Amounts of revenues accumulated for a period due to interest earned | Revenue |
| 520 | Advertising Expense | Costs due to all ads placed in newspapers, magazines, etc. | Expense |
| 530 | Office Supplies | Expenses for buying supplies needed for the office | Expense |

## Organization GL Account

Now that general ledger accounts have been established, they need to be related to the internal organizations that use them for reporting. Each INTERNAL ORGANIZATION may have many GENERAL LEDGER ACCOUNTs associated with it. Conversely, each GENERAL LEDGER ACCOUNT may be reused to satisfy the needs of many INTERNAL ORGANIZATIONs. The ORGANIZATION GL ACCOUNT shows which internal organizations use which general ledger accounts. The **from date** and **thru date** attributes on the ORGANIZATION GL ACCOUNT entity indicate when general ledger accounts were added to an internal organization's chart of accounts and for what period of time they were valid.

The ACCOUNTING PERIOD entity indicates the periods of time which the organization uses for its financial reporting. This may be to define a fiscal year, fiscal month, fiscal quarter, or any other time period which is available in the ACCOUNTING PERIOD TYPE. The **from day** and **thru day** attributes are character strings and not date domains, since they only specify part of a date such as the month and day for the start and end of the fiscal year period.

Table 7.2 illustrates examples of the chart of accounts for ABC Corporation and ABC Subsidiary. Notice that while many general ledger accounts are used within both organizations, some accounts are different. For example, ABC Corporation has a "trade show expense" account whereas the subsidiary doesn't have this account since it is not involved in trade shows.

Also, notice that each organization has its fiscal year accounting periods associated with it (Acctg Period From and Thru). The two organizations shown have the same fiscal year period; however, it is possible for internal organizations within the same enterprise to have different accounting periods. For example, an organization with a fiscal period from June 1 to May 31 may have been recently merged into an internal organization whose fiscal period is January 1 to December 31.

The GL account from and thru dates provide the ability to track which GL accounts existed at what periods of time. For example, Table 7.2 shows that on January 1, 1990, ABC Corporation divided its "marketing expense" account into two accounts: "advertising expense" and "trade show expense".

TABLE 7.2  *Organization GL Account*

| Internal Organization* | Acctg Period From Day* | Acctg Period Thru Day* | Acct Period Type* | General Ledger Account Type* | General Ledger Account* | GL Account From Date | GL Account Thru Date |
|---|---|---|---|---|---|---|---|
| ABC Corporation | Jan 1 | Dec 31 | Fiscal Year | Asset | Cash | Jan 1, 1988 | |
| | | | | | Accounts receivable | Jan 1, 1988 | |
| | | | | Liability | Notes payable | Jan 1, 1988 | |
| | | | | Owners Equity | Retained earnings | Jan 1, 1988 | |
| | | | | Revenue | Interest income | Jan 1, 1988 | |
| | | | | Expense | Marketing expense | Jan 1, 1988 | Dec 31, 1989 |
| | | | | | Advertising expense | Jan 1, 1990 | |
| | | | | | Trade show expense | Jun 1, 1990 | |
| | | | | | Office supplies | Jan 1, 1988 | |
| ABC Subsidiary | Jan 1 | Dec 31 | Fiscal Year | Asset | Cash | Jun 1, 1990 | |
| | | | | | Accounts receivable | Jun 1, 1990 | |
| | | | | Liability | Notes payable | Jun 1, 1990 | |
| | | | | Owners Equity | Retained earnings | Jun 1, 1990 | |
| | | | | Revenue | Interest income | Jun 1, 1990 | |
| | | | | Expense | Marketing expense | Jan 1, 1990 | |
| | | | | | Office supplies | Jun 1, 1990 | |

# ACCOUNTING TRANSACTION DEFINITION

Figure 7.2 illustrates a data model which cross-references transactions to the appropriate general ledger accounts. The ACCOUNTING TRANSACTION entity is a super-type that encompasses all the transactions which affect the financial statements of the enterprise. It includes INTERNAL TRANSACTION such as DEPRECIATION, CAPITALIZATION, AMORTIZATION, ITEM VARIANCE, and OTHER INTERNAL TRANSACTION which document adjustments to the internal organization's financial position. Accounting transactions may also be EXTERNAL TRANSACTIONs which involve either OBLIGATIONs between two PARTYs or PAYMENTs made between two PARTYs. Each PAYMENT may be of a certain PAY TYPE such as "electronic funds" or "cash". Each ACCOUNTING TRANSACTION is then described by a specific ACCOUNTING TRANSACTION TYPE and is broken down into various TRANSACTION DETAILs which are each allocated to an ORGANIZATION GL ACCOUNT.

## Accounting Transaction

In various parts of this book, some accounting transactions have already been modeled. For example, in Chapter 4, the creation of an INVOICE represents an accounting transaction. In Chapter 3, the identification of a ITEM VARIANCE to adjust INVENTORY ITEMs represents another accounting transaction.

Each accounting transaction generally has its own attributes and relationships; however, there are some similar characteristics among these transactions. This is the reason why Figure 7.2 models the super-entity ACCOUNTING TRANSACTION which incorporates the similar attributes and relationships among these transactions. Each ACCOUNTING TRANSACTION instance represents a *journal entry* in accounting terms.

The ACCOUNTING TRANSACTION entity has a **transaction ID** which uniquely identifies the particular transaction. The **transaction date** is the date upon which the transaction occurred. The **entry date** is the date upon which the entry was made into the system. The **amount** is the total amount of the transaction which occurred. Note that the **amount** is an optional attribute because certain types of accounting transaction amounts, such as INVOICE, can be calculated by summing the line items of the transaction. The **description** attribute describes the details behind the transaction.

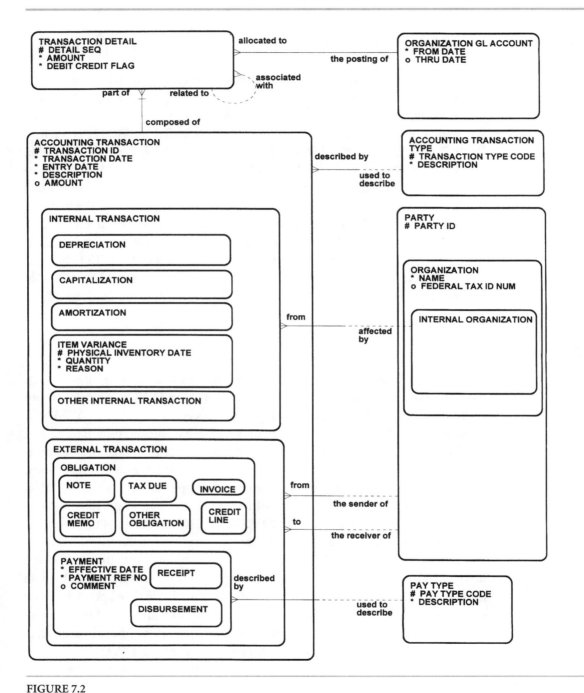

FIGURE 7.2

*Accounting transaction definitions.*

Accounting deals with two main types of transactions. An ACCOUNTING TRANSACTION may either be an INTERNAL TRANSACTION or an EXTERNAL TRANSACTION. The INTERNAL TRANSACTION identifies transactions which serve as adjustments to the books of an internal organization. Since there is only one organization involved in the transaction (namely, the internal organization whose books are being adjusted), there is a single relationship to an INTERNAL ORGANIZATION. The sub-types reveal examples of internal transactions such as DEPRECIATION, CAPITALIZATION, AMORTIZATION, ITEM VARIANCE, and OTHER INTERNAL TRANSACTIONs which adjust the financial position of the internal organization.

The EXTERNAL TRANSACTION sub-entity models accounting transactions that affect two parties. An EXTERNAL TRANSACTION may be either an OBLIGATION or a PAYMENT. An OBLIGATION represents a transaction where one party has recognized that it owes moneys to another party. Therefore, the *from* and *to* relationships identify the parties involved on both sides of a transaction.

The OBLIGATION sub-entity is broken down into various other sub-types that represent different forms of a party owing moneys to another party. One sub-type of OBLIGATION is a NOTE. It may be a note payable where the internal organization owes moneys or a note receivable where it is due moneys. Another sub-type is CREDIT MEMO which is a transaction where credit is given from one party to another party. TAX DUE is an obligation to pay taxes to government agencies. Chapter 4 covered the INVOICE entity which represents the obligation to pay for products sold. CREDIT LINE represents moneys actually borrowed from a line of credit extended from a financial institute to another party. There may be other forms of obligation depending on the business; therefore, the OTHER OBLIGATION sub-type is included.

The PAYMENT sub-entity represents collections of moneys received by an internal organization (RECEIPT) or payments of moneys sent by an internal organization (DISBURSEMENT). A payment made from one internal organization to another internal organization results in two PAYMENTs; one internal organization will record a RECEIPT and the other internal organization will record a DISBURSEMENT.

The PAYMENT sub-entity is related to the PAY TYPE entity whose description identifies the kind of payment such as "electronic" (for electronic transfers of moneys), "cash", "certified check", "personal check", or "credit card". The **payment ref no** references an external identifier such as a check number or electronic transfer identifier. The **effective date** documents when the payment can be made effective. For instance, an electronic transfer may be for a future period in time or a check may be postdated and take effect at a later period in time. The **comment** provides an attribute to fully describe any circumstances involved in the transaction such as "payment was made with a message which complimented the service provided".

The relationship from ACCOUNTING TRANSACTION to ACCOUNTING TRANSACTION TYPE provides a specific low-level categorization of each transaction. Types may include further breakdowns of the sub-types such as "Payment Receipt for Asset Sale" or "Payment Disbursement for Purchase Order".

Table 7.3 provides examples of various types of accounting transactions. The first row (transaction ID 32389) is an example of an internal transaction which records a depreciation expense for a piece of equipment. Only one party is affected—the internal organization that owns that piece of equipment, ABC Corporation. The rest of the transactions are different types of external transactions which involve a "to" party and a "from" party. For instance, transaction 39776 describes a revenue payment (incoming payment) to pay off $700 owed by ACME Company to ABC Corporation.

## Transaction Detail

As shown in Figure 7.2, each ACCOUNTING TRANSACTION must be composed of one or more TRANSACTION DETAILs which shows how each part of the transaction affects a specific ORGANIZATION GL ACCOUNT. A TRANSACTION DETAIL instance corresponds to a "journal entry line item" in accounting terms.

According to the principles of double-entry accounting, each transaction has at least two detail records, a debit and a credit. For instance, an ACCOUNTING TRANSACTION of type INVOICE may result in two TRANSACTION DETAIL instances: A debit to the general ledger account "accounts receivable" (showing that moneys are due) and a credit to the general ledger account "revenue" (showing that revenue is recognized). Table 7.4 illustrates the details of this transaction (transaction ID 38948 in the table).

Each transaction is related to the general ledger account within a specific internal organization which is why the **organization GL account** column of Table 7.4 references the "ABC Corporation" in parentheses. Appropriate business rules need to be put in place to make sure that the organization associated with the

**TABLE 7.3**  *Accounting Transaction*

| Transaction ID | To Party | From Party | Transaction Date | Transaction Amount | Transaction Type* | Description |
|---|---|---|---|---|---|---|
| 32389 | | ABC Corporation | Jan 1, 1995 | $200 | Depreciation | Depreciation on pen engraver |
| 38948 | ACME Company | ABC Corporation | May 31, 1995 | $900 | Invoice | Invoiced amount due |
| 39776 | ABC Corporation | ACME Company | Jun 13, 1995 | $700 | Payment Receipt For Invoices | Payment against invoice |
| 45783 | ACME Company | ABC Corporation | Jul 2, 1995 | $200 | Credit Memo | Credit to invoice # |
| 45894 | ABC Corporation | ACME Company | Aug 13, 1995 | $300 | Payment Receipt For Invoices | Payment made on account with no particular invoice in mind |
| 46325 | ACME Company | ABC Corporation | Oct 10, 1995 | -$300 | Payment Receipt for Invoices | Returned payment for moneys held on account with no invoice |
| 47874 | ABC Corporation | Johnson Recycling | Oct 11, 1995 | $1200 | Payment Receipt For Asset Sale | Payment received for sale of pen engraver |

ORGANIZATION GL ACCOUNT makes sense in relation to the PARTY associated with the ACCOUNTING TRANSACTION. For instance, if there is an INTERNAL TRANSACTION for ABC Corporation, then the TRANSACTION DETAIL records need to be related to ORGANIZATION GL ACCOUNTs of "ABC Corporation" and not of another internal organization.

The **transaction ID** and the **detail seq** uniquely identify the TRANSACTION DETAIL since it is a detail record which breaks down the ACCOUNTING

TABLE 7.4   *Transaction Detail*

| Transaction ID* | Transaction Description* | Detail Seq | Amount | Debit/Credit Flag | OrganizationGL Account* |
|---|---|---|---|---|---|
| 32389 | Depreciation on pen engraver | 1 | $200 | Debit | Depreciation expense (ABC Corporation) |
| | | 2 | $200 | Credit | Accumulated depreciation for equipment (ABC Corporation) |
| 38948 | Invoiced amount due | 1 | $900 | Debit | Accounts receivable (ABC Corporation) |
| | | 2 | $900 | Credit | Revenue (ABC Corporation) |
| 39776 | Payment against invoice | 1 | $882 | Debit | Cash (ABC Corporation) |
| | | 2 | $18 | Debit | Discount expense (ABC Corporation) |
| | | 3 | $900 | Credit | Accounts receivable |
| 47874 | Payment received for sale of pen engraver | 1 | $1000 | Debit | Cash (ABC Corporation) |
| | | 2 | $200 | Debit | Accumulated depreciation (ABC Corporation) |
| | | 3 | $800 | Credit | Asset (ABC Corporation) |
| | | 4 | $400 | Credit | Capital gain (ABC Corporation) |

TRANSACTION. The **debit/credit flag** indicates whether the transaction detail is posted as a debit or credit to the appropriate general ledger account. The **amount** indicates the amount of that portion of the transaction. Many *physical* database designs implement the **debit/credit flag** as a positive or negative sign within the **amount** field so that arithmetic functions can be easily used to offset debits and credits.

It was stated that an ACCOUNTING TRANSACTION has at least two TRANSACTION DETAIL records. In many cases, an accounting transaction may have more than two detail entries. Consider the third transaction in Table

7.4, transaction ID 39776. This transaction was a payment against an invoice with a 2 percent discount taken for early payment. The transaction resulted in three detail records, a credit to clear the accounts receivable of $900, a cash increase of $882, and a discount expense of $18.

The fourth transaction in Table 7.4 (transaction ID 47874) provides an example of an accounting transaction with four detail records. The sale of a piece of equipment, in this case the pen engraving machine, resulted in a debit to cash of the $1,000 received, a debit of $200 which clears the accumulated depreciation of the machine, a credit of $800 which was the book value of the asset, and a credit to record the capital gain on the transaction of $400 ($1,000 received minus the net value of the equipment of $600).

## Relationships between Accounting Transaction Details

Businesses need to answer questions regarding the relationships between certain transactions. For example, which invoices have been paid off through which payments and which invoices are still outstanding? Which invoices have been reduced via credit memos issued to customers? Which payments were subsequently sent back to the originating party since they did not correspond to an invoice or amount due?

The recursive relationship around TRANSACTION DETAIL provides the capability to track which accounting transaction details are associated with other transaction details. Using this recursive relationship, the model can provide the information to answer the previous questions.

Table 7.5 illustrates how the model can be used to relate different accounting transactions to one another. A very common type of related transaction is what payments are made against which invoices. Transaction ID 38948 shows that $900 is due as an accounts receivable. The next transaction shown (39776) is a payment that is applied to this invoice. The last column **Associated Transaction ID and Detail Seq** represents the recursive relationship from one transaction detail to another transaction detail. In this case, it identifies that the credit to accounts receivable is specifically regarding transaction 38948 which was the original invoice that was paid off.

Table 7.5 also shows that two invoices (transactions 50984 and 50999) were paid off via a single payment (transaction 60985). In this case, the transaction detail representing the "accounts receivable" entry was split into two detail records in order to identify the amounts allocated for each of the two invoices.

**TABLE 7.5**    *Transaction Detail Relationships*

| Transaction ID* | Transaction Description* | Detail Seq | Amount | Debit/Credit Indicator | Organization GL Account* | Associated Transaction ID and Detail Seq* |
|---|---|---|---|---|---|---|
| 38948 | Invoiced amount due | 1 | $900 | Debit | Accounts receivable (ABC Corporation) | |
| | | 2 | $900 | Credit | Revenue (ABC Corporation) | |
| 39776 | Payment against invoice | 1 | $882 | Debit | Cash (ABC Corporation) | |
| | | 2 | $18 | Debit | Discount expense (ABC Corporation) | |
| | | 3 | $900 | Credit | Accounts receivable (ABC Corporation) | 38948, 1 |
| 50984 | Invoiced amount due | 1 | $1000 | Debit | Accounts receivable (ABC Corporation) | |
| | | 2 | $1000 | Credit | Revenue (ABC Corporation) | |
| 50999 | Invoiced amount due | 1 | $2000 | Debit | Accounts receivable (ABC Corporation) | |
| | | 2 | $2000 | Credit | Revenue (ABC Corporation) | |
| 60985 | Payment against invoice | 1 | $3000 | Debit | Cash (ABC Corporation) | |
| | | 2 | $1000 | Credit | Accounts receivable (ABC Corporation) | 50984, 1 |
| | | 3 | $2000 | Credit | Accounts receivable (ABC Corporation) | 50999, 1 |

This model can accommodate any type of transaction relationship which occurs in accounting. For instance, it can provide the information to maintain credit memos which reduce invoice amounts (obligations related to other obligations), refunds of payments (payments related to other payments), partial payments applied to invoices (payments to obligations), and sales of depreciated equipment applied to the original purchase transaction (payments related to payments and to internal transactions; namely, depreciation).

## ASSET DEPRECIATION

There may be additional entities which are used to determine how certain accounting transactions are calculated. This section illustrates the means by which a common type of internal transaction, namely, depreciation, is calculated.

As shown in Figure 7.3, each DEPRECIATION transaction is specifically for one and only one FIXED ASSET (described in Chapter 6). A FIXED ASSET may be depreciated using DEPRECIATION METHODs. The same depreciation method may be used to depreciate more than one fixed asset and a fixed asset may have more than one DEPRECIATION METHOD over time, since a fixed asset's depreciation method may change (although this may be regulated by

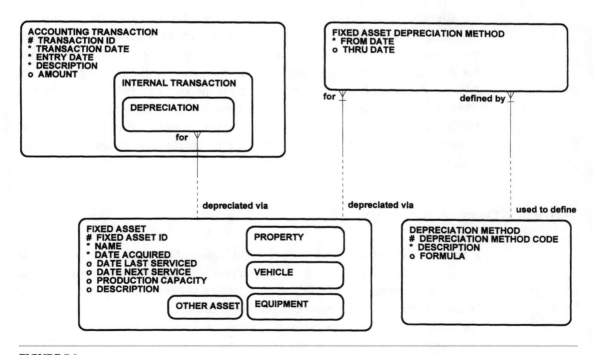

FIGURE 7.3

*Asset depreciation.*

TABLE 7.6    *Fixed Asset Depreciation Method*

| Fixed Asset Name* | Depreciation Method Description* | Depreciation Method Formula* | From Date | Thru Date |
|---|---|---|---|---|
| Pen Engraver | Double-declining balance depreciation | (Purchase cost – salvage cost)∗ (1/estimated life in years of the asset)∗2 | Jan 1, 1994 | Dec 31, 1994 |
| | Straight-line depreciation | (Purchase cost – salvage cost)/estimated life in years of the asset | Jan 1, 1995 | |

agencies such as the IRS). Therefore, the FIXED ASSET DEPRECIATION METHOD entity documents which depreciation method was used on each fixed asset during various periods of time.

The DEPRECIATION METHOD entity has a **description** attribute which specifies the type of depreciation such as "straight line depreciation" or "double declining balance depreciation". It also describes the **formula** for calculating depreciation. Table 7.6 illustrates examples of the type of information maintained for depreciation calculation purposes. In this example, the pen engraver used "double-declining balance" as a method for the year of 1994; then starting in 1995, it began using the "straight-line depreciation" method of depreciation. While it may be very interesting to describe the formulas behind these depreciation methods (for a very select breed), this information can be found in any accounting book and is beyond the scope of this book.

## BUDGET DEFINITION

Another aspect of financial control is budgeting. Figure 7.4 illustrates a data model that provides information on budgets which are set up to monitor the spending of moneys. A PARTY (which may be a person or an organization) may be the initiator of one or more budgets over time. The BUDGET entity describes the information about the amounts of moneys needed for a group of expense items over a certain period of time (represented by STANDARD TIME PERIOD). Each budget will usually go through a process whereby several BUDGET REVISIONs are created for the BUDGET. Each BUDGET REVISION must be com-

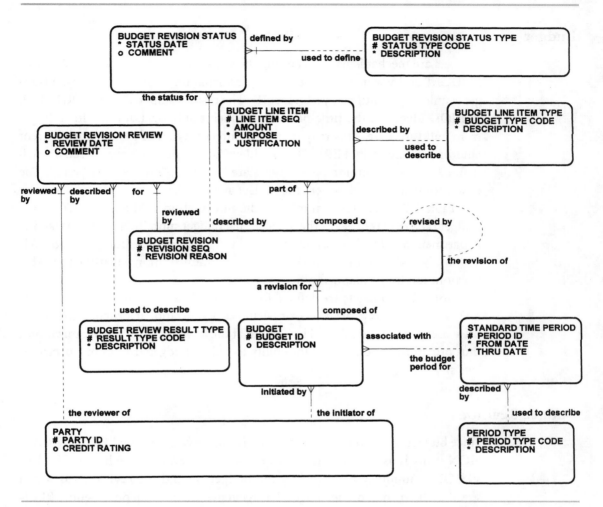

**FIGURE 7.4**

*Budget definition.*

posed of one or more BUDGET LINE ITEMs which describe the amounts allocated to various types of spending activities (or BUDGET LINE ITEM TYPEs). The model provides the capability to track the various statuses that each BUDGET REVISION has, over time, through the BUDGET REVISION STATUS entity which uses available status values from BUDGET REVISION STATUS TYPE. Budgets also have various PARTYs that are involved in BUDGET REVISION REVIEWs, each of which has a certain BUDGET REVIEW RESULT TYPE.

## Budget

Budgets are mechanisms for planning the spending of moneys. Figure 7.4 has a BUDGET entity which describes the key information regarding budgets. A budget is uniquely identified by a **budget ID**. The relationship to STANDARD TIME PERIOD identifies the time period for which the budget applies, including a from and thru date. This may represent different types of periods for different enterprises. The entity PERIOD TYPE identifies the particular type used by each defined period. Common period types are "month", "quarter", or "year". The **description** attribute describes the budget at a high level.

Table 7.7 illustrates examples of the information in the BUDGET entity. Budget ID 29839 represents the 1996 annual budget submitted by the marketing department of ABC Corporation for its marketing expenses. Budget ID 38576 is a monthly budget, for June of 1997, from the administration department of ABC Corporation for its planned office expenses.

Notice that budgets are defined for individual parties which may be departments, divisions, organizations, or whatever organizational structure the enterprise uses. The budget should be defined at the lowest level in the organizations, thus providing the enterprise the ability to roll up budgeted amounts to various levels.

## Budget Revision

Since budgets may go through many revisions or versions, the BUDGET REVISION entity is used to maintain each revision in its entirety. Each BUDGET REVISION is uniquely identified by the **budget ID** and the **revision seq** which specifies the version of the budget. The recursive relationship on the entity BUDGET REVISION identifies if the budget is a revision of a previous budget. Since the recursion is a one-to-one relationship, the model only tracks one previous budget revision, which is usually what's needed for most enterprises.

TABLE 7.7    *Budget Data*

| Budget ID | Party ID * | Budget Period * | Period Type* | Budget Description |
|---|---|---|---|---|
| 29839 | Marketing Department | 1/1/96–12/31/96 | year | Marketing budget |
| 38576 | Administration Department | 6/1/97–6/30/97 | month | Office expenses budget |

**TABLE 7.8**   *Budget Revision*

| Budget ID | Budget Description* | Revision Number | A Revision of | Revision Reason |
|-----------|---------------------|-----------------|---------------|-----------------|
| 29839 | Marketing budget | 1 | | |
| 29839 | Marketing budget | 2 | 29839, 1 | Needed to substantially cut budgeted amounts |
| 29839 | Marketing budget | 3 | 29839, 2 | A few changes needed to be made to budget line item justification |

Table 7.8 illustrates examples of the information in the BUDGET REVISION entity. This example shows that budget 29839 had three revisions. The initial budget (revision 1) was subsequently revised by revision 2. The second revision was needed to adjust amounts in the line items. The third revision was needed to modify some of the justifications for specific line items.

## Budget Line Item

Each BUDGET REVISION must be composed of one or more BUDGET LINE ITEMs since the line item defines the items within the budget revision. The **amount** attribute defines the total amount of funds required for the item within the time period. The **purpose** attribute identifies why the items are needed and the **justification** attribute describes why the budgeted amount of money should be expended. Each BUDGET LINE ITEM is described by a BUDGET LINE ITEM TYPE so that common budget line item descriptions can be reused. Table 7.9 provides two simple examples of budget line items within the budgets described in the previous section. Budgets defined within actual enterprises are likely to have many more budget line items per budget than the examples given (which of course is allowed in this data model).

## Budget Status

Each BUDGET REVISION generally moves through various stages as the budget process unfolds. A revision of a budget is typically created on a certain date, reviewed, submitted for approval, then either accepted, rejected, or sent back to the submitter for modifications, thus starting a new revision.

**TABLE 7.9**  *Budget Line item*

| Budget Id* | Budget Description* | Line Item Seq | Budget Line Item Description* | Amount | Purpose | Justification |
|------------|---------------------|---------------|-------------------------------|--------|---------|---------------|
| 29839 | Marketing budget | 1 | Trade Shows | $20,000 | Connect directly with various markets | Last year, this amount was spent and it resulted in 3 new clients |
|  |  | 2 | Advertising | $30,000 | Create public awareness of products | Competition demands product recognition |
|  |  | 3 | Direct Mail | $15,000 | To generate sales leads | Past experience predicts that one can expect 50 leads for every $5,000 expended |
| 38576 | Office expenses budget | 1 | Office Supplies | $5,000 | Supplies needed to perform office administration tasks | This is the amount expended last year and is required again |
|  |  | 2 | Furniture | $10,000 | For new facility on Benjamin Street | New facility needs some basic items of furniture |

Figure 7.4 shows that each BUDGET REVISION has one or more BUDGET REVISION STATUSes over time, each of which is described by a BUDGET REVISION STATUS TYPE. This structure provides for the tracking of the history of a budget through its various stages.

This budget model assumes that the enterprise tracks the status of a budget revision in its entirety. When a revision is required, another BUDGET REVISION and new BUDGET LINE ITEMs are created, even if some of the line items have not changed. In most enterprises, this information on the history of each revision is very important as it provides a proper auditing trail.

Table 7.10 illustrates examples of budget statuses. Notice that on November 15 when the budget was sent back to the submitter for modifications, it created the need for a new revision of the budget.

TABLE 7.10   *Budget Revision Status*

| Budget ID* | Revision Seq | Status Date | Budget Status Type Description* | Comment |
|---|---|---|---|---|
| 29839 | 1 | Oct 15, 1995 | Created | |
| 29839 | 1 | Nov 1, 1995 | Submitted | |
| 29839 | 1 | Nov 15, 1995 | Sent back for modifications | Management agreed with the types of items budgeted; however, it asked that all amounts be lowered. |
| 29839 | 2 | Nov 20, 1995 | Submitted | |
| 29839 | 2 | Nov 30, 1995 | Approved | |

## Budget Revision Review

In the budgeting process there may be several people involved in reviewing a budget revision for approval. The BUDGET REVISION REVIEW and BUDGET REVIEW RESULT TYPE entities in Figure 7.4 provide for the tracking of the parties involved in budget reviews.

The BUDGET REVISION REVIEW entity provides the information about which people were involved in the review process via the relationship from BUDGET REVISION REVIEW to PARTY. The **review date** identifies when they were involved in the review. The **comment** attribute allows any personal opinions about the review to be documented. Each person's decision regarding the budget review is indicated via the relationship to BUDGET REVIEW RESULT TYPE.

Table 7.11 illustrates the information that may be contained in the BUDGET REVIEW entity. The example provides information on the people involved in the budget review process and their comments and conclusions. This information serves as supporting information regarding budget revision statuses.

One may think that the BUDGET REVISION REVIEW entity is related to the BUDGET REVISION STATUS since the result of the reviews may affect the budget revision status. In reality, there is not really a direct data relationship between these entities, since reviews and statuses each exist independently for a budget revision. However, the enterprise may maintain business rules to determine what reviews constitute moving from one status to the next.

TABLE 7.11    *Budget Review*

| Budget ID* | Revision Seq | Party ID* | Review Date | Budget Review Result Description* | Comment |
|---|---|---|---|---|---|
| 29839 | 1 | Susan Jones | Nov 10, 1995 | Accepted | Budget seems reasonable |
|  |  | John Smith | Nov 15, 1995 | Sent Back | Budgeted figures are too high |
| 29839 | 2 | Susan Jones | Nov 22, 1995 | Accepted |  |
|  |  | John Smith | Nov 30, 1995 | Accepted |  |

## USE OF BUDGETED MONEY

Now that budgets have been set up, how does the organization monitor what commitments and expenses have been made to each budget line item? Figure 7.5 provides a data model to answer this question. Each ORDER LINE ITEM (from a purchase order) may be authorized via and allocated to a specific BUDGET LINE ITEM. A WORK ORDER (for projects) may be funded via many BUDGET LINE ITEMS (and vice versa) through the entity WORK ORDER BUDGET ALLOCATION. These relationships establish what commitments (and dollar amounts) have been made to various budget line items. The many-to-many relationship between DISBURSEMENT and BUDGET LINE ITEM is resolved by using a DISBURSEMENT BUDGET ALLOCATION entity. This entity models which disbursement payments are allocated to which budget line items, only for disbursements which *do not have* a corresponding order associated with them. For disbursements which have a purchase order, the DISBURSEMENT BUDGET ALLOCATION is not used since the budget line item allocation can be derived from relationships from the DISBURSEMENT to the corresponding ORDER LINE ITEM of the purchase order.

### Commitments against Budgets

Most enterprises involved in budgeting are interested in two types of comparisons against the budget: What commitments exist against a budget line item and what has been expended against a budget line item. This section addresses the information needed to track commitments against a budget.

After a budget is approved, enterprises are interested in tracking commitments against a budget. A line item on a purchase order may establish a commitment against a budget line item. Therefore, in Figure 7.5, the data model illustrates that each ORDER LINE ITEM may be allocated to one and only one BUDGET LINE ITEM. The order line item will generally be from a purchase order. For example, a purchase order line item for 20 "Johnson Elite Pens" may be recorded against an administration department's budget line item for "office supplies".

One may conclude that each purchase order line item is for a specific prod-

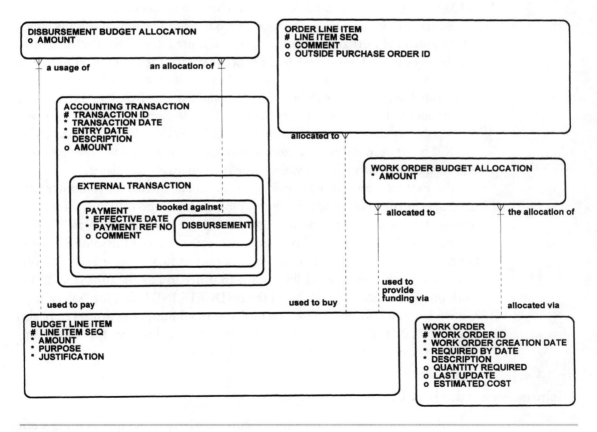

FIGURE 7.5

*Use of budgeted money.*

uct and each product corresponds to a particular budget line item. This would result in a PRODUCT to BUDGET LINE ITEM relationship instead of the ORDER LINE ITEM to BUDGET LINE ITEM. Although this may work in some circumstances, the allocation of a commitment is very dependent upon the particular situation and usually cannot be generalized.

Consider the purchase of a personal computer (PC). On one purchase order, the PC is used for a systems development project and is tied to the budget line item for that project. On another purchase order for a PC, the PC is for a particular employee and may be allocated to a computer equipment budget line item. Therefore, rather than perform budget allocations based upon the product being ordered, the ORDER LINE ITEM determines the allocation to a BUDGET LINE ITEM so that individual circumstances can be accommodated.

Budget line items may also be used to provide funding for WORK ORDERs. Even though the work order represents one or more internal work efforts, there is a single estimated cost to the work order that may need allocation to one or more BUDGET LINE ITEMs. Figure 7.5 shows that each WORK ORDER may be allocated to many BUDGET LINE ITEMs and that one BUDGET LINE ITEM may be used to fund more than one WORK ORDER. Hence, this many-to-many relationship is resolved with the entity WORK ORDER BUDGET ALLOCA-TION. The **amount** attribute is used to store the dollar allocation information so that total commitments for any given line item are easily calculated.

For example, an internal work order to repair a personal computer may have an estimated cost of $50 for the employee's time who is fixing it. This may represent a commitment toward a specific budget line item such as "PC Repairs". Over time, there could be many such orders against the same line item. On the other hand, a WORK ORDER for a project may require $100,000 total from several different budget line items. In order to pay the project staff, the work order may need $80,000 from the BUDGET LINE ITEM for "salary" that is included in a budget for research projects. In addition, the project may also need $20,000 for office supplies which comes from a line item for "office supplies" in the overhead budget for the enterprise.

## Disbursements against Budgets

In addition to knowing what commitments have been made against budget line items, organizations also want to know what disbursements have been made against each budget line item. The commitment, such as a purchase order line item, represents an obligation to pay, whereas the disbursement represents actual payments made against the budget line item.

The data model shown in Figure 7.5 provides the ability to capture disbursements against budgets under two different scenarios: when there is a purchase order prior to the disbursement and when there is an disbursement without a purchase order preceding it.

When there is a purchase order prior to the disbursement, the disbursement may be traced back to the corresponding purchase order line item. This is necessary to determine how much of the purchase order line item is now expended versus committed against the budget line item. In other words, the data model tracks disbursements against the corresponding purchase order which is tied to the budget line item. For instance, a $50,000 purchase order for an "office supplies" budget line item may have a $25,000 disbursement against it. The $50,000 represents the budget line item commitment. The $25,000 represents disbursements against that commitment.

The DISBURSEMENT is related back to the ORDER LINE ITEM through a series of data model transversals. The DISBURSEMENT is a type of PAYMENT which is related to the INVOICE entity through the TRANSACTION DETAIL. Then each INVOICE has one or more INVOICE LINE ITEMs which are related to either SHIPMENTS (for items) or directly to the ORDER LINE ITEM (for services purchased). The SHIPMENT LINE ITEM is then related back to an ORDER LINE ITEM of a purchase order.

Needless to say, the relationships from a disbursement back to the originating purchase order line item are very complex and require numerous business rules. For instance, disbursements may pay off partial orders or many orders for various shipments. The enterprise will need business rules regarding how to allocate the disbursements to the appropriate purchase orders.

While it may be complex to trace back a disbursement to a purchase order, it is also necessary if the budget is to accurately reflect committed and expended amounts against a budget line item. Whether the information is stored in the database or a person manually figures out the budget allocation, the same process needs to occur: The disbursement needs to be mapped to the corresponding invoice, mapped to the shipment, then mapped to the purchase order details, in order to figure out the proper budget allocation.

In some circumstances, a purchase order may not be in place before the disbursement is made. For example, an employee may go out to a store and pay for items with a check. Yet, this disbursement may still need to be allocated against a budget line item. The data model shown in Figure 7.5 accommodates this circumstance by using the DISBURSEMENT BUDGET ALLOCATION entity. This is an intersection entity between the BUDGET LINE ITEM and the DISBURSEMENT. The **amount** attribute records how much of each disbursement is allocated to each budget line item.

Table 7.12 gives an example of a disbursement budget allocation. In this case, an employee went out to an office supplies store and wrote out a check for $2,000 for the purchase of a chair and some office supplies. This payment needs to be allocated between two budget line items: office supplies and furniture. The first two columns of the table describe attributes of information in the budget entities. The next three columns describe information about the disbursement. The last column shows that $500 of the transaction was allocated to the "office supplies" budget line item and $1,500 was allocated to the "furniture" budget line item.

This budget data model is intended to illustrate only the purchase order commitment and disbursement side of budgeting. Sometimes, budgeting occurs for projected revenue and receipts of moneys. The model in Figure 7.5 can be modified to accommodate the use *and source* of moneys by changing the relationships slightly. The relationship from DISBURSEMENT BUDGET ALLOCATION to DISBURSEMENT would instead be related to ACCOUNTING TRANSACTION, thereby including sales invoices and receipts of moneys. Also, the relationship from BUDGET LINE ITEM to ORDER LINE ITEM should allow line items on sales orders as well as purchase orders. These changes would allow the enterprise to set up budgets for incoming and outgoing moneys. This model would also allow the organization to set up budgets for all types of accounting transactions including INTERNAL TRANSACTIONs.

TABLE 7.12  *Disbursement Budget Allocation*

| Budget ID* | Budget Line Item Description* | Disbursement Transaction ID* | Disbursement Transaction Description* | Disbursement Transaction Amount* | Disbursement Budget Allocation |
|---|---|---|---|---|---|
| 38576 | Office Supplies | 2903 | Payment by check for a chair and office supplies | $2000 | $500 |
| 38576 | Furniture | 2903 | Payment by check for a chair and office supplies | $2000 | $1500 |

# BUDGET RELATIONSHIP TO GENERAL LEDGER

Budgets are used for different purposes than general ledger accounts. Budgets are used to monitor disbursements; general ledger accounts are used to report the financial performance of an enterprise. Department managers may define budget line items in any fashion that helps them control costs. Accountants categorize their chart of accounts to meet tax needs and various financial reporting needs.

Therefore, budget line items may not correspond directly with general ledger accounts. However, it is very helpful (and sometimes required) to be able to tie budget line items to general ledger accounts. An enterprise may want to see how much was budgeted and expended for a specific general ledger account such as "marketing expense".

Figure 7.6 shows a data model which relates budget line item types to general ledger accounts. Each BUDGET LINE ITEM TYPE may be related to many GENERAL LEDGER ACCOUNTs and vice versa. Therefore, the GL BUDGET XREF entity resolves the many-to-many relationship.

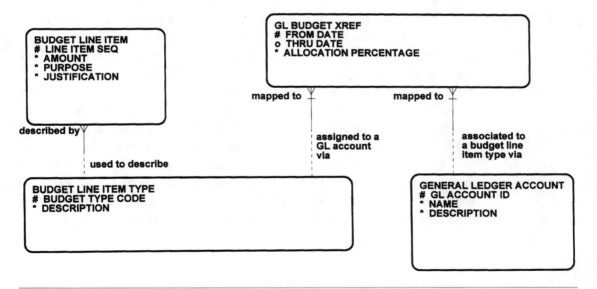

FIGURE 7.6

*Budget relationship to general ledger.*

TABLE 7.13    *General Ledger Budget Xref*

| General Ledger Account Name* | Budget Line Item Type Description* | GL Budget Xref Allocation Percentage | GL Budget Xref From Date | GL Budget Xref Thru Date |
|---|---|---|---|---|
| Office Supplies Expense | Office supplies | 100 | Jan 1, 1994 | |
| Salaries Expense | Sales Director | 100 | Jan 1, 1994 | |
| Salaries Expense | Sales Representative | 100 | Jan 1, 1994 | |
| Trade Show Expense | Marketing | 50 | Jan 1, 1994 | |
| Advertising Expense | Marketing | 50 | Jan 1, 1994 | |

Table 7.13 illustrates examples of relationships between budget line items and general ledger accounts. The first example illustrates a situation which accountants love! When a departmental manager uses the general ledger account name for budgeting purposes, then the budget line item ("office supplies") has a one-to-one mapping to the general ledger account ("office supplies expense").

The second example, illustrated by the second and third rows in Table 7.13, shows that many budget line item types may correspond to a single general ledger account (This is still easy for accountants to track and audit.) Budget line items were set up for a sales director position and for a sales representative. These are both mapped to a general ledger account "salaries expense".

The third example is the most complex and will require more work on the part of the enterprise to correctly maintain. The fourth and fifth rows of Table 7.13 show that "marketing" budget line items should be mapped 50 percent to "trade show" and 50 percent to "advertising expense" general ledger accounts.

The rules for how budget line items map to general ledger accounts may change over time. The **from date** and **thru date** attributes on the GL BUDGET XREF entity allow different mappings over time. This model assumes that the mappings will be the same for different organizations within an enterprise.

## SUMMARY

There are many similar accounting and budgeting information requirements among various enterprises. This chapter has included data models to establish chart of accounts for internal organizations, track accounting transactions, set up budgets, record commitments and disbursements against budgets, and cross-reference budgets to general ledger accounts.

Figure 7.7 shows an overall view of the accounting and budgeting models included in this chapter.

Refer to Appendix A for an alphabetical listing of entities and attributes along with attribute characteristics. For SQL scripts to build tables, columns, and primary and foreign keys derived from this logical model, please refer to the CD-ROM product, sold separately.

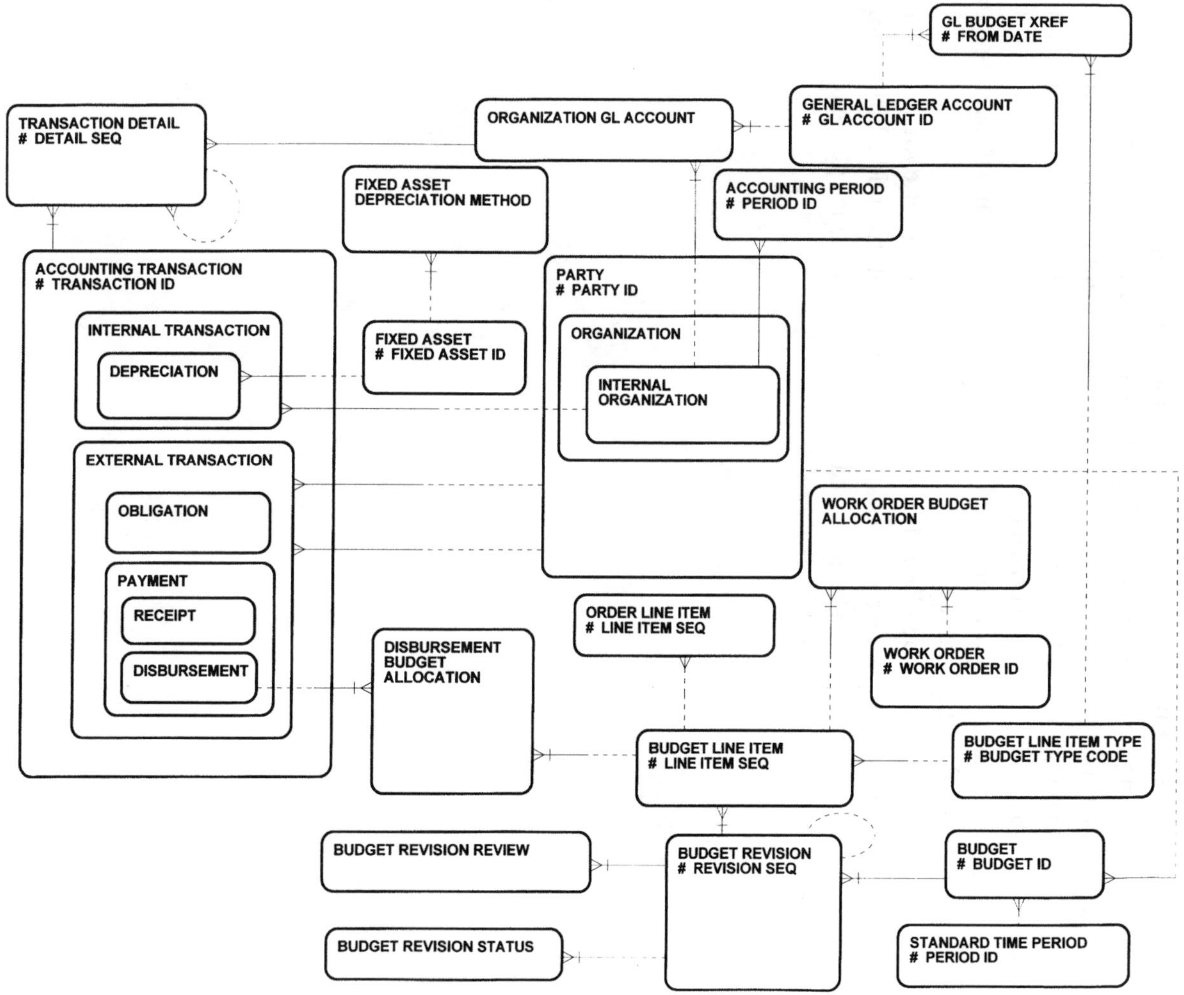

**FIGURE** 7.7

*Accounting and budgeting.*

# 8

## HUMAN RESOURCES

### INTRODUCTION

So far, this book has discussed models for handling much of the information an enterprise needs to conduct business: parties, products, orders, shipments, work efforts, and accounting. One critical section of the business remains for discussion: human resources or HR. Without human resources, an enterprise cannot operate or stay in business for long.

Information that an enterprise may want to keep includes:

What positions exist in the company?

Are they filled? If so, who has the position and what are his or her responsibilities?

Who reports to whom?

What is the rate of pay for these positions?

Who received raises and when?

What benefits does the enterprise provide and to whom?

What is the cost of these benefits?

In addition, the enterprise also needs to know certain information in order to process payroll.

Many enterprises implement a separate HR system, very often through a package that may not integrate well with other in-house systems. This chapter illustrates a model that allows an enterprise to track basic human resources information and have it tied to other models presented in this book. The models presented here are not meant to be all encompassing for HR and payroll systems; they will, however, provide a sound basis for building one if desired. The models presented include:

- Position definition
- Position type definition
- Position reporting relationships
- Position fulfillment and tracking
- Salary determination and pay history
- Benefits definition and tracking
- Payroll information

## POSITION DEFINITION

What is a position really? A POSITION represents a job slot in an enterprise that can be occupied by more than one person over time. In some enterprises, this may also be referred to as an FTE or full-time equivalent. For example, if the HR department of an organization was told that there were two positions (two FTEs) open for a junior programmer, that would indicate that they could hire two people. Each of these people may perform the same type of duties, but they would be filling two separate job slots. Over time, one of these people may resign and be replaced by a third person. This third person would fill the existing position that had been vacated. This would not constitute a new position. (This will be explained further in the section on position fulfillment.)

In Figure 8.1 the entities used to define a position are modeled. The POSITION entity contains the basic information to track about any given job slot. The POSITION TYPE entity provides information for further defining and categorizing a job, while the BUDGET LINE ITEM provides a possible means of authorizing a slot. The entities RESPONSIBILITY TYPE, VALID RESPONSIBILITY, and POSITION RESPONSIBILITY provide a mechanism for assigning and tracking what possible and actual responsibilities are for any position.

## Position

Some of the data an enterprise may wish to track about a POSITION is shown in Figure 8.1. The **estimated from date** and **estimated thru date** can be used for planning. This data is the first indication of when the enterprise expects to need a person to fill this role in the organization. If the position is for an indefinite period, the **estimated thru date** would remain blank.

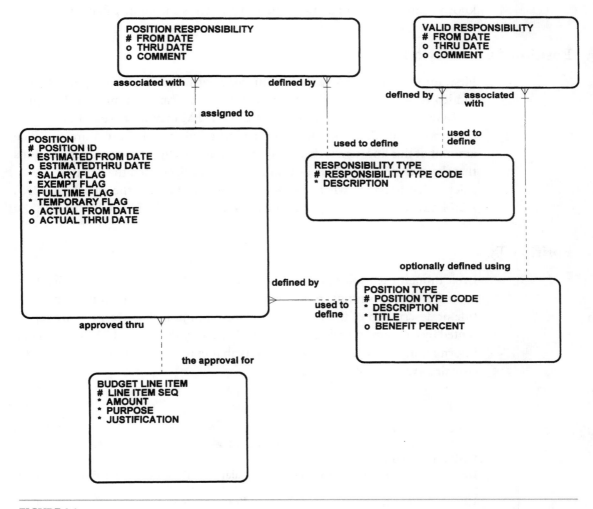

**FIGURE 8.1**

*Position definition.*

The various flags included in the entity help to define the particular circumstances under which a person hired for a position will be employed. Will the person be salaried or hourly? Is the position exempt or nonexempt under the Fair Labor Standards Act (FLSA)? Will this be a full-time or part-time position? Is it temporary or permanent? The answers to these questions will be very important for benefits administrators and payroll personnel. Additionally, the model includes an actual from and thru date to allow tracking of this data once it is known. Sample data for some of these attributes is shown in Table 8.1.

## Position Authorization

First, for a job to even exist in an enterprise, it must usually be approved and funded in some manner. In this model, positions can be approved through a BUDGET LINE ITEM. One BUDGET LINE ITEM may **approve** or fund one or more positions. For example, there may be a line item for programmers. The amount of this line item is then used to fund the multiple programmer positions that the enterprise has. If a position is tied to a budget, then the position is considered "authorized" when the BUDGET REVISION for the BUDGET LINE ITEM has been approved (see Chapter 7 for more on the BUDGET model).

## Position Type

Even though each job opening represents a single occurrence of POSITION, several of these openings could have some characteristics in common, such as a title or description of the type of job. Those common characteristics are represented by a common POSITION TYPE. The entity POSITION TYPE maintains information associated with all the slots that exist for a kind of job. Table 8.2 contains examples of this data.

TABLE 8.1   *Position Data*

| Position ID | Estimated From Date | Estimated Thru Date | Salary? | Exempt? | Full-time? | Temp? |
|---|---|---|---|---|---|---|
| 101 | Jan 1, 1996 | | Yes | No | Yes | No |
| 204 | Jun 1, 1996 | Aug 31, 1996 | Yes | Yes | Yes | Yes |

TABLE 8.2   *Position Type Data*

| Position Type Code | Description | Title | Benefit Percent |
|---|---|---|---|
| BUSAN | Recommend proper policies, procedures, and mechanisms for conducting effective business. | Business Analyst | 100 |
| ACLERK | Enter bookkeeping figures, file appropriate accounting papers, and perform administrative accounting tasks. | Accounting Clerk | 50 |

As shown in the data, each type of position will have a code for identification, a brief description, and a standard job title. Other data that could be stored is the **benefit percent.** This is used to store the percentage of benefits that an enterprise will pay for a particular type of position. For example, the data in Table 8.2 indicates that the enterprise has made a decision to pay 100 percent of the benefits for all "business analyst" positions.

## Position Responsibilities

Also shown in Figure 8.1 are the entities RESPONSIBILITY TYPE, VALID RESPONSIBILITY, and POSITION RESPONSIBILITY. These will allow for the definition of various job responsibilities, identification of which responsibilities are appropriate for the different position types, and finally for identifying responsibilities that are actually assigned to a given position. Notice that both VALID RESPONSIBILITY and POSITION RESPONSIBILITY have a **from date** and a **thru date.** These allow the enterprise to assign and track historically changing responsibilities for jobs and positions. In this way very specific and detailed job descriptions can be developed, while at the same time allowing for ongoing change.

In order to maintain a tightly integrated system, the enterprise may wish to establish business rules to control some of this data. Data checks could be developed to ensure that if a certain RESPONSIBILITY TYPE is assigned as a POSITION RESPONSIBILITY, that it is first identified as a VALID RESPONSIBILITY for the POSITION TYPE with which the POSITION is associated. For example, a new position for an "account representative" is created. One of the responsibilities is to "create monthly sales report". Before that could be assigned, "create monthly sales report" would have to already exist as a VALID RESPONSIBILITY associated with the POSITION TYPE of "account representative". In addition the **from date** and **thru date** in both entities could be compared to be sure that the assigned responsibility is actually valid for the assigned time period.

## POSITION TYPE DEFINITION

Some enterprises may need to further classify the types of positions they have. To help with this, the model shown in Figure 8.2 was developed. In it an optional entity POSITION TYPE CLASS is shown as an intersection between POSITION TYPE and POSITION CLASSIFICATION TYPE. Using these entities, additional

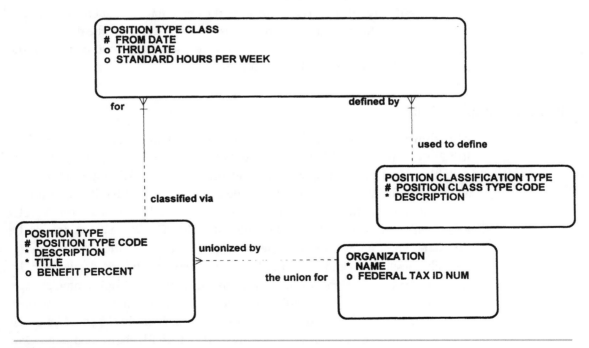

FIGURE 8.2

*Position type definition.*

groupings of types of positions can be done. Since it is possible that a POSITION TYPE could be reclassified over time, the attributes **from date** and **thru date** are included to support the one-to-many relationship to POSITION TYPE CLASS. An example of possible data is shown in Table 8.3.

The data shown indicates that for the enterprise in question, the position types "programmer", "system administrator", and "business analyst" were at one time all classified as "computer" positions. Then in 1995, the "business analyst" was reclassified to "MIS". In addition to the "computer" classification, "programmer" is also classified as "technical", while the "system administrator" is considered "admin support". In any of the cases where the **thru date** is not included, it is assumed that the classification is still valid. Using this model, the enterprise can develop a very detailed and flexible classification system to meet its needs.

There is an alternative use for this set of entities that some enterprises may wish to use. POSITION CLASSIFICATION TYPE could also include data such as "hourly", "salary", "exempt", "nonexempt", "part-time", "full-time", "regular", or "temporary". Then, the entity POSITION TYPE CLASS would act as an historical list of these base classifications for a POSITION. Note that the POSITION entity currently shows binary attributes for pairs of these classifications. If this use is implemented with the listed data, then these attributes could be removed from POSITION. (Although, in a physical model the enterprise may also want to implement this data as flags associated with a position slot for easier reporting of current data.)

**TABLE 8.3**  *Position Type Classification Data*

| Position Type* | Classification Type* | From Date | Thru Date |
|---|---|---|---|
| Programmer | Computer | Jan 1, 1990 | |
| | Technical | Jan 1, 1990 | |
| System Administrator | Computer | Jan 1, 1990 | |
| | Admin Support | Apr 1, 1992 | |
| Business Analyst | Computer | Jan 1, 1990 | Dec 31, 1994 |
| | MIS | Jan 1, 1995 | |

## Organization

Some other information that certain enterprises may need to track is whether certain types of positions are unionized. This is handled through the relationship to ORGANIZATION, since a union is one type of organization. This information could be of vital importance during salary and benefits negotiations or in the case of a pending strike. If a position is protected through a union relationship, then the enterprise may have certain guidelines regarding these type of positions.

## POSITION REPORTING RELATIONSHIPS

Most data models show people reporting to and managed by other people. As discussed in Chapter 2, common models for people and organizations are generally oversimplified. Many models show an EMPLOYEE entity with a recursive relationship for the manager. In a large and dynamic organization, this structure could result in a lot of updating and possible data inconsistencies.

The problem is that in reality the reporting structure is a function of the organizational structure of the enterprise, not of the people in the positions. If it really was a function of the person, then when a person gets promoted, everyone who was previously reporting to that person would still be reporting to that person after the promotion. This is usually not the case. In most instances, when a supervisor is promoted, the vacated supervisor position is filled by another person. The people who originally reported to the supervisor now report to a new person, but they still report to the same position. Instead of changing everyone's reporting relationships, the position reporting model handles this situation by changing one person's position assignment (further demonstrated later in the chapter).

Additionally, an enterprise may identify its position hierarchy before assigning people to the various positions. Certainly this is the case when an organization is first created. This situation also occurs when enterprises reorganize.

What happens when the simplified model is implemented is that usually only a picture of the organization structure at the current time is maintained. All history of reorganizations and promotions is lost. This can be a serious problem when, for example, an EEOC suit is filed against the enterprise and it becomes necessary to determine who occupied a position at a particular point in time and who was the supervisor. The model presented in Figure 8.3 solves this, and other challenges.

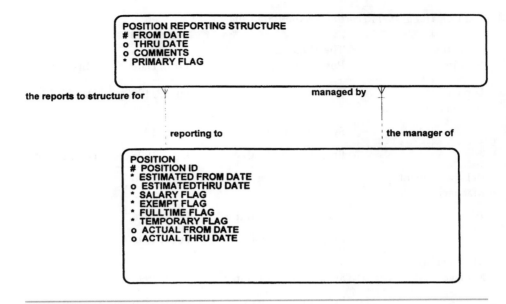

**FIGURE 8.3**

*Position reporting relationships.*

## Position Reporting Structure

The model above shows the entity POSITION REPORTING STRUCTURE, which links POSITION back to itself. The attributes **from date** and **thru date** are provided to allow for tracking organizational changes through time, as previously discussed. The **primary flag** attribute is included to help model flexible, matrix-type structures. In these cases, certain positions may report to more than one position at the same time. This indicator allows the enterprise to indicate which reporting relationship is the overriding one.

In the examples shown in Table 8.4, business analysts, system administrators, and programmer/analysts report to the director of IS. Suppose that the enterprise grows and subsequently creates an IS development manager position and a maintenance manager position which now report to the director of IS. Instead of changing the reporting relationship of each of the people, the old reporting relationships of the positions would be expired (using the **thru date**) and new records could be added to show the revised structure. In this way, the en-

**TABLE 8.4**  *Position Reporting Relationship Data*

| Reporting To Position* | The Manager Of Position* | From Date | Thru Date | Primary Flag |
|---|---|---|---|---|
| Director of Information Systems | Business Analyst | Jan 12, 1995 | Dec 30, 1995 | Yes |
| | Systems Administrator | Jan 1, 1995 | Dec 31, 1995 | Yes |
| | Programmer/Analyst | Jan 1, 1995 | Dec 31, 1995 | Yes |
| IS Development Manager | Business Analyst | Jan 1, 1996 | | Yes |
| | Systems Administrator | Jan 1, 1996 | | No |
| | Programmer/Analyst | Jan 1, 1996 | | Yes |
| Maintenance Manager | Systems Administrator | Jan 1, 1996 | | Yes |
| | Programmer/Analyst | Jan 1, 1996 | | No |

terprise can more easily implement the new reporting structure and at the same time retain an accurate history of previous structures.

Notice that in the sample data, the current reporting relationships are identified where the **thru date** is blank. Alternatively, a **thru date** in the future could also indicate a current relationship with a preplanned end date. Note also that with the new structure, the "programmer/analyst" and "systems administrator" positions now report to both the "IS development manager" and the "maintenance manager" (these positions represent actual slots within the enterprise and not position types). They have split duties. In the case of the "systems administrator", the **primary flag** is set to "yes" for the relationship to the "maintenance manager", while it is the opposite for the "programmer/analyst" position. In this way it is possible to identify which position each of these ultimately reports to.

In larger enterprises, these changes to organization structure may affect hundreds or thousands of people. By designing a system that merely changes the reporting relationship of the position instead of the actual parties involved, there will be much fewer updates required and presumably much cleaner data in the long run.

The point is that positions and people are separate entities. The next section will discuss how people and positions are actually related.

## POSITION FULFILLMENT AND TRACKING

Figure 8.4 shows a model which will allow the enterprise to track a person's movement within the organization. It includes entities for tracking POSITION FULFILLMENT and POSITION STATUS. The model needs the entities POSITION and PERSON for context. ORGANIZATION is also included to provide information on the hiring company and a possible trade union association.

## Position Fulfillment

A person can, of course, occupy more than one position either over time or at the same time. Conversely, a position may be filled by more than one person over time (and even at the same time through job sharing). The POSITION FULFILLMENT entity provides a very flexible way to retain the history of this activity. The attributes **from date** and **thru date** will allow the enterprise to keep historically accurate information about this data. It is a convenient and effective way to resolve the many-to-many relationship that really exists between PERSON and POSITION. Some possible data is shown in Table 8.5.

The data given shows the career path of Mike Johnson as he moved progressively up the corporate ladder from the position of "mail clerk" to "CEO". Since the **thru date** for the "CEO" entry is blank, it is assumed that he currently holds that position. Also shown is the career of Sue Jones. She started in the position of "programmer", then in 1994 took on the additional role of "business analyst". She was then promoted to "MIS manager" in 1994. Finally, she earned her current position as "CIO" ( Chief Information Officer).

A recent trend in industry is the concept of job sharing. In this situation, two people fill one position. Both work part-time and share the responsibilities of the position. This is where the concept of an FTE (full-time equivalent) is most useful. With a job-share situation, the enterprise has authorized only one full-time position (one FTE), which constitutes one "head count". One half-time person plus another half-time person equals one FTE! The number of FTEs is the information needed for resource allocation, budgeting, reporting relationships, and such. Again, the information is related to, or dependent on, the position not the person.

Another feature of the POSITION FULFILLMENT entity is that it can be used to record employee assignments in a job-sharing situation without confus-

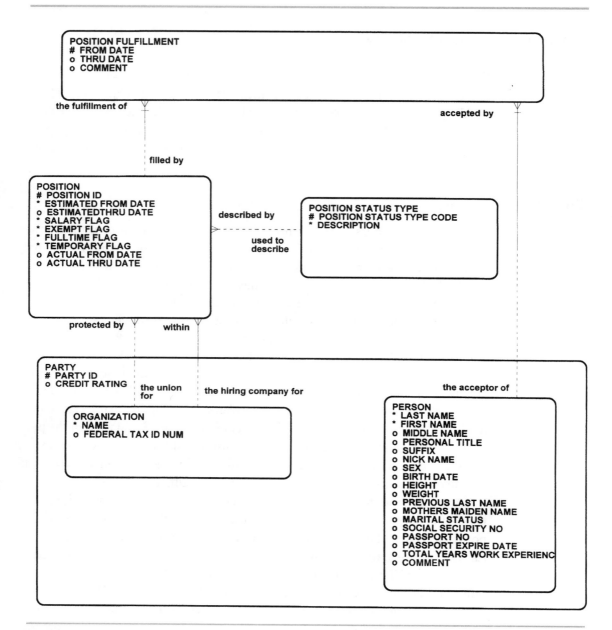

FIGURE 8.4

*Position fulfillment.*

**TABLE 8.5** *Position Fulfillment Data*

| Person* | Position* | From Date | Thru Date |
|---------|-----------|-----------|-----------|
| Mike Johnson | Mail Clerk | Jun 1, 1970 | May 31, 1975 |
| | Mail Supervisor | Jun 1, 1975 | Dec 31, 1978 |
| | Office Manager | Jan 1, 1979 | May 31, 1985 |
| | Regional Manager | Jun 1, 1985 | May 31, 1991 |
| | CEO | Jun 1, 1991 | |
| Sue Jones | Programmer | Mar 1, 1990 | Feb 27, 1994 |
| | Business Analyst | May 15, 1992 | Feb 27, 1994 |
| | MIS Manager | Mar 1, 1994 | Nov 1, 1995 |
| | CIO | Nov 2, 1995 | |

ing the FTE or head count. This is due to the fact that the primary key of this entity is the combination of an inherited key from POSITION (**position ID**), an inherited key from PERSON (**party ID**), and the attribute **from date**. With this three-part key, it is possible to record more than one person as having accepted the same position during the same time period. Of course, whether this was allowable could be controlled by implementing some business rules. If an enterprise never does job sharing, then the model could be changed to enforce this by removing the relationship to PERSON and hence removing the **party ID** from the compound key. If that were done, then the model would allow one and only one person to occupy a position during the same time period (even in this case, some business rules will be needed).

Note that it is also possible that a person from outside of the organization could fill a position that was authorized, such as a contractor. Since this model shows that POSITION FULFILLMENT must be accepted by a PERSON and not an EMPLOYEE, it is much more flexible than standard models and can handle this situation. To determine if the person is an employee or a person external to the enterprise the PARTY RELATIONSHIP entity may be used (refer to Chapter 2). Since it contains this information, PARTY RELATIONSHIP could also be used to enforce business rules such as whether positions may be filled by non-employees.

## Position Status Type

The POSITION STATUS TYPE identifies the current state of a position. When a position is first identified, it is in a state of "planned for". When the enterprise decides to pursue fulfillment of the position, it may then change to a state of "active" or "open". If the enterprise then decides that it no longer needs that position, the status may be "inactive" or "closed". A "fulfilled" status would not be a value since this information can be derived from the POSITION FULFILLMENT entity. That is why the relationship is optional.

## Organization

Who is the hiring company? This is easily tracked via a relationship between POSITION and ORGANIZATION. Without the enterprise, there would be no need for a position. Notice also in Figure 8.4 that there is a second relationship between these two entities. This relationship represents the actual union, perhaps a local chapter, by which a particular position is protected. This is an optional relationship since not all positions, or in some cases none, within an enterprise are unionized.

## Other Considerations

Some other information not obvious in this model concerns how a person actually gets offered an open position. In fact, the interview process can be tracked through the PARTY CONTACT model. An interview is a CONTACT TYPE with interview notes stored in the entity CONTACT NOTE. See Chapter 2 for more details on this model.

By using the POSITION FULFILLMENT model combined with the model for position reporting, an enterprise can retain and access a complete picture of its organization and structure at any point in time.

# SALARY DETERMINATION AND PAY HISTORY

The model presented in this section is an extended compensation model which handles both highly structured organizations such as the government or less structured organizations such as small private businesses (see Figure 8.5). This is

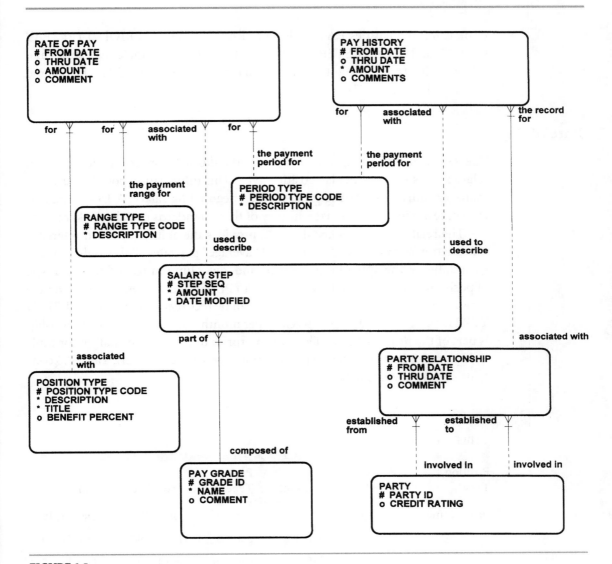

FIGURE 8.5

*Salary determination and history.*

done using the entities RATE OF PAY, RANGE TYPE, PERIOD TYPE, PAY GRADE, and SALARY STEP. In addition, this model also includes entities and relationships to allow the tracking of salary history (i.e., PAY HISTORY and PARTY RELATIONSHIP).

## Rate of Pay

The RATE OF PAY entity is used to record the allowable or acceptable salary and salary ranges for a particular position type. This information could be used by managers during the hiring process when negotiating salary. A **from date** and **thru date** are included so that a history of these standards can also be kept.

The relationship to RANGE TYPE provides the ability to record reference information such as "high", "low", and "average" pay rates. This would indicate such things as the upper limit, average, and lower limit ranges of pay for a type of position. The relationship to PERIOD TYPE will allow an enterprise to define various pay period types for which rates can be recorded. Examples of PERIOD TYPE include "per year", "per week", "per month", and so on. This relationship is part of the primary key to allow an enterprise to record information for multiple period types (i.e., average per hour and average per month). Table 8.6 contains sample pay rate data.

TABLE 8.6    *Rate of Pay Data*

| Position Type* | Range Type* | Amount | Period Type* | From Date | Thru Date |
|---|---|---|---|---|---|
| Programmer | Average | $25,000 | per year | Jan 1, 1985 | Dec 31, 1994 |
| | High | $50,000 | per year | Jan 1, 1985 | Dec 31, 1994 |
| | Low | $15,000 | per year | Jan 1, 1985 | Dec 31, 1994 |
| | Standard | $10.00 | per hour | Jan 1, 1985 | Dec 31, 1994 |
| | Average | $45,000 | per year | Jan 1, 1995 | |
| | High | $80,000 | per year | Jan 1, 1995 | |
| | Low | $30,000 | per year | Jan 1, 1995 | |
| | Standard | $35.00 | per hour | Jan 1, 1995 | |

Looking at the sample data indicates that the enterprise in question has only updated rate information for the position type "programmer" once in 10 years. The rate of pay stayed the same from 1985 through 1994, then was increased in 1995. This organization kept information on the average, high, and low annual salary that it was willing to pay to programmers. It also kept track of a standard rate which was used to establish hourly pay.

## Pay Grade and Salary Step

Additional information stored in this entity could also include a pay grade and step equivalence for use in enterprises which have a predefined, highly structured pay system (such as the federal government). This is done by reference to a structured pay schedule. These types of schedules normally have two levels: a grade and a step. The SALARY STEP entity includes an **amount** attribute and is generally described in the context of a PAY GRADE. Table 8.7 includes part of a sample grade schedule.

Notice that there is an overlap in the pay scale between "GG-1" and "GG-2". Step #1 for GG-2 falls between step #3 and step #4 of GG-1. This is not uncommon in these types of pay systems. It allows HR administrators some flexibility in negotiating pay for new employees. Since the grades are basically "set in

TABLE 8.7　*Pay Grade System Sample*

| Grade ID | Pay Grade Name | Step Seq | Salary Step Amount |
|----------|----------------|----------|--------------------|
| 1 | GG-1 | 1 | $10,000 |
| | | 2 | $10,200 |
| | | 3 | $10,400 |
| | | 4 | $10,500 |
| | | 5 | $10,800 |
| 2 | GG-2 | 1 | $10,450 |
| | | 2 | $10,780 |
| | | 3 | $11,200 |
| | | 4 | $11,650 |

**TABLE 8.8**  *Rate of Pay Sample #2*

| Position Type* | Range Type* | Amount | Grade* | Step Seq | Period Type* | From Date | Thru Date |
|---|---|---|---|---|---|---|---|
| Programmer | Average | | GG-6 | 6 | per year | Jan 1, 1985 | |
| | High | | GG-8 | 10 | per year | Jan 1, 1985 | |
| | Low | | GG-5 | 1 | per year | Jan 1, 1985 | |

stone" and tied to specific position types, the administrators are restricted as to what grades can be offered for any given position. To compensate for these restrictions, the range of pay covered by the steps of a grade are often very wide. Table 8.8 gives sample data for RATE OF PAY where a grade system is used.

There are several things to notice in the data shown in Table 8.8. First, there are no values in the **amount** column because, when using a pay grade system, the amount is taken directly from SALARY STEP. Business processes would, of course, need to be implemented to ensure that **amount** was not filled in; otherwise, there could be conflicting information. In implementing this model for use with a pay schedule, this attribute could be dropped. Conversely, when implementing the model for an enterprise that *will not* use a schedule, the **amount** attribute should be mandatory.

Second, note that the **thru date** is also blank. This is to illustrate the concept that, over time, the dollar amount for a selected pay grade and step may increase, but the step assignment in the RATE OF PAY does not need to change. In this case, nothing needs to be changed in the pay rate records to indicate the increase in pay. In other words, there is no need to enter a **thru date**, then create a new record to show the pay increase, since the pay increase is reflected via an update to the SALARY STEP information.

## Pay History and Actual Salary

Actual salary or pay, represented by PAY HISTORY, is related to a person, *not* POSITION or POSITION TYPE. In fact, it is really related to the PARTY RELATIONSHIP which exists between the PERSON and an ORGANIZATION. The relationship that is represented should be that of employer and employee.

Salary history is *not* related to POSITION because the position the person occupies can change over time, but that doesn't mean the salary will automatically change as well. Sometimes, a person is given more responsibility and placed in a higher-level position, but is not given the salary raise until he or she demonstrates the capability of performing the duties appropriately. Also, consider again the job-sharing scenario. If the pay was tied to the position, both people would have to be paid the same. This would limit the flexibility of the enterprise to pay one party more than the other based on differing levels of skill or experience.

Depending on the nature of the enterprise, salary is represented by actual dollar amounts and optionally by the relationship to SALARY STEP. Unlike RATE OF PAY, **amount** is always recorded in PAY HISTORY to ensure that there is no confusion on what the person was paid during a given time period. Also, note that since this is a record of the actual rate of pay for a person, not a list of possible rates, there can only be one record for the person for any selected time period. The PERIOD TYPE associated with this record is determined based on how the enterprise wants to see this data. See Table 8.9 for examples of this data.

The data shown gives the record of pay for John Smith who works for ABC Corporation. It shows his salary and increases over the past six years. Where the **thru date** is missing, again assume that this indicates his current annual salary. With this kind of data, an enterprise can accurately track the salary history of its employees. It is also possible to track the pay of outside parties, such as contractors, by relating the PAY HISTORY to a PARTY RELATIONSHIP of contractor and contractee.

## BENEFITS DEFINITION AND TRACKING

In addition to salary or pay, most enterprises provide compensation through a benefits package. This could include vacation, health or life insurance, sick leave, or a retirement plan. The cost of these benefits may be partly or completely ab-

TABLE 8.9   *Pay History Data*

| Employer* | Employee* | From Date | Thru Date | Amount | Period Type |
|-----------|-----------|-----------|-----------|--------|-------------|
| ABC Corporation | John Smith | Jan 1, 1990 | Dec 31, 1992 | $45,000 | per year |
| | | Jan 1, 1993 | Dec 31, 1995 | $55,000 | per year |
| | | Jan 1, 1996 | | $62,500 | per year |

sorbed by the enterprise. Figure 8.6 demonstrates a simplified model for benefits tracking. It includes the information on PARTY RELATIONSHIP, PARTY BENEFIT, PERIOD TYPE, and BENEFIT TYPE.

## Party Relationship

Like PAY HISTORY, PARTY BENEFIT is also related to the PARTY RELATIONSHIP, not the PARTY or PERSON because the benefits are associated with a particular employer and employee relationship. In a large multicompany enterprise people may move from one company to another, so sometimes their benefits may come from different organizations at different times in their career. If the enterprise wants to track benefits costs at the lower levels of the organization, then associating the costs simply with the employee will not be sufficient. Why not associate the benefit with the employee and the organization directly? By using PARTY RELATIONSHIP, the enterprise can enforce business rules that would prevent such things as contractors accidentally being given benefits.

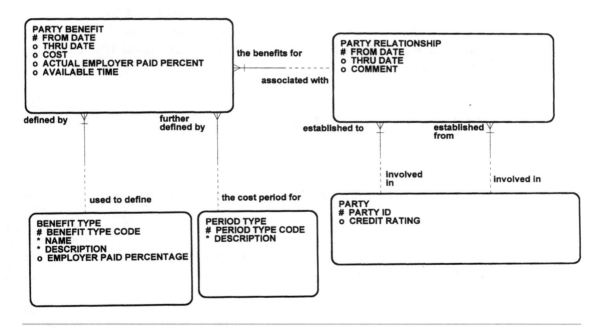

FIGURE 8.6

*Benefits definition and tracking.*

In the case of an insurance provider, there is a need to determine the benefits for a person and within an organization (through the PARTY RELATIONSHIP entity). Some of its customers may have two part-time jobs; it may be important to know the benefits offered by each job to avoid duplication of benefits. This is also useful for determining which insurance policy should pay for an illness. The information could be critical to assist the insurance company in controlling its costs.

## Party Benefit

In PARTY BENEFIT there can be several pieces of information that the enterprise may wish to track. First is the **from date** and **thru date**. These allow the tracking of benefits through time. Additionally, the enterprise may want to track the actual **cost** of the benefit and the **actual employer paid percentage**. With the information it would be possible to calculate not only the cost to the employee but to the enterprise as well. Another attribute, **available time**, is also included for tracking allowable time off such as vacation and sick leave. Example benefit data is shown in Table 8.10.

The examples given again deal with John Smith who works for ABC Corporation. Over the years, the cost of his health insurance has risen from $1,200 to $1,500 per year. During that time ABC Corporation initially paid 50 percent of the cost for him, but now pays 60 percent. The data also shows that he has 15 vacation days and 10 sick days as a current balance, and that the company absorbs the full cost of that time off. Mr. Smith also has a 401K plan that he started when he was eligible in 1991. The information indicates that the plan cost is $50 per year (for administration) with the company picking up 100 percent of the cost.

**TABLE 8.10**  *Party Benefit Data*

| Employer* | Employee* | Benefit Type* | From Date | Thru Date | Cost | Period Type* | Employer % | Available Time |
|---|---|---|---|---|---|---|---|---|
| ABC Corporation | John Smith | Health | Jan 1, 1990 | Dec 31, 1991 | $1200 | per year | 50 | |
| | | | Jan 1, 1992 | | $1500 | per year | 60 | |
| | | Vacation | | | | days | 100 | 15 |
| | | Sick Leave | | | | days | 100 | 10 |
| | | 401K | Jan 1, 1991 | | $50.00 | per year | 100 | |

## Period Type

Notice that Table 8.10 includes **Period Type.** This is the result of the resolution of the relationship to the entity PERIOD TYPE (see Figure 8.6). This information is used primarily to modify the **cost** attribute. Without it, there would be no context for the dollars reported, and thus no way to determine accurately the enterprise's costs. Additionally, it could also be used as the context for types like "vacation" and "sick leave", as shown in the table.

## Benefit Type

The various types of benefits provided by the enterprise are listed in the entity BENEFIT TYPE. Samples of that data were included in Table 8.10. In addition to the identification of the benefit, this entity may also store a standard **employer paid percentage** that can be used to calculate costs related to all employees with a particular benefit.

Percentages for employer contribution are included not only in BENEFIT TYPE, but also in PARTY BENEFIT and POSITION TYPE to allow recording this information at various levels of detail. Because of this, certain business rules need to be put in place. A likely set of rules would be as follows:

- If **actual employer paid percent** exists in PARTY BENEFIT, that number takes precedence.
- If that is blank, then **benefit percent** on the POSITION TYPE associated with the person's current position (as indicated in POSITION FULFILL-MENT) is used.
- If both of these values are blank, then the **employer paid percentage** in BENEFIT TYPE would be the override.

Note that a complete benefits schedule is very complex; it will not be modeled here since it is specific to a particular industry (i.e., insurance) and is, therefore, outside the scope of this book. In general, a model of a benefits schedule would relate the benefit type to specific costs based on various characteristics associated with individuals. The characteristics of interest would vary according to the benefit type. The model described here was concerned only with the tracking of general employee benefits.

# PAYROLL INFORMATION

The last item to consider for an overview model of Human Resources is payroll (see Figure 8.7). Without payroll, there won't be many human resources working for the enterprise for long! This model considers what to many people will be the most critical portion of payroll: getting paid correctly. Information about payroll is included in the entities PARTY RELATIONSHIPS, PAY TYPE, PAYROLL PREFERENCE, PAYCHECK, DEDUCTION, and DEDUCTION TYPE.

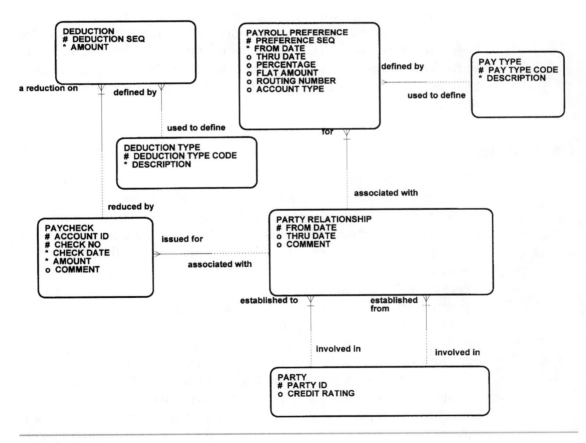

FIGURE 8.7

*Payroll information.*

## Party Relationship

As with benefits and salary, all payroll information is related to PARTY RELA-TIONSHIP. The reason is the same: If there was no employer and employee, or similar relationship, there would be no need for a paycheck. By using the relationships as a base, business rules can be used to ensure that not just any party within the system can be issued a paycheck.

## Pay Type

In today's world of convenience and electronic commerce, getting paid is not as simple as it once was. Now there are many options employers can choose to offer their employees when it comes to methods of receiving their pay. The basic form of these options is described by the entity PAY TYPE. In it could be stored data such as "cash", "check", and "electronic". Depending on the capabilities of an enterprise's payroll department, any or all of these options may be offered to employees.

## Payroll Preference

It is possible that an employee may want part of his or her pay in check form and the rest in cash. Others may want their money split up and electronically deposited to several different banks. In order to handle this type of information, the model includes the entity PAYROLL PREFERENCE. Since an employee may change preferences over time, the attributes **from date** and **thru date** are included. Other information that is needed includes the **percentage** of total pay or a **flat amount** that the employee wants designated to a particular pay type. If the type of pay selected is "electronic", then the **routing number** and **account type** are also required to successfully complete the transaction. Business rules would need to be implemented to enforce this since these attributes are not required for other forms of payment. Sample data is included in Table 8.11.

As in previous examples, assume that the employer is still ABC Corporation and the employee is John Smith. The sample data contains what is a very common scenario that payroll departments encounter today. When Mr. Smith starts with the company, he chooses to have his paycheck deposited electronically. As indicated in the data, he wants it split between a checking and a savings account.

**TABLE 8.11**  *Payroll Preference Data*

| Preference Seq | Pay Type* | From Date | Thru Date | Percentage | Flat Amount | Routing No | Account Type |
|---|---|---|---|---|---|---|---|
| 1 | Electronic | Jan 1, 1990 | Nov 1, 1994 | 50 | | 99986-99 | checking |
| 2 | Electronic | Jan 1, 1990 | | 50 | | 99986-98 | savings |
| 3 | Electronic | Nov 2, 1994 | | 50 | | 11111-22 | checking |

Then in 1994, he decides to close one checking account and open a new one at a different bank. So, the payroll department is informed, and the first preference is then expired, and a new one is entered to take effect on November 2.

Note that the primary key for PAYROLL PREFERENCE is a simple sequence number compounded with the primary key from PARTY RELATIONSHIP. This is needed because the PAY TYPE combined with the inherited key would not uniquely identify an occurrence in this entity (as seen in the sample data). Adding the **from date** still would not produce a unique key. Since all the other attributes are not required, there are no additional candidates to add to the primary key; therefore, an independent attribute is needed to ensure uniqueness.

## Paycheck

Now that method of payment has been established, it is time to consider the actual payment itself. The PAYCHECK entity contains basic information an enterprise needs to record about the checks it writes to its employees. As seen in Figure 8.7, this entity contains an **account ID, check no, check date, amount,** and optionally, a **comment.**

The **account ID** and **check no** will contain the information to uniquely identify a particular paycheck. Even electronically deposited checks need a source account and a check number, which show up on the paper confirmation. The **check date** is the actual date the check was issued. In the case of electronic deposit, this may or may not correspond to the bank posting date. The **amount** recorded as part of the PAYCHECK entity is the gross amount of pay. The net amount deposited can be *calculated* by subtracting the amounts recorded in the associated records stored using the DEDUCTION entity.

## Deduction and Deduction Type

The DEDUCTION entity stores information about the various deductions that occur on a particular check. The DEDUCTION TYPE entity contains a list of the valid types of deductions that are allowed by the enterprise or are required by law. Some of these include: "federal tax", "FICA", "state tax", "401K", "retirement", "insurance", or "cafeteria plan". Table 8.12 contains examples of this payroll data.

Again, assume that the sample data is related to John Smith and ABC Corporation. The data shows an example which would be typical in most organizations. The check number 10001 is cut on January 1, 1996, with a gross amount of $2,000. The deductions include the standard ones that everybody sees, plus an additional deduction for insurance. The total deductions add up to $459.50, making the net amount for the check $1,540.50.

So where did the $1,540.50 go? It should be deposited or distributed based on what was recorded in the PAYROLL PREFERENCE occurrence that is associated with the same PARTY RELATIONSHIP that the PAYCHECK is associated with (i.e., if a paycheck is issued for John Smith at ABC Corporation, then the preferences for John Smith at ABC Corporation should be used). If there were no preference records, then what happens? Is a paper check cut by default or is the check processing held up until preferences are declared? Again, more business rules need to be in place to make these decisions and ensure that the entire transaction is completed correctly.

TABLE 8.12   *Payroll Data*

| Account ID | Check No | Check Date | Amount | Deduction Seq | Deduction Type | Amount |
|---|---|---|---|---|---|---|
| 20001111 | 1001 | Jan 1, 1996 | $2000 | 1 | Fed Tax | $200.00 |
| | | | | 2 | FICA | $54.50 |
| | | | | 3 | State Tax | $80.00 |
| | | | | 4 | Insurance | $125.00 |

# SUMMARY

This chapter has discussed one of the more complex aspects of operating a business: the tracking and management of human resources and payroll information (see Figure 8.8). The models presented allow an enterprise to more efficiently track positions and assignments associated with its employees and contractors. In addition, the models contain elements for determining pay rates and tracking the salary history of those people associated with the enterprise. Also included are the basic components needed to record benefits and payroll information.

Refer to Appendix A for an alphabetical listing of entities and attributes along with attribute characteristics. For SQL scripts to build tables, columns, and primary and foreign keys derived from this logical model, please refer to the accompanying CD-ROM product, which is sold separately.

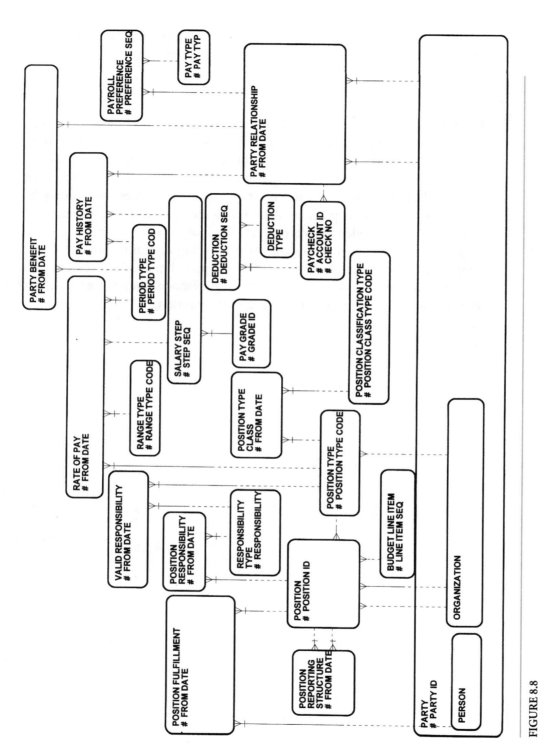

FIGURE 8.8

*Human resources model.*

# Creating the Data Warehouse Data Model from the Corporate Data Model

## Introduction

Each of the previous chapters focused on the data model for a specific subject data area, namely parties, products, orders, shipments, work efforts, accounting, and human resources. These data models are essential for building not only a data warehouse but also *any* type of system, since it is critical to understand the nature of the data and their relationships.

So what is the process for using these data models to build a data warehouse? This chapter not only describes the transformation process, but also provides examples of each type of transformation by using the logical data models from the previous chapters as a basis.

# THE DATA WAREHOUSE ARCHITECTURE

Before discussing how to convert the logical data models into a data warehouse, it is important to understand the three types of models involved in the transformation process from the operational environment to a decision support system:

- The corporate data model
- The data warehouse data model
- The departmental data warehouse design

## The Corporate Data Model

The corporate data model is an enterprise-wide view of the data and its relationships. It normally includes a high-level model which is an overview of each subject data area and the relationships between them, as well as logical data models for each subject data area. These models are the basis for developing both the enterprise's online transaction processing (OLTP) systems and data warehouses. The models presented in the previous chapters could serve as a starting point for an enterprise's corporate data model.

## The Data Warehouse Data Model

The data warehouse data model is sometimes referred to as an enterprise data warehouse model or data warehouse design. It represents an integrated, subject-oriented, and very granular base of strategic information which serves as a single source for the decision support environment. This allows an architecture where information is extracted from the operational environment, cleansed, and transformed into a central, integrated enterprise-wide data warehouse environment. The data warehouse data model maintains this integrated, detailed level of information so that all the departments and other internal organizations of the enterprise can benefit from a consistent, integrated source of decision support information.

## The Departmental Data Warehouse Design

The departmental data warehouse design is used to maintain departmental information that is extracted from the enterprise data warehouse. This is sometimes referred to as lightly and highly summarized data or as data marts. An example of a departmental data warehouse is the maintaining of a particular department's sales analysis information such as its product sales by customer, by date, and by sales representative. This department can create a departmental data warehouse and pull the information into its own data warehouse (or data mart) from the enterprise data warehouse.

Another department of the corporation, for example, the marketing department, may be interested in higher-level sales information across the enterprise such as sales by month, by product, and by geographic area. This department can create a departmental data warehouse design for its own purposes. Rather than building its own extraction, transformation, and cleansing routines against the operational systems to gather this information, it can rely on the enterprise data warehouse.

## An Architected Data Warehouse Environment

By using this architected approach as illustrated in Figure 9.1, the enterprise will avoid the pitfall of having each department extracting different views of the enterprise's information, thus creating more unintegrated and inconsistent data. After all, the primary goal of decision support is to provide strategic, meaningful management information. The most ideal method of doing this is by focusing on developing integrated data, then once this is done, passing it on to different departments who have various information needs.

It is important to note that as the enterprise moves from the corporate data model to the data warehouse data model to the departmental data warehouse, the models become more dependent on the particular enterprise. For instance, many parts of the logical data models in the prior chapters can be used by many different enterprises. The data warehouse data model is more specific to an enterprise since it is based upon numerous assumptions concerning the type of decision support information that is considered useful to the enterprise. The departmental data warehouse is even more dependent on the specific needs of a department. Therefore, the data warehouse models presented later in this chapter and in subsequent chapters serve only as examples since each enterprise's data warehouse designs will be highly dependent on its own specific business needs.

This chapter will focus specifically on the transformation of the corporate data model to the data warehouse data models. Chapter 10 provides an example of a data warehouse data model containing several subject areas. Chapters 11

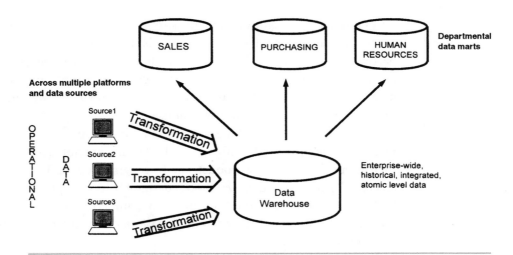

FIGURE 9.1

*Data warehouse architecture.*

and 12 provide examples of *departmental* data models and illustrate various designs for structuring the departmental warehouse using the **star schema** representation for multidimensional analysis.

## THE CORPORATE DATA MODEL

The point of departure for the design and construction of the data warehouse is the corporate data model. Without a data model it is very difficult to try to organize the structure and content of data in the data warehouse.

The corporate data model may cover a very wide scope; when it does, it is sometimes called the enterprise data model. On the other hand, the corporate data model may cover a restricted scope. When this is the case, it is usually called the corporate data model. Either case—that of the enterprise data model or the corporate data model—is adequate for starting the process of creating the data warehouse data model.

Many organizations have recognized the importance of the data model over the years and have invested the time and effort to build such a model. One of the problems with classical data modeling techniques is that there is no distinction between modeling for the operational and decision support environments. Classical data modeling techniques gather and synthesize the informational needs of the entire enterprise without consideration for the context of the information. The result of such a model is the corporate data model which tends to be very normalized.

The corporate data model is a very good place to start the process of building a data warehouse. It provides a foundation for integration and unification at an intellectual level. But because the corporate data model is not built specifically for the data warehouse, some amount of transformation is necessary to adapt it to the design that must be done in order to build the data warehouse data model.

## Transformation Requirements

To do the transformation from the corporate data model to the data warehouse data model, the corporate data model must have identified and structured—at least—the following:

- Major subjects of the enterprise
- Relationships between the subjects
- Definitions of the subject areas
- Logical data models for each subject data area (sometimes referred to as entity relationship diagrams)

Also, for each major logical data model, the following must be identified and structured:

- Entities
- Key(s) of the entity
- Attributes of the entity
- Sub-types of the entity
- Relationships between entities

Figure 9.2 identifies the minimum components of the corporate data model.

The logical models in the previous chapters can be used as a starting point toward the development of a corporate data model. The models presented represent many of the major subject data areas within enterprises. However, each enterprise needs to select the appropriate subject data areas for its specific business and add any other subject data areas needed.

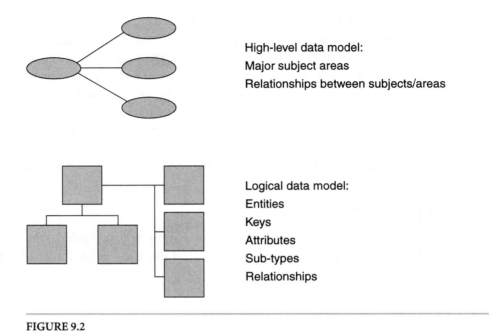

High-level data model:
Major subject areas
Relationships between subjects/areas

Logical data model:
Entities
Keys
Attributes
Sub-types
Relationships

**FIGURE 9.2**

*The components of a data model.*

## Process Models

There may be many more design and modeling components that are used in conjunction with a corporate data model. For example, the enterprise may model the design and synthesis of processes as well. Process analysis typically consists of:

- Functional decomposition
- Data and process matrices
- Data flow diagrams
- State transition diagrams
- HIPO charts
- Pseudocode

These are generally included in a corporate *process* model as opposed to being part of the corporate data model. While these corporate process models are interesting to some, the process model usually is not of much interest to the data warehouse designer because the process analysis applies directly to the operational environment, not the data warehouse or the Decision Support System (DSS) environment. It is the corporate data model that forms the backbone of design for the data warehouse, not the process models.

## High-Level and Logical Data Models

As stated previously, the corporate data model is usually divided into multiple levels—a high-level model and logical data models for each subject area. The high level of the corporate data model contains the major subject areas and the relationship between the subject areas. Figure 9.3 shows a simple example of a high-level corporate data model.

In Figure 9.3 there are five subject areas: party, order, product, shipment, and work effort. A direct relationship exists between party and order, order and work effort, order and shipment, and order and product. Of course, there are many indirect relationships which are inferred from the high-level data model, but only the direct relationships are shown. Note that the high-level corporate data model does not contain any amount of detail at all; at this level, detail only clutters up the model unnecessarily.

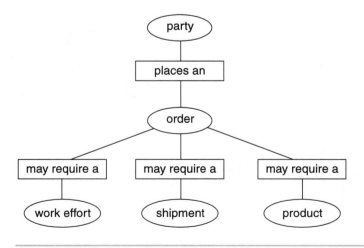

FIGURE 9.3

*A simple example of a high-level model.*

The next level of modeling found in the corporate data model is logical data modeling. Here is where much of the detail of the model is found. These models contain entities, keys, attributes, sub-types, relationships, and are fully normalized. Each of the previous chapters generally corresponds to a subject data area and includes a normalized logical data model for that area. There is a relationship between each subject area identified in the high-level model and the logical data models. For each subject area identified, there is a single logical data model, as shown in Figure 9.4.

Note that in many organizations the logical data model is not fleshed out to the same level of detail. Some logical data models are completely designed and fully attributed, while other models are only sketched out, with little or no detail.

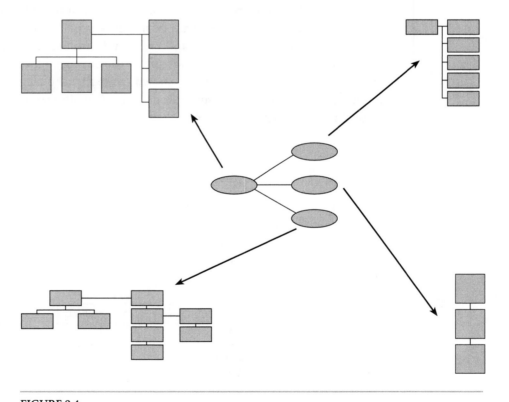

FIGURE 9.4

*Each major subject area has its own mid-level model.*

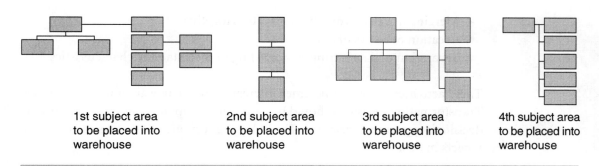

1st subject area to be placed into warehouse

2nd subject area to be placed into warehouse

3rd subject area to be placed into warehouse

4th subject area to be placed into warehouse

**FIGURE 9.5**

*Each major subject area will be integrated one step at a time.*

The degree of completion of the larger corporate data model is of little concern to the data warehouse developer because the data warehouse will be developed iteratively, one stage at a time. In other words, it is very unusual to develop the data warehouse on a massive frontal assault, where all logical data models are developed at once. Therefore, the fact that the corporate data model is in a state of differing degrees of readiness is not a concern to the data warehouse developer. Figure 9.5 shows that the data warehouse will be built one step at a time. First one logical data model is transformed and readied for data warehouse design, then another logical data model is transformed, and so forth.

## MAKING THE TRANSFORMATION

Once the enterprise has a corporate data model, the transformation process into the data warehouse data model can begin. Following are a few basic activities that make up the corporate data model to data warehouse model transformation:

- Removal of purely operational data
- Addition of an element of time to the key structure of the data warehouse if one is not already present
- Addition of appropriate derived data
- Transformation of data relationships into data artifacts
- Accommodating the different levels of granularity found in the data warehouse

- Merging like data from different tables together
- Creation of arrays of data
- Separation of data attributes according to their stability characteristics

These activities serve as guidelines in creating the data warehouse data model. Transformation decisions should be based largely upon the enterprise's specific decision support requirements. The following sections will discuss each of these aspects in detail.

## Removing Operational Data

The first task is to examine the corporate data model and remove all data that is purely operational, as illustrated in Figure 9.6. The figure shows that some data found in the corporate data model finds its way into the data model for the data warehouse. However, some attributes of data such as **message, description,** and **status** usually apply to the operational environment. These attributes should be removed as a first step in building the data warehouse data model. However, they are *not* removed from the logical data models; they are simply not useful in the data warehouse.

The removal of operational data is seldom a straightforward decision. It always centers around the question, "What is the chance the data will be used for DSS?" Unfortunately, circumstances can be contrived such that almost *any* data

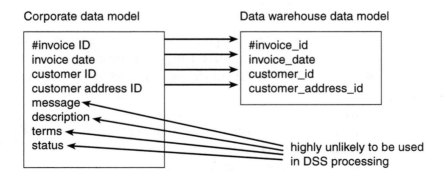

**FIGURE 9.6**

*Removing data that will not be used for DSS processing.*

can be used for DSS. A more rational approach is to ask "What is the *reasonable* chance that the data will be used for DSS?"

The argument that can always be thrown up is that one never knows what is to be used for DSS, since it always involves the unknown. On that basis, *any* and *all* data should be kept. However, the cost of managing volumes of data in the data warehouse environment is such that it is patently a mistake not to weed out data that will be used for DSS only in farfetched or contrived circumstances.

## Adding an Element of Time to the Warehouse Key

The second necessary modification to the corporate data model is the addition of an element of time to the data warehouse key if one does not already exist, as shown in Figure 9.7.

In the figure, **snapshot_date** has been added as a key to the customer record. The corporate data model has specified party information with only a party ID as the key. But in the warehouse, snapshots of customer-related party data are made since customer demographics may change over time. The effective date of those snapshots is added to the key structure. Note that there are many different ways to take these snapshots and a few common ways to add an element of time to the data warehouse key. The technique shown in the example is one common technique.

Another common technique is the addition of a from and through date to the key structure. This technique has the advantage of representing continuous data rather than snapshots at a specified point in time. An example of this technique is illustrated in the sample data warehouse data model in Figure 10.2.

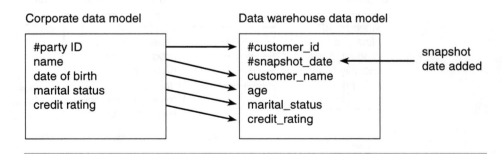

**FIGURE 9.7**

*Adding an element of time to the data warehouse data model.*

If data identified in the logical data model already has an element of time—such as a date—as part of the key structure, then there is no need to add another element of time to the data warehouse key structure.

## Adding Derived Data

The next transformation to the logical data models is the addition of derived data to the data warehouse data model where it is appropriate, as shown in Figure 9.8.

As a rule data modelers do not include derived data as part of the data modeling process. Logical models only show the data *requirements* of an enterprise. The reason for the omission of derived data in logical data models is that when derived data is included, certain processes are inferred regarding the derivation or calculation of that data. Derived data is only added to the *physical* database design for performance or ease of access reasons.

It is appropriate to add derived data to the data warehouse data model where the derived data is popularly accessed and calculated once. The addition of derived data makes sense because it reduces the amount of processing required upon accessing the data in the warehouse. In addition, once properly calculated, there is little fear in the integrity of the calculation. Said another way, once the derived data is properly calculated, there is no chance that someone will come along and use an incorrect algorithm for the calculation of the data, thus enhancing the credibility of data in the data warehouse.

Of course, any time that data is added to the data warehouse, the following question must be asked: "Is the addition of the data worth it?" The issue of volume

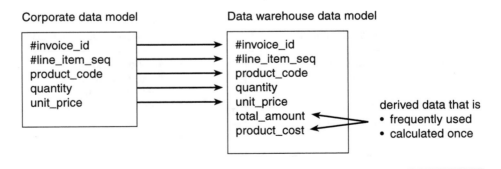

FIGURE 9.8

*Adding appropriate derived data.*

of data in a data warehouse is such that every byte of data needs to be questioned. Otherwise, the data warehouse will quickly grow to unmanageable proportions.

## Creating Relationship Artifacts

The data relationships found in classical data modeling assume that there is one and only one business value underlying the relationship (i.e. there is only one primary supplier for a product). For the assumption that data is accurate as of the moment of access (i.e., operational data), the classical representation of a relationship is correct. However, a data warehouse usually has *many* relationship values between tables of data, because data in a warehouse represents data over a long spectrum of time; therefore, there will naturally be many relationship values over time (i.e. there are many product suppliers for a product, overtime). Thus, the classical representation of relationships between tables as found in classical data modeling is inadequate for the data warehouse. Relationships between tables in the data warehouse are achieved by means of the creation of *artifacts*.

An artifact of a relationship is merely that part of a relationship that is obvious and tangible at the moment the snapshot of data is made for the data warehouse. In other words, when the snapshot is made the data associated with the relationship that is useful and obvious will be pulled into the warehouse table.

The artifact may include foreign keys and other relevant data, such as columns from the associated table, or the snapshot may include only relevant data and no foreign keys. This subject is one of the most complex subjects facing the data warehouse designer. Consider the simple data relationship shown in Figure 9.9.

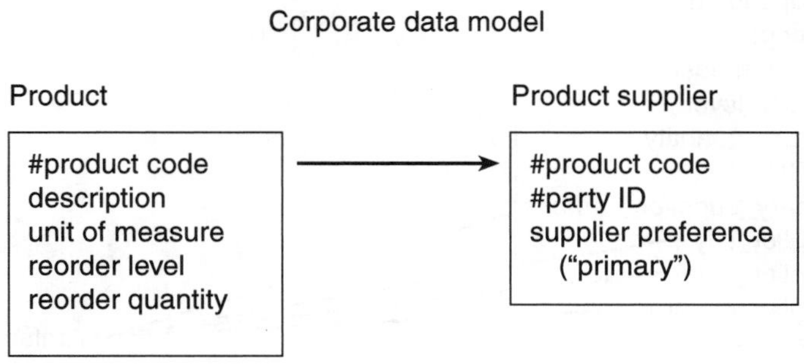

Corporate data model

Product                                    Product supplier

```
┌──────────────────┐          ┌──────────────────────┐
│ #product code    │─────────▶│ #product code        │
│ description      │          │ #party ID            │
│ unit of measure  │          │ supplier preference  │
│ reorder level    │          │   ("primary")        │
│ reorder quantity │          └──────────────────────┘
└──────────────────┘
```

FIGURE 9.9

*An operational relationship between product and supplier.*

Figure 9.9 shows that there is a relationship between a PRODUCT and a SUPPLIER. This information is shown in Chapter 3, Figure 3.2, in the entities PRODUCT, PRODUCT SUPPLIER, and PRODUCT SUPPLIER PREFER-ENCE. In the example, each PRODUCT has a primary SUPPLIER (a preference of *primary*). Integrity constraints dictate that if a SUPPLIER (or organization) is deleted, no PRODUCT SUPPLIER record may exist that has that SUPPLIER as the primary source. In other words, the information about who was the primary supplier is lost since the supplier record was deleted. The relationship represents an ongoing relationship of data that is active and accurate as of the moment of access.

Now consider how snapshots of data might be made and how the relation-ship information might be captured. Figure 9.10 shows a snapshot of PROD-UCT and SUPPLIER data that might appear in the data warehouse.

The PRODUCT snapshot table is one that is created periodically—at the end of the week, the end of the month, and so on. Much detailed information about a PRODUCT is captured at this time. One of the pieces of information that is cap-tured is **primary supplier** as of the moment of snapshot. Other artifact informa-tion is the supplier location and other information about the supplier which is extracted from the supplier information found in the operational system at that

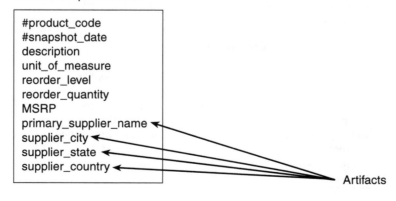

FIGURE 9.10

*Artifacts of the operational data relationship.*

point in time (see Chapter 2). Even if the enterprise stops doing business with a supplier and the supplier record is deleted, the data warehouse still maintains a history of the primary suppliers for the product. This, then, is an example of an artifact of a relationship being captured. Note that the relationship is accurate as of the moment of capture. No other implications are intended or implied.

The snapshot previously discussed has one major drawback: It is incomplete. It shows only the relationship as it exists as of some moment in time. Major events may have occurred that are never captured by the snapshots. For example, suppose the PRODUCT SNAPSHOT is made every week. A product may have had three primary suppliers during the week, yet the snapshot would never reflect this fact.

Snapshots are easy to make and are an essential part of the data warehouse, but they do have their drawbacks. To capture a complete record of data, an historical record rather than a snapshot is required for data in the data warehouse. Figure 9.11 shows an example of historical data in a data warehouse.

In the PRODUCT HISTORY table, a shipment has been received at the loading dock and relevant information is recorded. Among other things, the SUPPLIER of the PRODUCT is recorded. This is another form of artifact relationship information being recorded inside a data warehouse. Assuming that *all* deliveries have an historical record created for them, the record of the relationship between the two tables, over time, is complete.

Data warehouse data model

Product history table

```
#product_id
#shipment_id
date_received
supplier_id
supplier_name
unit_of_measure
condition
received_by
storage_container
```

FIGURE 9.11

*Another form of warehouse data is discrete historical data where all activities are captured.*

## Changing Granularity of Data

One of the features of a data warehouse is the different levels of granularity. In some cases, the level of granularity does not change as data passes from the operational environment to the data warehouse environment. In other cases, the level of granularity does change as data is passed into the data warehouse. When there is a change in the level of granularity, the data warehouse data model needs to reflect those changes, as shown in Figure 9.12.

In the figure, the corporate data model shows shipment activity data that is gathered each time a shipment is made. Due to the requirements specified by end users, data granularity is changed as the data passes into the data warehouse. Two summarizations of shipment data are made—the monthly summarization of total shipments and the summarization of shipments made by the **shipped from** location.

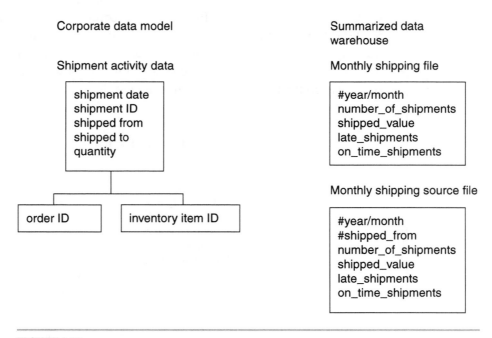

FIGURE 9.12

*Accommodating the different changes in granularity in going from the operations environment to the data warehouse environment.*

The issues in the changing of granularity (insofar as the data warehouse data modeler is concerned) revolve around:

- What period of time should be used to summarize the data (i.e., summarized by day?, by week?, by month?, etc.)?
- What elements of data should be in the summarized table?
- Will the operational environment support the summarized data elements (i.e., has the data warehouse designer specified data in the warehouse which cannot be calculated from the operational data source)?
- What is the trade-off between keeping lower levels of granularity for detailed analysis versus the cost of storing those details? The costs include disk space, performance, and database management overhead, especially for very large databases (VLDB).

## Merging Tables

The next transformation consideration involves merging corporate tables into one data warehouse table, as illustrated in Figure 9.13.

The figure shows two tables, INVOICEs and INVOICE_LINE_ITEMs (the top 2 boxes), from an operational environment (see Chapter 5). The tables are

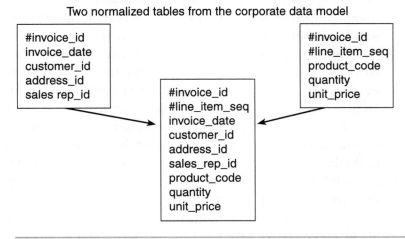

FIGURE 9.13

*Merging corporate data tables into a warehouse data model.*

normalized. As they are placed in the data warehouse environment, they are merged together. The merger can greatly improve query performance and simplifies the data structure by eliminating a commonly required join.

The conditions under which a merger makes sense are when:

- The tables share a common key (or partial key)
- The data from the different tables is used together frequently
- The pattern of insertion is roughly the same

If any one of these conditions is not met, it makes sense to *not* merge the tables together.

In the example given, the common portion of the key is **invoice_id.** In many situations the information in the two tables is used together and the pattern of insertion is exactly the same (i.e., there would be no need for an invoice without line items).

## Creation of Arrays of Data

The next transformation activity is the consideration of the creation of arrays of data in the data warehouse data model. Data in the corporate data model is usually normalized. This means that repeating groups are not shown as part of the data model. But, under the proper conditions, the data warehouse can and should contain repeating groups. Figure 9.14 shows an example creating a data warehouse data model containing arrays of data.

The corporate data model has shown that the budget record (from BUD-GET and BUDGET_LINE_ITEMs in Chapter 7) is created on a month-by-month basis. But as data goes into the data warehouse, it is organized into an array so that each month of the year is an occurrence of the array.

There are several benefits to this structuring of data. One is that by not having individual records of data for each month, a certain amount of space is saved. In the data warehouse case, the values **budget_id** and **year** appear once for each year, while in the case of the corporate data model, the values appear 12 times for each year (assuming that the **budget period** is monthly). The savings of this space may not be trivial at all. In some cases, it amounts to as much as 25 percent of the total space required for the table. In addition, the data warehouse structuring of data requires one twelfth the index entries as the corporate data model structuring of data.

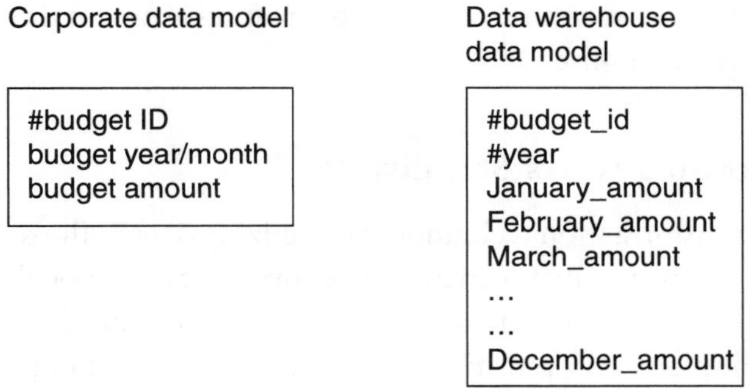

```
Corporate data model          Data warehouse
                              data model

┌─────────────────────┐      ┌─────────────────────────┐
│ #budget ID          │      │ #budget_id              │
│ budget year/month   │      │ #year                   │
│ budget amount       │      │ January_amount          │
└─────────────────────┘      │ February_amount         │
                             │ March_amount            │
                             │ ...                     │
                             │ ...                     │
                             │ December_amount         │
                             └─────────────────────────┘
```

**FIGURE 9.14**

*Under the right conditions, creating an array of data in the data warehouse data model is the correct design choice.*

The other advantage is the possibility of organizing all yearly occurrences of data in a single physical location, creating the possibility of performance enhancement. This is due to a reduction in the number of physical inputs/outputs (I/Os) needed to retrieve the same data, since many logical records are stored in one physical record. Whether this turns out to be a significant factor depends on many considerations, such as the use of data, which database management system (DBMS) is being used, the physical organization of the records within the DBMS, and so forth.

The creation of arrays of data is not a general-purpose option. Only under the correct circumstances does it pay off to create arrays of data in the data warehouse data model. Those conditions are:

- When the number of occurrences of data are predictable
- When the occurrence of data is relatively small (in terms of physical size)
- When the occurrences of data are frequently used together
- When the pattern of insertion and deletion is stable

One of the interesting aspects of the data warehouse is that since the key structure of the data in the warehouse often contains an element of time and since the units of time occur predictably, then the techniques of arrays of data in a data warehouse table are peculiarly appropriate. In other words, there is a strong affinity between the technique of creating arrays of data in a single table and the data warehouse.

## Organizing Data According to Its Stability

The final transformation technique is organizing data in the data warehouse according to its propensity for change. The corporate data model makes little or no distinction in the rate of change of the variables contained inside a table. But a data warehouse is very sensitive to the rate of change of data within the warehouse. The optimal organization of data inside a data warehouse is where data in one table all changes slowly and data in another all changes rapidly.

An illustration of how this transformation works is shown in Figure 9.15. The figure shows that the corporate data model has gathered some data for customer. That data is then divided into three categories—data that rarely changes, data that sometimes changes, and data that often changes. The data warehouse data structure finally ends up with structures that are compatible, in terms of volatility.

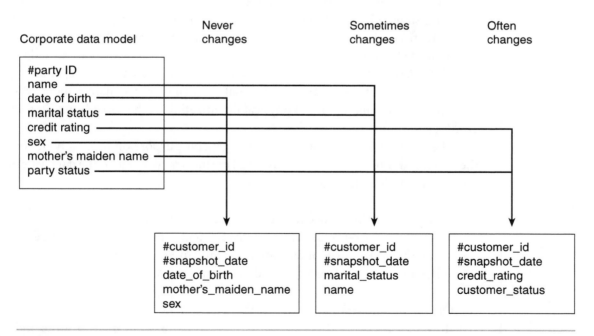

FIGURE 9.15

*Data in the corporate data model may be further divided according to its propensity for change.*

## THE ORDER OF APPLYING THE TRANSFORMATION CRITERIA

The order in which the transformation criteria are applied is as previously presented, with the removal of purely operational data first and the grouping of data according to stability last. Of course, as with every design process there is a certain amount of iteration that occurs. The order that the transformation criteria are applied is not set in concrete. However, as a general guideline, the criteria should be applied as presented.

## SUMMARY

The corporate data model is the basis for building the data warehouse. But the corporate data model needs a fair amount of design activity as it is turned into a design for the data warehouse. The data warehouse data model is created from the corporate data model by going through the following design activities, as they relate to user requirements:

- Removing all purely operational data
- Adding an element of time to the warehouse key if one isn't already there
- Adding appropriate derived data
- Creating relationship artifacts
- Accommodating the granularity changes in warehouse data
- Merging tables where appropriate
- Specifying arrays of data where appropriate
- Organizing data according to its stability

The next chapter will illustrate the design of a sample data warehouse data model using these principles.

# 10

## A Sample Data Warehouse Data Model

### Introduction

Each enterprise has its own unique requirements regarding the types of information that are valuable for decision support. Generally, the decision support environment provides information to illustrate trends, depict performance, and provide key business indicators in order to make informed strategic decisions.

There are a variety of decision support questions that many different departments across an enterprise may need to have answered, such as:

How did sales representatives perform over different periods of time?

What products are most popular to whom and when?

What types of customers are buying what types of products?

How much are the various internal organizations spending on what products?

What were the variances between the amounts budgeted and the amounts spent?

What positions are being filled by people with what types of backgrounds?

What is the average pay for people within different age brackets or Equal Employment Opportunity Commission (EEOC) categories?

This chapter provides a sample data warehouse data model which answers these types of questions. The model was developed using the logical data models from Chapters 2 through 8 as a basis, then utilizing the principles outlined in Chapter 9 to perform the appropriate transformations. The model in this chapter will serve as the source for the data in the departmental models in Chapters 11 and 12.

This data warehouse data model serves as the enterprise-wide source of decision support information. It is an integral piece for an architecture as described in Chapter 9 that allows a central process for the extraction, cleansing, and transformation of data from the operational environment into the data warehouse environment. Using this approach, various departments with differing needs can use an integrated, consistent source of information to build departmental data warehouses or data marts.

## TRANSFORMATION TO CUSTOMER INVOICE

There are two key factors needed in describing the transformation of data from the operational environment to the data warehouse environment: the selection (or nonselection) of data and the transformation rules describing how the data is moved into the data warehouse.

This section gives an example of the transformation process used to develop the CUSTOMER_INVOICES subject data area of an enterprise-wide data warehouse data model (see Figure 10.1). Selection criteria and algorithms for extracting the data are provided solely for the purpose of illustrating the process. Remember, these selection criteria and algorithms may vary across enterprises based upon business requirements.

The information in the CUSTOMER_INVOICES table is the result of transforming INVOICE and INVOICE_LINE_ITEM (see Chapter 5) according to the principles described in Chapter 9. Details of this process are outlined in the following sections.

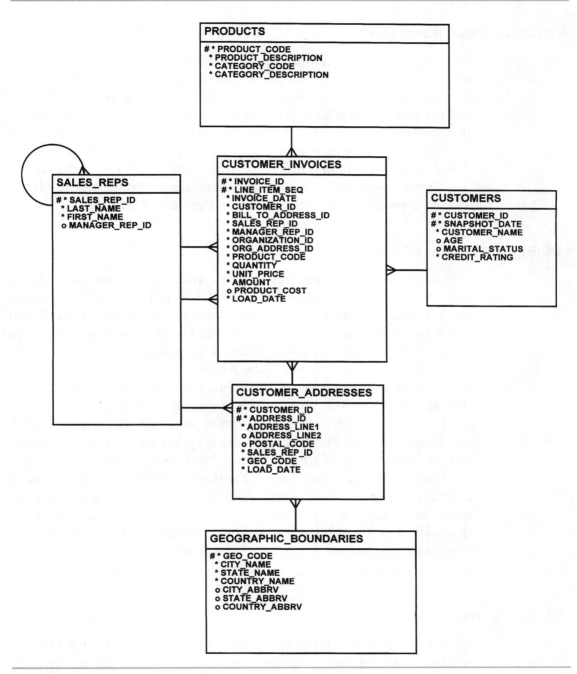

**FIGURE 10.1**

*Customer invoice data warehouse data model.*

## Removing Operational Data

First, any operational information such as messages, descriptions, status, and invoice terms, was removed from INVOICE. This left **invoice_id** and **invoice_date** as part of the CUSTOMER_INVOICES data warehouse table. The column **invoice_id** was left to allow the user to do analysis on a specific transaction. Looking at the line items, **taxable_flag** was removed in this model, since it was deemed as not important for strategic sales management decisions (although some organizations may deem this as valid decision support information—again these decisions are dependent on the enterprise involved). Therefore, **product_code**, **quantity**, and **unit_price** were left.

## Adding an Element of Time

In order to make sure that the element of time is present, the **invoice_date** was left from the INVOICE entity. Since the table CUSTOMER_INVOICES represents particular line item transactions, it is not necessary to include the **invoice_date** as part of the key. The transaction itself is identified uniquely by the **invoice_id** and the **line_item_seq** and is not time-variant; in other words, the transaction information will not change over time. (This model assumes that the enterprise has a business rule that prevents invoice line items from being updated once they are sent out. Any adjustments must be made as separate line items.)

The CUSTOMERS table includes demographics about a customer which *can* change over time. This table includes a **snapshot_date** as part of the key to provide for the storage of historical data and is discussed later in this chapter.

The POSITION table in Figure 10.2 later in this chapter illustrates the use of another common technique to represent changes to data over time. It includes an effective date range as part of the key by using the columns **from_date** and **thru_date**. This is an appropriate technique when the data changes less frequently and changes over time need to be recorded. (The snapshot method only gives information at specific points in time, not for time intervals.)

## Adding Derived Data

The **amount** column in the CUSTOMER_INVOICES table is included as a derived value. It was added because it can be calculated once and will be commonly accessed. The formula for calculating this field is **unit_price\* quantity**.

## Creating Relationship Artifacts

Where did the **customer_id** and **bill_to_address_id** in CUSTOMER_INVOICES come from? They were derived through the resolution of the various **bill to** relationships described in the logical model. Those relationships ultimately point to a **party ID** either through a BILLING ACCOUNT, a PARTY CONTACT MECHANISM, or a PARTY ADDRESS (see Chapter 5 for details). In any case, for the purposes of *this* decision support model, the information required is the **who** and **where** portion of these relationships. In order to make the design more understandable for the DSS analyst or other end users, the column is called **customer_id** rather than **party_id**.

The **customer_id** and **bill_to_address_id** identify the customer and location of the party invoiced. For this model it was decided that the definition of a customer would be based on who was billed for the transaction. Other enterprises could have different rules, such as using the party to whom the order was shipped as the customer. This model could have included additional artifact information about the customer and address in this entity; however, another design decision was made to store this information in the CUSTOMER ADDRESSES and CUSTOMERS tables, since this would reduce the overall storage space required (by reducing the amount of redundantly stored data).

Another question the DSS analyst may need to answer is: Who was the sales representative involved in the transaction? To answer this, the **sales_rep_id** is included in the CUSTOMER_INVOICES table. The sales person can again be derived from the PARTY RELATIONSHIP information. In this case, a relationship similar to customer/sales rep between an external organization (i.e., customer), and an internal person (i.e., sales rep or employee) needs to be traced. This is an example of inclusion of a relationship artifact because there is a need to record who the sales rep was *at the time* of this particular sale. Since this relationship could change with time, it is necessary to capture and store this detail in the warehouse table.

The **sales_rep_last_name** and **sales_rep_first_name** columns *could* be included in CUSTOMER_INVOICES as data artifacts to allow for the occasions when the sales rep perhaps has left the enterprise. This model, however, assumes that sales person records are never deleted from the system. Additionally, if user requirements indicated that the names of the sales reps would be used frequently, then it would make the analysis simpler and more efficient by including these columns with the details and eliminating the need for a join to

SALES_REPS to find the rep's name. In this way the DSS analyst could more easily access the sales information by the sales rep's name. However, it would require more disk space for storage.

Who was the manager of the sales rep at the time of the transaction? The column **manager_rep_id** provides this data. This column indicates the **party id** for the sales rep's manager at the current time. Since this relationship can change over time, the **manager_rep_id** is kept as an artifact with the invoice data just as the **sales_rep_id** is. To make analysis easier, the **manager_last_name** and **manager_first_name** *could* have also been stored as artifacts in the CUSTOMER_ INVOICE, if user requirements so indicated. However, these fields were omitted from the data warehouse data model to reduce storage requirements.

Assuming the models from this book have been implemented, the manager ID can be obtained from the operational data by examining the POSITION REPORTING STRUCTURE (see Chapter 8). This data can be derived by determining the **party ID** of the person holding the position which is "reported to" by the position that the sales rep is currently filling. The recursive foreign key shown on the SALES_REP table is meant to indicate that the **manager_rep_id** will exist as a **sales_rep_id** in the SALES_REP table. This model assumes then, that all sales rep managers are also sales reps themselves. In addition, this recursive relationship could be used for a higher-level grouping by which sales data could be summarized (i.e., a salesperson may report to a local manager who may report to a regional manager). Since the only information stored by this model is **first_name** and **last_name**, this relationship also saves the overhead of having an additional table for the manager information (this may or may not be a benefit, depending on the DBMS being used).

The **organization_id** and **org_address_id** columns in CUSTOMER_ INVOICES provide a mechanism for tracking which internal organization is responsible for the sale. The information is derived from tracing the **billed from** relationship from INVOICE to PARTY ADDRESS in Chapter 5, Figure 5.7. If internal organizational information changes quickly, the designer may also consider storing artifacts of additional internal organization information in the CUSTOMER_INVOICES table.

The **product_cost** is a derived field based upon relationship artifacts. It represents what the actual product cost was at the time of the sale. Some of the information for item costs can be selected by traversing the relationships between the INVOICE LINE ITEM, SHIPMENT INVOICE, SHIPMENT LINE ITEM, and INVENTORY ITEM entities in Chapter 5 and applying a costing method [i.e., First In First Out (FIFO), Last In First Out (LIFO), or average cost] to determine the product cost. The INVOICE LINE ITEM entity stores the **quantity** and **unit price** as well as any INVOICE ADJUSTMENTS which provide some of the information necessary to determine the costs of purchased items. While this example provides some of the selection criteria involved, the algorithms involved in determining product costs can be quite complex and are beyond the scope of this book.

## Accommodating Levels of Granularity

By storing sales information at an invoice line item level in the CUSTOMER_ INVOICES table, the enterprise has chosen to maintain the lowest level of granularity in its enterprise data warehouse. In other words, the data is stored at the transaction level and cannot be further subdivided. This allows departmental data warehouses the ability to summarize the sales information at whatever level of detail is required, since the most detailed level of data (sometimes referred to as *atomic level*) is present in the data warehouse data model.

In some cases, it may be prudent to store multiple levels of granularity in an enterprise warehouse. This should only be done if there are good business reasons and requirements available to define the additional levels. However, if real requirements are not known, then the space required to store these extra levels, and the resources to build them, may be wasted. When it is known that the warehouse will be used to feed departmental warehouses, it is best to defer the definition of higher levels of granularity to the designers of these data marts. Then the specific requirements of the department can be used in producing meaningful summaries.

## Merging Tables

As implied from the previous sections, the basis for CUSTOMER_INVOICES was the merging of the INVOICE and INVOICE LINE ITEM entities. This was done on the basis that the two tables shared a common key (i.e., **invoice_id**), the data from the different tables is used together frequently, and the pattern for insertion is the same for both tables.

## Separation Based upon Stability

In the CUSTOMERS table, the **snapshot_date** column, which is part of the primary key, provides the ability to maintain a history of some of the more volatile demographics associated each customer. If some of this data was more volatile such as age and credit rating, it could have been separated into a CUSTOMER_DEMOGRAPHICS table to save space. This would have illustrated the concept of separation of data attributes according to its stability.

The customer information can be directly extracted from the operational systems of the enterprise. In terms of the models presented in this book, this data comes from the PARTY entity as described in Chapter 2. The data could be extracted by gathering all the parties that had a PARTY RELATIONSHIP to the internal organization of the type "customer/vendor". In the case of a customer that is an organization or company, the column **name** is derived from **organization name**. If the customer is a person, then the **first name** and **last name** would be combined into the **name** column (in which order will need to be determined by detailed *enterprise-specific* transformation rules).

## Other Considerations

The **load_date** in CUSTOMER_INVOICES identifies the date that data was loaded into the data warehouse. This provides the ability to replace some records in the data warehouse with more up-to-date information if there are changes in the operational environment that affect past history.

As may be obvious by the discussion so far, even though the design of the tables for the warehouse may be simple in nature, getting the data into the proposed format could be quite an ominous task. Considering that the data may be coming from many separate source systems, there could be a need to scrub (or clean) the data and integrate it, as well as transform it into the warehouse model. For example, customer data may exist in two operational systems running on different platforms. To get this information into one warehouse table will require careful examination of the data to see where the two systems match and where they do not. Then processes must be developed to convert that data into a common format that fits in the warehouse.

This point is precisely why a properly designed data warehouse can be of such incredible benefit to executives and analysts in an enterprise. It can allow them to view data and trends in ways that were not possible before without a substantial amount of time and effort on the part of the IS staff. With the data prearranged as described, the amount of time and system resources needed to process the various reports is also reduced.

## THE SAMPLE DATA WAREHOUSE DATA MODEL

Figure 10.2 illustrates an example of a data warehouse data model to support the information needs across an enterprise. This model illustrates the idea that while a data warehouse data model may start with a single subject data area, other subject areas may be integrated as time moves forward.

This sample data warehouse model builds upon the previous section's customer invoicing model and integrates other subject data areas into the model. In particular human resources, budget and purchasing information have been added to the model.

Notice that while this model may contain a large part of the information that an enterprise may find useful for decision support, it is not all-inclusive. For instance, it doesn't cover all financial information, work efforts, ordering and shipment information. This model illustrates the principle that the data warehouse is developed iteratively and other subject areas may be integrated, one at a time, into this model over time. Three subject data areas are integrated and included in this model:

- *Sales analysis:* This decision support information is primarily provided via the PRODUCTS, CUSTOMER_INVOICES, SALES_REPS, CUSTOMER_ ADDRESSES, CUSTOMERS, and GEOGRAPHIC_BOUNDARIES tables.
- *Budgeting and purchasing:* This decision support information is provided via the PRODUCTS, PRODUCT_SNAPSHOTS, PURCHASE_INVOICES, SUPPLIER_ADDRESSES, BUDGET_DETAILS, INTERNAL_ORG_ ADDRESSES, and GEOGRAPHIC_BOUNDARIES tables.
- *Human resources:* This decision support information is provided through the INTERNAL_ORG_ADDRESSES, POSITIONS, and EMPLOYEES tables.

### Common Reference Tables

Notice in Figure 10.2 that certain tables span subject data areas and are useful for several departmental views of data. The GEOGRAPHIC_BOUNDARIES table is useful to identify the types of boundaries included in different types of analysis.

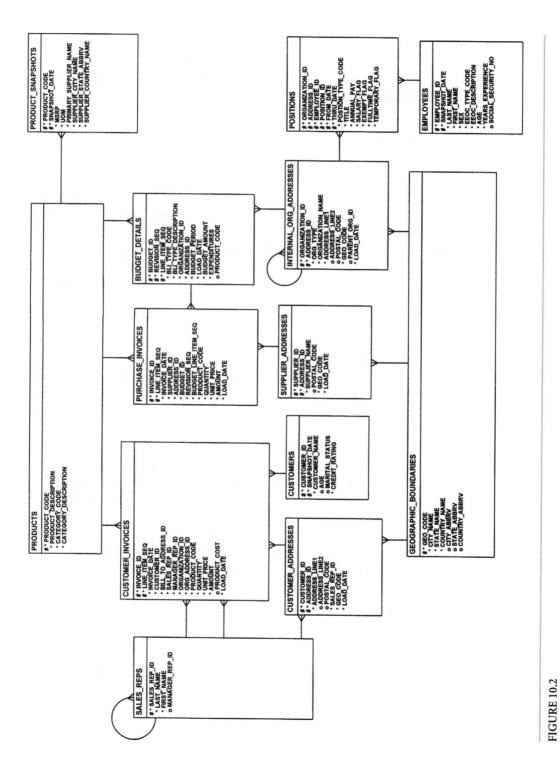

FIGURE 10.2

*Sample data warehouse data model.*

Notice that **geo_code** is present in several tables such as the CUSTOMER_AD-DRESSES, SUPPLIER_ADDRESSES, and INTERNAL_ORG_ADDRESSES. The GEOGRAPHIC_BOUNDARIES table provides the look-up information linked to **geo_code**. This table can be used for extracting data based on city, state, or country (this will be discussed in future chapters). Because this information is maintained in a central prescrubbed decision support environment, it can be easily extracted into various departmental data marts (thus ensuring consistency across the data marts).

The PRODUCTS table is another example of standard information which may be used in purchasing, sales, and budgeting departmental data marts. The products sold are very often the products purchased, especially in retail and distribution organizations. For instance, a distributor may purchase a certain type of pencil in order to resell it. The fact that this information is being transformed only once from the operational environment to the data warehouse can save a great deal of development time in the long run and can lead to better quality decision support information.

## SUMMARY

This chapter has discussed details of the design of a sample data warehouse built to support the enterprise's needs. The methods discussed in Chapter 9 for transforming a corporate data model to a data warehouse model were applied specifically to the logical data models related to invoicing as presented in this book. The resulting data warehouse design contains some denormalization and various levels of granularity to assist in answering questions posed by the enterprise. The data warehouse data model as presented could be used as a starting point for developing departmental models for use in DSS, on-line analytical processing (OLAP), and multidimensional analysis. Some examples of these models are presented in the next two chapters.

It should be noted that what has been presented is one of many possible warehouse designs that could result from transforming the logical data models. The structure of a data warehouse will be influenced greatly by the questions it is designed to answer. If the corporate end users are asked enough questions during analysis, then the resulting design should provide the enterprise with the information it needs. If this does not occur, then more questions must be asked and another design developed. This is why it has been said that building a data warehouse is an *iterative* process.

Detailed table and column definitions for the sample data warehouse data model are included in Appendix B. In addition, the detailed SQL scripts to build this model can be found on the CD-ROM product, which is sold separately.

# 11

## STAR SCHEMA DESIGNS FOR SALES ANALYSIS

### INTRODUCTION

Suppose that ABC Corporation has built the data warehouse depicted in Chapter 10. Excited about the opportunity to get meaningful sales analysis information, the eastern regional sales manager has approached the IS department to see how and when the data would be available. The IS department, knowing that nothing is as simple as it seems, went out and gathered some specific requirements. After a review of the real requirements, it was obvious that the sales manager did not need access to the entire warehouse. In fact, that would be too much information and ultimately result in confusion and dissatisfaction. So, IS decided the best solution was to develop a departmental data warehouse (or *data mart*).

As pointed out in the previous chapters, a data warehouse is generally developed one subject area at a time. This chapter will briefly discuss possible star schema structures for a departmental warehouse containing the first of two subject areas to be transformed: sales analysis.

The purpose of the designs in this chapter is to provide an example of a departmental-specific data warehouse (or data mart) which could be developed from the data warehouse. Each enterprise may choose to modify this sales analysis departmental warehouse to meet its own specific needs. The models are presented in a standard *star schema* format to allow for multidimensional analysis. A star schema is a database design that contains a central table, called a *fact* table, with relationships to several look-up tables called *dimensions*. When the schema is diagrammed, it often forms a pattern resembling a star, thus the name *star* schema.

The models in this chapter will allow the DSS analyst to answer questions such as the following:

What was the sales volume for a product during a specific time period?

What was the sales volume for a category of products for a specific time period?

How much of each product did various customers buy?

How much of each product category did a selected customer buy?

How much are the sales reps selling? To whom are they selling?

Which products or product categories are they selling?

When were sales the best? When were sales the worst?

During those times who was buying and who was making the sale?

Which products and/or customers are most profitable?

The specific schemas presented in the following pages include:

- Detailed customer sales information
- Sales by product, sales rep, customer, and location
- Sales by sales rep, customer, and location
- Sales by product and geographic area

## DETAILED CUSTOMER SALES INFORMATION

Continuing with the example, the requirements analysis determined that the eastern region sales manager needs to see sales information by product, customer, sales representative, and geographic area. All this information must be available for analysis over daily, weekly, monthly, quarterly, and yearly time periods. In addition, the sales manager needs the ability to view information at a transaction level when supporting detail is required.

Figure 11.1 shows the star schema that contains the lowest level of granularity contained in the warehouse—transaction level. The diagram shows a simple database star schema containing a central fact table and several dimension tables.

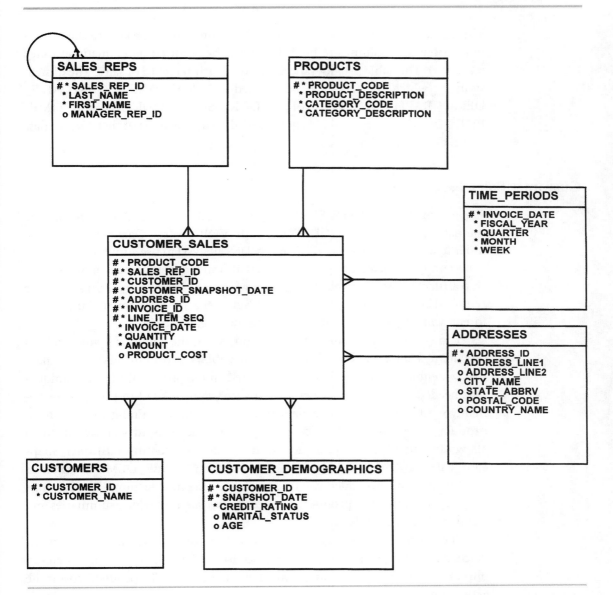

FIGURE 11.1

*Sales data warehouse—detailed customer sales.*

The fact table is CUSTOMER_SALES, which contains all the keys to the various dimensions and columns to hold the data to be reported on (sometimes called *measures*). This table provides the detailed historical record of sales. The dimensions by which the facts can be queried are CUSTOMERS, CUSTOMER_ DEMOGRAPHICS, SALES_REPS, ADDRESSES, PRODUCTS, and TIME_ PERIODS. This schema will likely be loaded on a daily basis so that current data is available every 24 hours.

## Customer Sales Facts

The information in the CUSTOMER_SALES table is the result of transforming the data warehouse table CUSTOMER_INVOICES (see Chapter 9). First, in order to allow the sales manager (or any DSS analyst) to use a multidimensional analysis approach, all non-key columns that resulted from inclusion of relationship artifacts were removed. Next the **organization_id** and **org_address_id** were removed because it was assumed that this model is for departmental use; therefore, it will only contain data for one internal organization.

Though not represented by dimension tables, the columns **invoice_id** and **line_item_seq** were left to allow analysts the ability to drill through to the main data warehouse if further details are required and to provide the level of uniqueness needed for the primary key. The **invoice_date** was left to provide the element of time required for a data warehouse. The remaining key columns, **product_code**, **sales_rep_id**, **customer_id**, and **address_id** were included to allow sales analysis based on these dimensions. The column **customer_snapshot_date** was added to allow joining to the CUSTOMER_DEMOGRAPHICS dimension (how it is added will be discussed in the next section). The columns **quantity**, **amount**, and **product_cost** are the *measures* on which summaries and trend analysis will be done.

The **quantity** column represents the actual product quantity that was invoiced. The **amount** is the extended price for a line item: unit price* quantity plus or minus any adjustments related to that line item. The **product_cost** is the actual product cost.

No actual data transformation is needed to move data from the warehouse model into CUSTOMER_SALES since these values were already calculated when the main warehouse was loaded. There could, however, be a restriction on the data selected. For example, as previously indicated, the process to extract the warehouse data may only include customer invoice data for a particular department or division. This would be done by limiting the selection process to specific organization IDs. Other possible restrictions could be on sales representatives, customers, or a date-range basis. *The particular algorithm used must be based on the specific business analysis requirements of the enterprise using the data.*

## Customer and Customer Demographics Dimensions

To allow the analyst to get more detail on a particular customer, the CUS-TOMERS and CUSTOMER_DEMOGRAPHICS tables are included. If the analyst is interested in seeing sales data for all customers over the age of 20, that could be done with this data using a restrictive query against CUSTOMER_ DEMOGRAPHICS (e.g., select all customer IDs where the age is greater than 20). The same approach could be used to gather data based on **marital_status** or **credit_rating** as well.

The data for both tables can be directly extracted from the CUSTOMERS table found in the enterprise data warehouse. During the user interviews, the IS department learned that the sales manager was *not* interested in historical customer names so the name field was separated into the CUSTOMERS dimension table along with **customer_id**. The data selected from the warehouse into this table should be the most current data available on each customer.

In order to get meaningful information, the sales manager did indicate a need for demographic data *as it was* when the sale was made. It does not matter what age the customer is this month. The important information is what age was the customer last year when the sale was closed. In order to provide this level of detail, the CUSTOMER_DEMOGRAPHICS table was built using the columns **age**, **marital_status**, and **credit_rating**. Note that **age** and **marital_status** are optional columns since not all customers are people. The column **credit_rating** is required because it is possible to get a rating on people and organizations.

As in the enterprise warehouse, the key to this dimension is **customer_id** and **snapshot_date**. The table could be loaded by inserting records with a snapshot date that is greater than the date of the last load. Putting the appropriate date (via **customer_snapshot_date**) in the CUSTOMER_SALES table to complete the foreign key is a matter of selecting the most recent **snapshot_date** that is less than or equal to the **invoice_date** (**snapshot_date** indicates the date that the values were changed). In this way, the sales information can access the historically accurate demographics without having to store the demographics redundantly on every transaction, thus saving space and load time.

## Sales Rep Dimension

Another question the DSS analyst may need answered is: What was the sales volume attributed to each sales representative during a certain time period? To answer this need, the **sales_rep_id** column is included in CUSTOMER_SALES. With this data the DSS analyst can easily group, sum, and sort the sales information by sales rep.

The details about a particular rep, including his or her name, are included in the dimension table SALES_REPS. This table is an exact duplicate of the corresponding table in the warehouse. The only possible restriction to consider when populating this table would be to select only those reps that are involved in the required sales data. If the warehouse table is small, copying the entire table may be simpler and pose no performance impact. (Note that the definition of "small" varies from one enterprise to another.)

## Address Dimension

Another component, or dimension, commonly required in DSS and multidimensional analysis is geographic area, region, or location. For example, the eastern region sales manager needs to know sales volume not only by the various geographic areas, but also by the various customer locations or sites. In some cases, it may be critical to know the actual address where sales were made. This will provide the region with information to assess how well different products are selling at various customer locations.

The **address_id** columns and the ADDRESSES dimension will provide that information for this model. This data is extracted from the warehouse table CUSTOMER_ADDRESSES. The values for **city_name**, **state_abbrv**, and **country_name** will be extracted from the warehouse table GEOGRAPHIC_BOUNDARIES using the column **geo_code** in the CUSTOMER_ADDRESSES table. Because of this, the column **geo_code** will not be included in the dimension table since it adds no additional value. As with customer and sales rep data, the only restriction to consider would be to pull only addresses referenced by the selected sales data.

Also dropped was the **customer_id** column. Since the identifiers for an address are unique and the characteristics of an address rarely change, it was determined (through user interviews) that this dimension needed unique address records only. In other words, the extraction process from the enterprise warehouse needs to pull information for a particular **address_id** only once, regardless of how many customers are associated with it. This serves to save some space in the departmental warehouse because redundant data is eliminated.

Notice that the ADDRESSES table includes not only the city, state, country, and postal code but also includes **address_line1** and **address_line2**. This allows the regional sales manager to compare sales for a single customer that may have several locations within the same city. While some DSS analysts may be interested in performance at specific customer locations, others may be more interested in grouping sales by the large geographic areas like city, state, and country; so both levels of detail are included.

## Product Dimension

The PRODUCTS table provides description and category information about the various items which have been sold. Using this dimension, the DSS analyst can determine product sales by product or product category for higher level analysis. The data in this table is a direct extract or copy of the PRODUCTS table found in the enterprise warehouse model.

## Time Dimension

An accepted standard in the industry is that most star schema designs will have a time dimension. To accommodate this, the table TIME_PERIODS is used. It includes **fiscal_year, quarter, month**, and **week**. In this way, the data in the warehouse can be accessed and summarized to accommodate any of these time periods, not just a single period such as year. Table 11.1 contains examples of the data that could fill the TIME_PERIODS table.

As indicated by the data, the table key, **invoice_date**, references the date of the invoice in the fact table. These dates are then associated with the appropriate year, month, quarter, and week. What dates are loaded into this table are again dependent on the time periods over which the enterprise wishes to do analysis.

At this point it should be noted that this time data could mean several things depending on the rules of the enterprise. The table can be used to store organizationally defined time periods. Since many businesses operate on a fiscal year basis, the column for year is called just that: **fiscal_year**. This allows analysts to work within the bounds of their companys' standard time frames without too

**TABLE 11.1** *Time Period Data*

| Invoice Date | Fiscal Year | Quarter | Month | Week |
|---|---|---|---|---|
| 01-JAN-90 | 1990 | 1 | 1 | 1 |
| 02-JAN-90 | 1990 | 1 | 1 | 1 |
| 27-JAN-90 | 1990 | 1 | 1 | 4 |
| 02-MAY-96 | 1996 | 2 | 5 | 1 |

much confusion. If the year stored was only a calendar year, there is a possibility for confusion to occur when interpreting the data and trends as there would be a mismatch between the time codes in the dimension table and the time periods expected on company reports. A column for calendar year could be added if both year values are needed for analysis. Other extensions could be made to the model to categorize days into other classifications such as work days, weekends, or holidays.

Using this construct, it is possible to summarize the detailed data in CUSTOMER_SALES, by the time element **invoice_date**. It could be summarized by fiscal year so that annual trends could be observed, or by month so that the trends within a year could be observed or seasonal trends could be analyzed (e.g., compare gross sales for June, July, and August, for 1990 through 1995). Likewise, summary data by quarter or week could also be constructed. This would be done by selecting data associated with time code values that have a particular year, month, or week (the actual mechanics of this will vary according to the DSS tool being used). This model is very flexible because one time dimension table could be used to produce many different summaries.

Note that this may or may not provide fast query retrieval, depending on many factors such as the DBMS and amount of data. If performance becomes an issue, then separate tables could be constructed to hold data summarized by the various time periods. For example, a *highly* summarized table containing this sales data by year could be built simply by substituting the column **year** for **invoice_date**. Then a different time dimension table would be required that simply contained the list of years available. (If this was done, then the **quantity**, **amount**, and **product_cost** fields would represent the sum of those values over a year's worth of invoices.)

# Sales by Product, Sales Rep, Customer, and Location

Another principle in transforming a logical model to a data warehouse model is that of accommodating different levels of granularity. This means that the data warehouse should include different levels of summarization as appropriate to the needs of the DSS analyst and other users. As previously written (W.H. Inmon, *Building the Data Warehouse,* 1992, QED Technical Publishing Group), these levels include *lightly* summarized and *highly* summarized data.

Interviews with the eastern sales manager indicated that some presummarized data would indeed be useful. The model shown in Figure 11.2 contains a fact table called CUSTOMER_REP_SALES which represents a *light* summarization of data. This table provides a construct for presummarizing sales information by sales rep, customer, product, and location, on a daily level instead of an individual transaction level (as in CUSTOMER_SALES, Figure 11.1). In it, the dollar amount of the sales (**gross_sales**) and the physical volume of sales (**quantity**) are both included as data elements which have been summarized for an entire day. This schema would also likely be loaded daily.

## Customer Rep Sales Facts

In the table CUSTOMER_REP_SALES, notice that **invoice_id** and **line_item_seq** have been removed. This is to allow data to be summarized above the transaction level. In this case, it will be summarized to a daily level instead of the transaction line item level. Since it is possible for one customer to have several invoices in a day, this will allow the regional sales manager to easily determine total daily sales based on all the previously discussed dimensions.

How is this new level of summarization derived? There are two possible options. First, the data could be gathered from the enterprise warehouse as before and grouped according to date, customer, sales rep, address, and product. Alternatively, if the CUSTOMER_SALES fact table is available, then the data from that table could be summarized to form the facts for this table. If this is the case, the building of the CUSTOMER_REP_SALES table could be completed more quickly since CUSTOMER_SALES already contains a subset of the warehouse data and therefore has fewer rows to summarize. If this schema needs to be populated for a different internal organization than was used for CUSTOMER_SALES, the summary needs to be built from the enterprise-wide data warehouse.

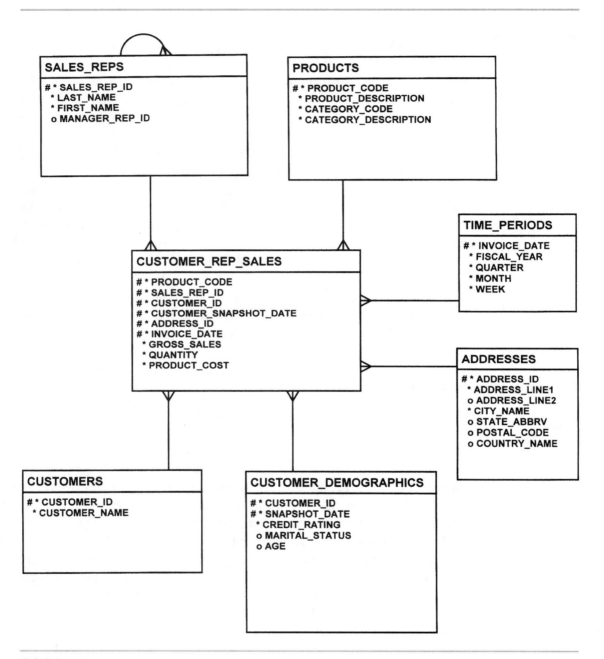

FIGURE 11.2

*Sales by product, sales rep, customer, and location.*

The dimension tables for this schema are arrived at as described in the previous section (and may be shared if both schemas are being used by the same internal organization).

Using the table CUSTOMER_REP_SALES, some questions the regional sales manager (or a DSS analyst) might answer are:

What was the sales volume for a product for a specific customer over the last 12 months?

Which sales representative had the highest volume for several products for a specific time period?

What was the distribution of sales between various customers for a sales representative?

In which state was the greatest volume of a specific product sold? Which had the least?

## SALES BY SALES REP, CUSTOMER, AND LOCATION

Some departmental data marts may have very specific goals. Take for example the need to analyze the performance of sales reps on a monthly basis. This may be done by the previously mentioned regional sales manager or, in other enterprises, by a human resources manager. These managers may need to evaluate the performance of the sales reps that report to them or develop and monitor sales incentive plans. They generally do not care what products are being sold, nor about customer demographics. Their concern is sales performance and perhaps how much is sold to various clients to determine how diverse the sales rep's market is. To answer these needs, the table SALES_REP_SALES (see Figure 11.3) was designed. This table provides presummarized data by sales rep, customer, and location, by month.

### Sales Rep Sales Facts

Notice that there is no longer a PRODUCT dimension table because the table SALES_REP_SALES is a summarization of data about the performance of the sales reps, regardless of the individual products. Customer demographics are also deemed as unimportant and the CUSTOMER_DEMOGRAPHICS dimen-

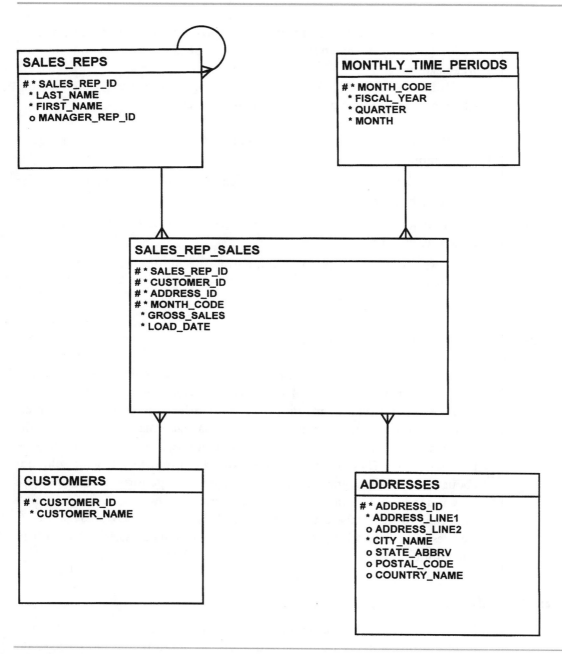

FIGURE 11.3

*Sales by sales rep, customer, and location.*

sion has also been dropped. This table then represents a slightly higher level of summarization than the previous ones described since two of the dimensions have been eliminated. The measures **quantity** and **product-cost** have also been dropped since their values are dependent on product and cannot be summarized correctly in this context.

The column **load_date** has been added so that analysts know how current the data is. This will be especially important when doing year-to-date or month-to-date analysis. Suppose the sales manager wants to know how a certain rep is progressing toward this month's goals. If the revenue figures indicate that rep has only reached 50 percent of the goal, and the load date is the 25th of the month, then there may be cause for concern; but, if the load date is the 15th of the month, the rep is right on target. This assumes that the sales data for the current month is updated on a daily basis.

## Time Dimension

In this star schema, there is a slight variation in the time dimension table. It is now called MONTHLY_TIME_PERIODS. When the sales manager was interviewed by the IS department, it became clear that daily information was not required to answer the questions posed; however, a monthly view of the data would be most useful. Therefore, the fact table has a column (**month_code**) that contains the code to uniquely identify a specific month within the enterprise's fiscal year. This is matched in the time dimension table.

Since the data is only to be summarized by month, the time dimension only needs the columns **month**, **quarter**, and **fiscal_year**. The column **week** is no longer needed as it makes no sense in a monthly summary view of the data. Another point to note is that summarizing data to the monthly level also represents another higher level of summarization.

This schema can be used to easily answer questions such as:

What was the sales volume for a specific sales rep over the last 12 months?

Which customer bought the highest volume through a particular sales rep for a specific month?

What was the distribution of sales across a sales rep's customers?

How much does each sales rep sell across each of his or her assigned states?

Within each state, which city had the greatest volume?

Thus, this table can provide the DSS analyst or department manager with another very flexible means of viewing the data.

## SALES BY PRODUCT AND GEOGRAPHIC AREA

Suppose a product analyst for ABC Corporation needs information to assess product performance. The information will be used to make strategic decisions on product offerings for various geographic areas. Interviews with the analyst determine that specific customer, customer address, or customer demographic information is unimportant for this type of analysis. It is also determined that monthly summaries will provide an appropriate level of granularity.

Figure 11.4 shows a schema containing PRODUCT_SALES as the central fact table. This is considered more highly summarized because it contains fewer dimensions than the previously discussed tables and records are summarized by month. Thus, this table can be used to hold presummarized data for product sales by geographic area by month. While previous tables also included customer and sales rep information, this one does not (as the analysis indicated it was not required). Thus, the columns **sales_rep_id**, **customer_id**, and **address_id** are not included in this table. The only dimensions tables needed in this schema are GEOGRAPHIC_BOUNDARIES, PRODUCTS, and MONTHLY_TIME_PERIOD.

### Product Sales Facts

The measures in this table are again the **quantity, gross_sales,** and **product_cost.** Data in this table could be created by summing all the information in CUSTOMER_REP_SALES by **product_code, city_name** (from the ADDRESSES dimension), month, and year. The cities selected would be referenced by a new column **geo_code.** As in the previous examples, this data could also be taken directly from the main warehouse by selecting and summing data from CUSTOMER_INVOICES for the products of interest. An additional restriction on the data extracted would need to be made through a join to CUSTOMER_ADDRESSES with a summarization based on the **city name** via the column **geo_code.** (Note that the column **load_date** is also included in this fact table for the reasons discussed in the previous section.)

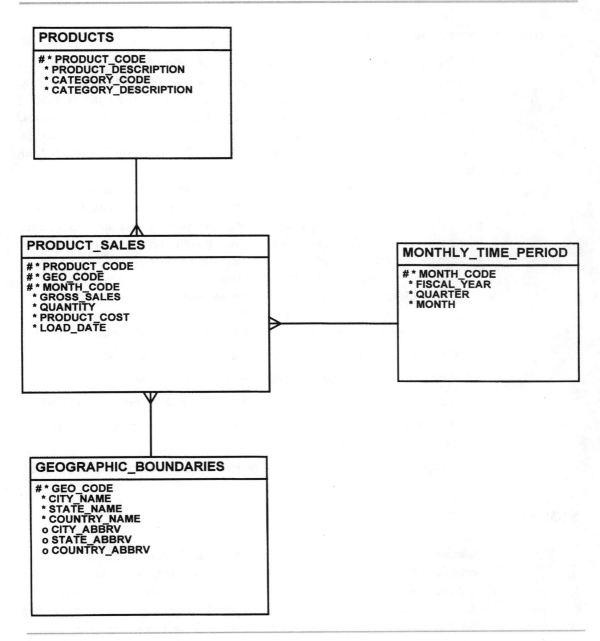

FIGURE 11.4

*Sales by product and geographic area.*

## Geographic Boundaries Dimension

So what is this **geo_code**? In the case of this warehouse, these codes are tied to city names, so the data can be summed to the level of city-related data. The table GEOGRAPHIC_BOUNDARIES can be used much the same as TIME_ PERIODS. It contains a hierarchy of geographic areas—namely, cities, states, and countries. By using this dimension, an analyst could gather data for all the cities within a selected state or country. Additionally, data could be selected for multiple states or countries.

Thus, for each product for a city, all the sales dollars and quantities for that product would be added up to give a grand total by product and city. Once compiled, this data could be very useful for product analysts and other executives who need a quick, high-level view of how their products are performing with respect to the various geographic areas. Even getting a view of total sales by product would be quick using this table, since there are far fewer rows to sum.

Questions that could be answered from this data include:

What was the sales revenue from a specific product over the last 12 months?

What was the highest volume of a product for a specific month?

Which product had the greatest revenue across all sales?

Within that product, which geographic region had the greatest revenue?

What was the profitability for each product or product category in a certain country for a specific year?

Which country has generated the greatest average annual revenue by product?

## SUMMARY

This chapter presented details of the design of sample star schemas built to support sales analysis. The movement of data from the enterprise data warehouse to a data mart was discussed. The resulting design contained various levels of granularity to assist in answering the questions posed. The models presented could be effectively used to support DSS, OLAP, and multidimensional analysis.

It should again be noted that what has been presented is one of many possible designs that could result from building departmental warehouses based on the enterprise warehouse. The structure of a schema will be influenced greatly by the questions it is designed to answer. With a thorough end-user interview process the resulting design should provide the departmental analyst with useful information. When this is not the case, more questions must be asked and another design developed. Again, this is why building a data warehouse or data mart *must* be an iterative process.

As may be obvious by the discussion so far, even though getting the data into the enterprise data warehouse may have been difficult, once in place, the warehouse provides an excellent basis for developing departmental data marts (star schemas). All the major transformation and integration work has already been done *and documented*. To state again, this is why a properly designed data warehouse can be of such incredible benefit to executives and analysts in an enterprise. It allows them to more easily get data extracts for viewing trends in ways that were not possible before without a substantial amount of time and effort on the part of the IS staff. With the data prearranged as described, the amount of time and system resources needed to produce various data marts can be reduced. The accuracy of data is also increased since there is an integrated source (from the data warehouse data model) allowing for consistent decision support information which may be useful in many departmental data warehouses.

For details on the table and column definitions for these schemas, refer to Appendix C. For the SQL scripts to implement these tables, including primary and foreign key definitions, refer to the CD-ROM product, which augments this text but is sold separately.

# 12

# STAR SCHEMA DESIGNS FOR HUMAN RESOURCES ANALYSIS

## INTRODUCTION

As in the previous chapter, the design of another proposed departmental data warehouse will be discussed. The EEOC (Equal Employment Opportunity Commission) Compliance Division of the Human Resources Department of ABC Corporation has been hearing how happy the eastern regional sales manager is with the data mart that was produced for that group. The division has heard that the data mart has drastically reduced the time and energy required to get reports on strategically important data and that with some appropriate DSS tools, it is fairly easy to effectively analyze trends.

Not wanting to be behind the times, and having a real need, the EEOC division manager asks the IS department for assistance in producing a small data warehouse for the division. Elated that the data mart concept is catching on, the IS manager is more than willing to assign some people to the task. After a series of interviews, the IS team determines what questions the EEOC team is most interested in answering and develops a few star schemas for the data mart to specifically address those questions. This chapter will examine the structure for that data mart.

As stated before, the purpose of the models in this chapter is to provide examples to demonstrate the concepts of building a departmental data warehouse. This model may be tailored to fit a specific enterprise's needs; however, it should be understood that the design of this departmental data warehouse is highly dependent on the enterprise implementing it.

This model will, however, allow the DSS analyst in the EEOC division to answer questions such as the following:

How many programmer/analysts are African-American or Hispanic?

What is their annual salary in comparison to those who are white?

What is the average salary for female versus male workers?

Over time, how often do most workers get raises?

Is there any group that has a higher, or lower, rate of salary increase compared to others?

How do annual salaries compare with respect to years of experience or years employed by the company?

How many minority workers are there in total? What percentage does this represent?

The specific schemas presented in the following pages include:

- Employee pay history
- Average annual pay

## EMPLOYEE PAY HISTORY

Given the results of the interviews of the EEOC staff, the IS department determined that initially it would be very useful to be able to look at annual salaries for all employees, across all departments, and to group them by position, EEOC category (white, Hispanic, African-American, Asian, Native American, etc.), and sex. In addition, information on length of employment and years of experience could also be important. Discussions with the staff indicated that daily information would not be needed, but that a picture of the organization at month-end would allow for observation of some meaningful trends.

The star schema depicted in Figure 12.1 was developed—based on the data in the enterprise data warehouse—to address these needs. The central fact table, PAY_HISTORY_DETAILS, contains not only the keys to the various dimensions, but also the important measures to be analyzed and some non-key dimensions. The dimensions for this star schema include ORGANIZATIONS, POSITIONS, EEOC_TYPES, EMPLOYEES, and MONTHLY_TIME_PERIODS. As indicated, the data for this schema will likely be loaded at the end of each month.

## Pay History Details

The information in the PAY_HISTORY_DETAILS table is the result of transforming data from the POSITIONS table of the warehouse (see Chapter 10/Figure 10.2) to this departmental data warehouse. As in previous examples (see Chapter 11), several of the non-key columns were removed. This included **salary_flag, exempt_flag, fulltime_flag**, and **temporary_flag**. This information was deemed unnecessary for the required analysis. The **address_id** key column was removed because the users were not interested in looking at any geographic factors. The **organization_id** was left in this case because the analysis needed to be done across all internal organizations. The **position_type_code** and **title** were moved to a POSITIONS dimension table in order to reduce redundancy and save space (since there were far fewer positions than employees).

Since the requirements indicated that data was needed on a monthly basis, the **from_date** and **thru_date** columns were replaced with the column **month_code**. In order to get the correct data into this data mart, the extraction program needs to select records from the POSITIONS table in the data warehouse data model (Chapter 10) based on the from and thru dates for a given position. This means that the **from_date** must be on or before the first day of the selected month and the **thru_date** is either on or after the last day of the month. If both dates fall within the current month, those records are also needed. In addition, any records where one of the two dates falls within the month should also be loaded to the data mart. The only records that should *not* be loaded to the departmental warehouse are those where both dates occur either before or after the month of the extract.

The **month_code** column acts as the link to the time dimension. This information then represents the pay history facts for each month the enterprise does business. The load for this departmental data warehouse takes place at the end of the month so the **month_code** also indicates a specific point in time (i.e., the end of a particular month) when the data was captured.

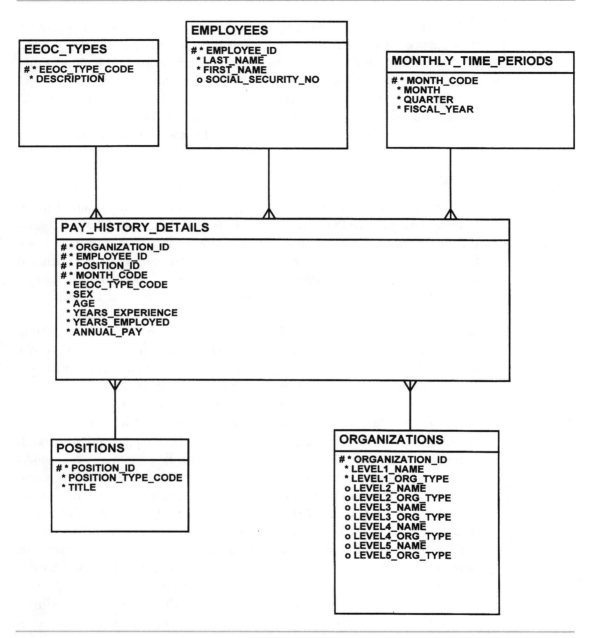

FIGURE 12.1

*Employee pay history.*

The remaining key column in the fact table is **employee_id**. Since the EEOC staff is looking for information about job types and the characteristics of those in the job, why is this needed? For one, **position_id** is not enough to ensure uniqueness in the table because of the potential for job sharing (as discussed in Chapter 8). The combination of **position_id** and **employee_id** is unique on a monthly basis. It is also needed to allow the data to be traced back to an actual employee should any questions about the information need further research.

Besides the keyed dimensions, this schema has several non-key dimensions that represent additional factors by which the data could be sliced but are not required for ensuring the uniqueness of the records in the table. The columns in this example are **eeoc_type_code** and **sex**. Both of these columns are critical to the type of analysis that the EEOC compliance staff needs to do and, as such, there is a reasonable expectation that they will be accessed often. To make this easier, these columns were pulled into the fact table as artifacts of the relationship to EMPLOYEES. Notice that there is no dimension table for the column **sex**. This was intentionally left out to save storage space since this column is easily interpreted (e.g., *M* or *F*) and has no other characteristics associated with it.

The main measure for this table is **annual_pay**. This represents the annualized salary for a given employee as of the end of the month in question. In other words, at the point in time when the snapshot was taken, this is the amount of money that an employee would make over the period of one year if the current pay rate remained the same.

Other non-key columns in this table are **age** and **years_experience**. These are also artifacts of the relationship to EMPLOYEES. The column **years_experience** indicates the total number of years of work experience both in and outside ABC Corporation. The column **years_employed** is a calculated column based on the **from_date** and **thru_date** of all the positions an employee has held for the company as indicated in the enterprise warehouse. Even though these columns have changing values for employees, the fact that month is part of the key provides a history of what these values were at various points in time (in this case, at each month end).

Are these columns measures or dimensions? They could be used as both. As measures, the analysts can find out such things as the average age of employees in the company or the total years experience within a position type in a department. As dimensions, questions such as what is the average salary for those between the ages of 55 and 60 compared to those between 25 and 30, or what is the salary for those with over 15 years of experience (or employment) within each position type or each department, can be asked.

## Organization Dimension

Information about the internal organizations is taken from the warehouse table INTERNAL_ORG_ADDRESSES. Since no geographic information was required for this data mart, only the unique organization identifiers and names were selected to be moved from the enterprise warehouse. In addition, the column **org_type** was also extracted to allow analysts to select the organizations to be analyzed based on a type such as department, division, or branch.

The structure of this table is somewhat different from the other tables seen so far. It has been denormalized to store the organizational hierarchy which is represented in the main warehouse by the column **parent_org_id**. The "level 1" information represents the data associated directly with the position records that were extracted. "Level 2" is the name and type of the parent organization to the "level 1" organization. "Level 3" is the parent of "level 2", and so on.

The "level 2" and higher levels do not include an ID as that information is not needed. Each dimension record is defined by its **organization_id** which is a "level 1" or lowest level unit. For instance, a dimension record may show that the "accounting department" is a "level 1" which is within a "level 2" finance division which is within a "level 3" eastern region which is within a "level 4" ABC Subsidiary which is part of "level 5" ABC Corporation. The inclusion of only five levels of structure was a decision based on the levels of organization found in ABC Corporation. This model could easily be adapted to other organizations by adding or subtracting levels as required.

Table 12.1 gives examples of the data which may be found in the organization dimension. It is only shown to "level 3" for illustration purposes. The key point is that each organization dimension represents the lowest level in an enterprise structure, allowing analysis to be summarized to any level desired. The flat structure of this table serves to enhance performance and simplify queries, rather than imposing a recursive structure on end users.

## Position Dimension

This information is extracted directly from the POSITIONS table in the enterprise warehouse. It is a *unique* list of all positions represented along with the po-

**TABLE 12.1**  *Organization Dimension*

| Organization ID | Level 1 Name | Level 1 Org Type | Level 2 Name | Level 2 Org Type | Level 3 Name | Level 3 Org Type |
|---|---|---|---|---|---|---|
| 10929 | Accounting | Department | Finance | Division | Eastern | Region |
| 23948 | Investments | Department | Finance | Division | Eastern | Region |
| 29039 | Sales | Department | Marketing | Division | Western | Region |

sition_type_code and **title**. It was assumed that for any given position that there was one and only one position type associated with it throughout time. Using this dimension, an analyst can select from PAY_HISTORY_DETAILS by **position_type_code** or a job title. This is similar in construct to the PRODUCTS dimension (discussed in the previous chapter) which includes both a **product_description** and **category_description** columns.

## EEOC Type Dimension

This dimension is built by gathering the unique **eeoc_type_code** and **eeoc_description** values from the EMPLOYEES table in the enterprise warehouse. Based on the analysis requirements, it was critical that this information be included as a dimension, even though it is actually a characteristic of the employee. This eliminates the need for analysts to constantly start their queries from the EMPLOYEES dimension table. It should result in a performance improvement overall, especially considering that there are many more employee records than there are EEOC types.

## Employee Dimension

As may be obvious, the EMPLOYEES dimension is a direct extract from the EMPLOYEES warehouse table. It contains information about an employee that doesn't change very often. It should contain only those employees that are included in the data mart. In the initial load of the data mart, the majority of the records will undoubtedly be loaded. However, in subsequent loads, only the employee records added to the warehouse since the last monthly load to the data mart need to be added. These records can be found easily by selecting records that have a **snapshot_date** greater than the last load date and an **employee_id** that does not already exist in the dimension table.

Depending on the analysis needs, this table could actually be dropped from the schema. The reason it is included is that analysts may want to select records based on a common name, or require the name or social security number of the specific employees returned in a query. If this is not a requirement, then the data warehouse designer may want to drop this dimension from the design.

## Time Dimension

The MONTHLY_TIME_PERIODS table used for this schema is the same table used in the sales analysis data mart discussed in Chapter 10. To review, it contains a **month_code** which uniquely represents a fiscal year and month combination. The data loaded in this table should represent all time periods covered by the data in the fact table. It provides the EEOC analysts with the ability to gather data not only by month, but by quarter and year as well. In this way they should be able to easily comply with their reporting requirements.

## AVERAGE ANNUAL PAY

As previously stated, another principle in data warehousing is that of accommodating different levels of granularity. As in the sales analysis model, interviews with EEOC compliance staff members did indeed indicate that there were some common averages they needed for reporting to the federal government. They needed to evaluate average annual salaries based on the position type, EEOC category, and sex, across the organization. To accommodate this need, the IS department developed the schema based around the PAY_SUMMARIES table (see Figure 12.2).

## Pay Summary Facts

As may be expected, the keys to this new fact table are somewhat different from the previous one because it represents a higher level of summarization. The key still includes **organization_id** and **month_code** to meet some of the reporting requirements. However, **employee_id** and **position_id** have been removed. Instead, the columns **position_type_code**, **eeoc_type_code**, and **sex** are included

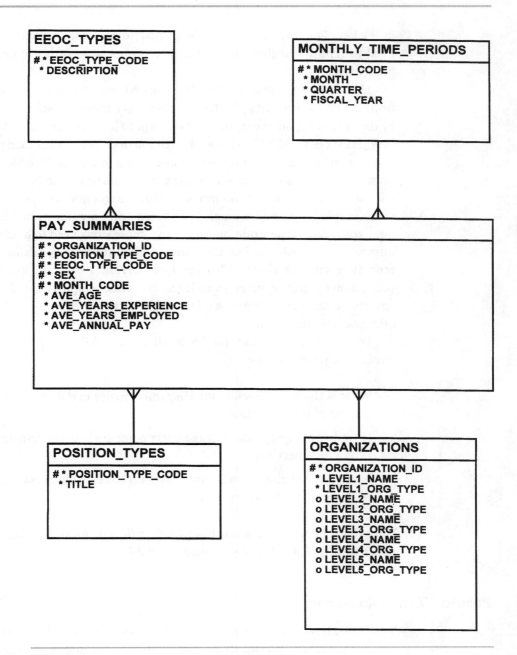

FIGURE 12.2

*Average pay by organization, type, EEOC, sex.*

in the key. These values provide the primary dimensions by which the analysts need to report and they ensure that the summary records are unique at this higher level.

How is this table loaded? It could be loaded from the enterprise warehouse or from the PAY_HISTORY_DETAILS table. Since these two schemas will be used by the same division, it may be most efficient to load the summary data from the PAY_HISTORY_DETAILS table after completing the monthly load process (this saves having to scan the entire warehouse—data in the details table is essentially preselected). If this is the case, then the table would be loaded by selecting the detail data for a month, then summing each of the columns **age**, **years_experience**, **years_employed**, and **annual_pay** based on **organization_id, position_type_code, eeoc_type_code**, and **sex**. Next, those sums need to be divided by the number of records having the same **organization_id, position_type_code, eeoc_type_code**, and **sex**. This produces averages that are loaded into the columns **ave_age, ave_years_experience, ave_years_employed**, and **ave_annual_pay**. (Note that in most relational DBMSs, there will likely be a SQL function that calculates averages easily.)

With this data in hand, the EEOC division at ABC Corporation can easily answer such questions as:

What is the average salary for Hispanic females in data modeling positions compared to white males?

How do average age and average salary compare between female supervisors and male supervisors?

Is there any obvious trend comparing years of experience, salary, and EEOC category within a particular division?

With this schema, the analysts have another flexible means for examining their data that was probably not previously available.

## Position Type Dimension

The POSITION_TYPES table is a new dimension for this schema while the others are the same as previously discussed. How is this dimension arrived at? It is simply an extract from either the POSITIONS table in the warehouse or the POSITIONS dimension from the previous schema. In either case, the data is extracted by gathering the unique occurrences of **position_type_code** along with the corresponding title. The extraction process needs to add to it any time a record for a new position has been added to the warehouse. Alternatively, it may be loaded once manually if the position types are static within the organization.

## SUMMARY

This chapter contained details of the design of two sample star schemas built to support analysis of human resources data—specifically EEOC-related data. In addition to principles illustrated in Chapter 11, the additional features of non-key dimensions were also explored. A creative approach to using some measures as dimensions was also introduced. The resulting design demonstrated some additional denormalization and several levels of summarization to assist in answering the questions revealed during end-user interviews.

As previously noted, what has been presented are several of the many possible schemas that could be derived from an enterprise data warehouse. The structure of a departmental model is in a large part determined by the questions it is designed to answer. It cannot be over emphasized that that end users of the data must be interviewed to determine their *real* business and information needs if a data warehouse strategy is going to be successful.

As illustrated, it is not uncommon for one department to wait to see how successful another department's venture is before it is willing to commit time and money to the effort. Once the methodology and technology have been proven, by producing not only data marts but *happy and satisfied* users, then others will soon want to join in that success.

For details on the table and column definitions for these schemas, refer to Appendix D. For the SQL scripts to implement these tables, including primary and foreign key definitions, refer to the CD-ROM product which is sold separately.

# 13

## USING THESE MODELS IN THE REAL WORLD

Now that many common logical data models and data warehouse designs have been illustrated, how can they be used most effectively to build information systems? This chapter gives some suggestions regarding the use of the models presented in this book.

## USING THE LOGICAL DATA MODELS

This section provides practical advice regarding the usage, customization, and implementation of the logical data models from Chapter 2 through Chapter 8.

### Purposes for the Logical Data Models

The logical data models in this book can be used to:

- Provide a starting point in developing a logical data model
- Add a new section of a data model to an enterprise's existing data model
- Validate an enterprise's existing logical data models and provide ideas for additions or modifications
- Help build a corporate data model that illustrates the interrelationships between information in various applications

- Help systems developers to understand the nature of various pieces of data and possible options and examples

## Customizing the Logical Data Models

The logical data models in this book were designed to give an enterprise a head start in designing a system or in developing a corporate data model. As noted in many sections of this book, enterprises will invariably have specific business needs which are not addressed by these models. This will necessitate changes to the models presented.

There are varying degrees of changes which may be made to these data models. The changes range from very easy modifications to more difficult data model changes. An example of an easy change is adding additional attributes to one or more entities in the model. The reason that this is considered a very easy change is that the structure of the data model is kept in tact and it is not necessary to evaluate the impact that this change has on other parts of the model. However, care should be taken not to introduce attributes that represent the denormalization of existing structures.

A slightly harder modification is adding a new entity or relationship to the data model. In this case, it is necessary to determine if the new entity or relationship already exists in some other portion of the model. For instance, if there is a proposal to add an entity named PRODUCT PACKAGING, does that information already exist within the PRODUCT COMPONENT entity? This depends on how the enterprise defines PRODUCT PACKAGING and therefore requires careful analysis.

Data modelers need to be a little more cautious when modifying or deleting entities and relationships in the data models. Since the data models are highly integrated, many entities and relationships in these data models are reused in many different diagrams and for many different purposes. There should be some consideration and analysis of how the change may affect other portions of the model. For example, if the enterprise decides to model ORGANIZATION and PERSON as two separate entities instead of as sub-types of PARTY, how this change affects other portions of the model must be considered. Some changes may be dramatic while other changes to entities and relationships may have lesser impacts on the whole model. If the enterprise is only using a small, specific portion of these data models, the impact of proposed changes may not be as significant.

While care should be taken when modifying these models, one purpose of these models is to provide a starting point for data modelers. If the models are used for this purpose, modifications to the models *should be expected* and encouraged in order to meet the information requirements of each enterprise.

Since these data models are integrated and many changes may require impact analysis, the systems development team should consider the use of appropriate change control and data administration procedures. These procedures include, but are not limited to, defining: Who is responsible for maintaining the models; how change requests are documented, prioritized, evaluated, and approved; how data model versions are maintained; and what mechanisms are provided to support the change control process (i.e., regular review meetings, systems, forms, etc.).

## Creating a Physical Database Design

The logical data models in this book do not represent physical database designs; they illustrate the information needs of an enterprise. The physical database design converts the information requirements represented by the logical data model into a design for the database which can be implemented.

The main difference between the logical data models and the physical database design is that the latter may be optimized for performance. The physical database designer uses the logical database design as a starting point for the database design and denormalizes the structures where appropriate for performance and ease-of-access reasons. For instance, derived data may be included, tables may be merged, and arrays of data may replace one-to-many relationships in certain circumstances.

Several different ways exist to convert the same logical data model into various physical database designs. Much of the design decisions depend on transaction frequencies, use of the data, data volume statistics, and the chosen relational database management system (RDBMS).

Additionally, super-types and sub-types may be implemented in many different ways in a physical database design:

- The entire super-type with its sub-types may be implemented as a single table.
- Each sub-type may be established as a separate table with the super-type columns included in each table.
- The super-type and one sub-type a may be merged into one table and the other sub-types may be merged into another table.

- The super-type may be implemented as one table and each sub-type may be implemented in separate tables.

The physical database designer needs to make these and other decisions to arrive at a physical database design.

The CD-ROM which may be ordered to supplement this book includes a physical database design of the book's logical data models using a very straight-forward conversion process. No denormalization has taken place and each super-type with its sub-types is generally implemented as a single table. This should provide a good starting point for the physical database design of these models. Also, the standard SQL statements included in the CD-ROM enable developers to create the physical database design in most RDBMSs. After the database is created, the database design may be reverse-engineered into a Computer Aided System Engineering (CASE) tool which supports reverse engineering in that RDBMS (most mainstream CASE tools support this feature). Then, the design can be modified as needed.

## USING THE DATA WAREHOUSE MODELS

The data warehouse models presented in this book serve to illustrate examples of how to move from the corporate or logical data models to an enterprise-wide data warehouse data model, then to departmental data models. The most important point of these chapters is to show the transformation process so that enterprises can understand the importance of setting up an appropriate data warehouse architecture.

Chapter 9 presented the transformation steps for converting a corporate data model into a data warehouse data model. Chapter 10 then provided a sample data warehouse data model which was developed using these transformation concepts. These transformation steps should be used selectively; it is not necessary to use all of these steps when developing the data warehouse data model. They merely serve as guidelines.

For instance, denormalizations such as including derived data, merging tables, and creating arrays of data may not always be required or they may be postponed until later. They should be included only when it is obvious that there are enterprise-wide requirements for the information provided by these transformations. Reducing the amount of denormalization can simplify the initial transformation process and reduce initial disk storage space.

There has been much debate in the data warehouse community regarding the architecture involved in moving data to a data warehouse environment. Specifically, there seems to be two schools of thought. Some say that it is necessary to first extract data into an enterprise-wide data warehouse, then move it to departmental data warehouses. Others contend that they can simply move the information directly from the operational systems to departmental data warehouses.

Certainly, it is initially easier to move the data directly into the departmental data warehouses. Only one transformation is needed instead of moving the data to an intermediate stage first, then to the departmental data warehouse. Business managers want information quickly and easily. There is an urgent need to provide the user community with the information it needs. This is exactly why the data warehouse concept has caught on. So why not take the direct route and provide the information directly to the departmental warehouse?

There is a major drawback in moving the information directly into the departmental warehouse. The drawback is *not* on the first implementation of the departmental data warehouse but on subsequent departmental implementations. If each department moves the data from the operational systems directly into its own departmental data warehouse, there is a great exposure in creating more inconsistent data sources than already exist in the operational systems.

Most enterprises which are creating data warehouses are faced with complex transformation routines which need to cleanse and consolidate data from several operational systems. The largest challenge in creating data warehouses is in deciphering the source of the most reliable data of the enterprise. This is complicated by the fact that the same data is often stored redundantly and inconsistently in most organizations (see the introduction for a discussion on separate and redundant data in enterprises). Therefore, in the transformation process, the data inconsistencies need to be dealt with.

To illustrate the problems of inconsistent data, a project engagement comes to mind where data was being transformed into a new database. When the database design was reviewed, it was noticed that there were two fields for **blood type** in the person table. The obvious question, "How can there be two blood types for a single person—a person of course has only one blood type!" created some concern. When the problem was tracked down, there actually *were* two blood types for each person; one from system A and the other from system B! It was extremely difficult to find out which system held the most accurate information for each person, so the enterprise decided to keep both values in the system. This is only one example showing the challenge of trying to consolidate information from several sources.

If each department uses its own transformation routines, think of the potential for inconsistent management information. Many of the departments may use the same information regarding people, organizations, products, sales, purchases, projects, and so forth in their decision support environment. The transformation routines are bound to be different for each department, if they are done separately, leading to inconsistent and confusing results. For instance, it is conceivable that a marketing organization may produce executive decision information which may be inconsistent with the data produced by the order processing department if it used different sources or transformations to gather its sales information. This can have devastating effects on an enterprise. Either the enterprise eventually questions the credibility of the information or worse, they act upon incorrect information.

The entire enterprise can capitalize on sharing the results behind this difficult process of transforming data. The only way this can happen is by having *one central* transformation process for decision support. By building an enterprise-wide data warehouse data model, common transformation routines can be built which serve the needs of the entire enterprise. In addition, the enterprise can identify data inconsistencies which are discovered in the transformation process and make *one* decision on how these inconsistencies will be handled. This knowledge can help the enterprise move toward more integrated operational systems by pinpointing existing problems. Finally, the enterprise can save time and money in the long run by doing the transformation process once for the enterprise instead of transforming similar types of data for each departmental data warehouse.

The enterprise needs to be willing to make an investment in its data and information architecture in order to be successful with data warehousing in the long run. An analogy is that it often seems easier to jump in and develop a program without taking the time to formally analyze the requirements or design. However, experience has shown that the lack of up-front investment will usually lead to increased programming and maintenance costs over the life of the program.

If an enterprise wants to get a quick head start into the data warehouse arena, another strategy would be to use the models presented to create a prototype departmental data warehouse, then load it with a limited amount of data. This allows the enterprise to evaluate the benefits of a decision support environment and make strategic decisions regarding its data warehouse environment. After an initial prototype is built, the enterprise may want to consider building an enterprise-wide data warehouse to support future departmental information needs.

## SUMMARY

This book provides numerous examples of different models. However, it is not a "how-to" book of data modeling. It was designed to be a very practical *resource* book to allow data modelers, database designers, data warehouse designers, and other systems professionals to be more productive by building upon the logical data models and data warehouse models presented.

We hope that this is just the beginning of efforts toward *universal data models* and that the information systems (IS) industry will continue to develop reusable models. If the IS industry can develop more common sharable models over time, systems development professionals will be able to shorten systems development cycles and produce higher quality information systems at a reduced cost for the user community at large.

We encourage and would be appreciative of any suggestions to enhance these models. To contribute toward improving or adding to these models, please feel free to e-mail us at **lsilvers@qdbc.com**.

# DETAILED ATTRIBUTE
# LISTINGS FOR THE
# LOGICAL DATA
# MODELS

Listed here are the entity and attribute definitions for the logical data models presented in Chapters 2 through 8. The **entity name** and **attribute name** columns are those shown on the diagrams and are presented in alphabetical order. The **datatype** column indicates the database data type for a column. The **length** column indicates the maximum size of the attribute, **prec** indicates the number of digits to the right of a decimal point, and **optional** indicates if the column is required ("N") or optional ("Y"). Note that entities without attributes are *not* listed here.

The attribute sizes presented here are only *recommendations.* These should be adjusted to fit actual business requirements. SQL code to implement a physical design for these models (along with foreign and primary key constraints) can be found on the CD-ROM product, which is sold separately.

**TABLE A.1**  *Attribute Listing for Logical Data Models*

| Entity Name | Attribute Name | Datatype | Length | Prec | Optional |
|---|---|---|---|---|---|
| Accounting Period | Period ID | Number | 8 | | N |
| | From Day | Varchar | 10 | | N |
| | Thru Day | Varchar | 10 | | N |
| Accounting Period Type | Period Type Code | Varchar | 10 | | N |
| | Description | Varchar | 40 | | N |
| Accounting Transaction | Transaction ID | Number | 8 | | N |
| | Transaction Date | Date | | | N |
| | Entry Date | Date | | | N |
| | Description | Varchar | 40 | | N |
| | Amount | Number | 9 | 2 | Y |
| Accounting Transaction Type | Transaction Type Code | Varchar | 10 | | N |
| | Description | Varchar | 40 | | N |
| Addendum | Addendum Seq | Number | 4 | | N |
| | Addendum Creation Date | Date | | | Y |
| | Addendum Effective Date | Date | | | Y |
| | Addendum Text | Varchar | 2000 | | N |
| Address | Address ID | Number | 8 | 0 | N |
| | Postal Code | Integer | 9 | | N |
| | Address1 | Varchar | 35 | | N |
| | Address2 | Varchar | 35 | | Y |
| | Directions | Varchar | 2000 | | Y |
| Adjustment | Amount For Order | Number | 9 | 2 | Y |
| | Amount Per Unit | Number | 9 | 2 | Y |
| | Percentage For Order | Number | 5 | 3 | Y |
| | Percentage Per Unit | Number | 5 | 3 | Y |
| Adjustment Type | Adjustment Type Code | Varchar | 10 | | N |
| | Description | Varchar | 40 | | N |
| Agreement | Agreement ID | Number | 8 | 0 | N |
| | Agreement Date | Date | | | N |
| | From Date | Date | | | N |
| | Thru Date | Date | | | N |
| | Description | Varchar | 40 | | N |
| Agreement Line Item | Line Item Seq | Number | 4 | 0 | N |
| Agreement Line Item Price | Line Item Price Seq | Number | 4 | 0 | N |
| | From Date | Date | | | N |

**TABLE A.1** *Continued*

| Entity Name | Attribute Name | Datatype | Length | Prec | Optional |
|---|---|---|---|---|---|
| | Thru Date | Date | | | N |
| | Price | Number | 9 | 2 | N |
| | Percent | Number | 5 | 2 | Y |
| | Comment | Varchar | 240 | | Y |
| Agreement Line Item Term | From Date | Date | | | N |
| | Thru Date | Date | | | N |
| | Term Value | Varchar | 240 | | N |
| Agreement Term | From Date | Date | | | N |
| | Thru Date | Date | | | N |
| Agreement Term | Term Value | Varchar | 240 | | N |
| Agreement Type | Agreement Type Code | Varchar | 10 | | N |
| | Description | Varchar | 40 | | N |
| Benefit Type | Benefit Type Code | Varchar | 10 | | N |
| | Name | Varchar | 40 | | N |
| | Description | Varchar | 240 | | N |
| | Employer Paid Percentage | Number | 6 | 3 | Y |
| Billing Account | Billing Account ID | Number | 8 | 0 | N |
| | From Date | Date | | | N |
| | Thru Date | Date | | | Y |
| | Description | Varchar | 40 | | Y |
| Budget | Budget ID | Number | 8 | | N |
| | Description | Varchar | 240 | | Y |
| Budget Line Item | Line Item Seq | Number | 4 | | N |
| | Amount | Number | 9 | 2 | N |
| | Purpose | Varchar | 30 | | N |
| | Justification | Varchar | 2000 | | N |
| Budget Line Item Type | Budget Type Code | Varchar | 10 | | N |
| | Description | Varchar | 40 | | N |
| Budget Review Result Type | Result Type Code | Varchar | 10 | | N |
| | Description | Varchar | 40 | | N |
| Budget Revision | Revision Seq | Number | 4 | | N |
| | Revision Reason | Varchar | 2000 | | N |
| Budget Revision Review | Review Date | Date | | | N |
| | Comment | Varchar | 240 | | Y |

**TABLE A.1**  *Continued*

| Entity Name | Attribute Name | Datatype | Length | Prec | Optional |
|---|---|---|---|---|---|
| Budget Revision Status | Status Date | Date | | | N |
| | Comment | Varchar | 240 | | Y |
| Budget Revision Status Type | Status Type Code | Varchar | 10 | | N |
| | Description | Varchar | 40 | | N |
| City | City ID | Number | 8 | | N |
| Contact Mechanism | Contact Mechanism ID | Number | 8 | | N |
| Contact Mechanism Type | Contact Mechanism Type Code | Varchar | 10 | | N |
| | Description | Varchar | 40 | | N |
| Contact Note | Contact Note ID | Number | 8 | 0 | Y |
| | Date | Date | | | N |
| | Note | Varchar | 2000 | | Y |
| Contact Type | Contact Type Code | Varchar | 10 | | N |
| | Description | Varchar | 40 | | N |
| Container | Container ID | Number | 8 | | N |
| Container Type | Container Type Code | Varchar | 10 | | N |
| | Description | Varchar | 40 | | N |
| Cost Component Type | Cost Component Type Code | Varchar | 10 | | N |
| | Description | Varchar | 40 | | N |
| Country | Country ID | Number | 8 | 0 | N |
| County | County ID | Number | 8 | | N |
| Customer | Customer ID | Number | 8 | | N |
| | Invoicing Message | Varchar | 2000 | | Y |
| | Special Invoicing Instructions | Varchar | 2000 | | Y |
| Deduction | Deduction Seq | Number | 4 | | N |
| | Amount | Number | 9 | 2 | N |
| Deduction Type | Deduction Type Code | Varchar | 10 | | N |
| | Description | Varchar | 40 | | N |
| Deliverable | Deliverable ID | Number | 8 | | N |
| | Name | Varchar | 40 | | N |
| | Description | Varchar | 40 | | Y |
| Deliverable Type | Deliverable Type Code | Varchar | 10 | | N |
| | Description | Varchar | 40 | | N |

**TABLE A.1**  *Continued*

| Entity Name | Attribute Name | Datatype | Length | Prec | Optional |
|---|---|---|---|---|---|
| Depreciation Method | Depreciation Method Code | Varchar | 10 | | N |
| | Description | Varchar | 40 | | N |
| | Formula | Varchar | 240 | | Y |
| Dimension Type | Dimension Type Code | Varchar | 10 | | N |
| | Description | Varchar | 40 | | N |
| Disbursement Budget Allocaton | Amount | Number | 9 | 2 | Y |
| Electronic Address | Electronic Address String | Varchar | 30 | | N |
| Estimated Product Cost Component | From Date | Date | | | N |
| | Thru Date | Date | | | Y |
| | Cost | Number | 9 | 2 | N |
| Exhibit | Exhibit Seq | Number | 4 | | N |
| | Exhibit Text | Varchar | 2000 | | N |
| | Exhibit Image | Varchar | 2000 | | Y |
| Fixed Asset | Fixed Asset ID | Number | 8 | 0 | N |
| | Name | Varchar | 40 | | N |
| | Date Acquired | Date | | | N |
| | Date Last Serviced | Date | | | Y |
| | Date Next Service | Date | | | Y |
| | Production Capacity | Number | 10 | 2 | Y |
| | Description | Varchar | 40 | | Y |
| Fixed Asset Assignment | Start Date | Date | | | N |
| | End Date | Date | | | Y |
| | Comment | Varchar | 240 | | Y |
| Fixed Asset Assignment Status Type | Status Type Code | Varchar | 10 | | N |
| | Description | Varchar | 40 | | N |
| Fixed Asset Depreciation Method | From Date | Date | | | N |
| | Thru Date | Date | | | Y |
| Fixed Asset Type | Asset Type Code | Varchar | 10 | | N |
| | Description | Varchar | 40 | | N |
| General Ledger Account | Gl Account ID | Number | 8 | | N |
| | Name | Varchar | 40 | | N |
| | Description | Varchar | 40 | | N |

**TABLE A.1**  *Continued*

| Entity Name | Attribute Name | Datatype | Length | Prec | Optional |
|---|---|---|---|---|---|
| Geographic Boundary | Geo Code | Varchar | 10 | | N |
| | Name | Varchar | 40 | | N |
| | Abbreviation | Varchar | 4 | | Y |
| Gl Account Type | Acct Type Code | Varchar | 10 | | N |
| | Classification | Varchar | 40 | | N |
| Gl Budget Xref | From Date | Date | | | N |
| | Thru Date | Date | | | Y |
| | Allocation Percentage | Number | 5 | 2 | N |
| Identification Type | ID Type Code | Varchar | 10 | | N |
| | Description | Varchar | 40 | | N |
| Inventory Assignment | Quantity | Number | 12 | 2 | N |
| Inventory Item | Inventory Item ID | Number | 8 | 0 | N |
| | Quantity On Hand | Number | 11 | 0 | N |
| | Serial No | Varchar | 30 | | N |
| Invoice | Invoice ID | Number | 8 | 0 | N |
| | Invoice Date | Date | | | N |
| | Message | Varchar | 2000 | | Y |
| | Description | Varchar | 40 | | Y |
| Invoice Adjustment | Amount | Number | 9 | 2 | N |
| Invoice Line Item | Line Item Seq | Number | 4 | 0 | N |
| | Taxable Flag | Varchar | 1 | | N |
| Invoice Status | Status Date | Date | | | N |
| Invoice Status Type | Status Type Code | Varchar | 10 | | N |
| | Description | Varchar | 40 | | N |
| Invoice Term | Term Value | Varchar | 240 | | N |
| Item | Reorder Level | Number | 11 | 0 | Y |
| | Reorder Quantity | Number | 11 | 0 | Y |
| Item Identification | ID Value | Varchar | 40 | | N |
| Item Line Item | Estimated Ready Date | Date | | | Y |
| Item Variance | Physical Inventory Date | Date | | | N |
| | Quantity | Number | 10 | 3 | N |
| | Reason | Varchar | 240 | | N |

**TABLE A.1**    *Continued*

| Entity Name | Attribute Name | Datatype | Length | Prec | Optional |
|---|---|---|---|---|---|
| Lot | Lot ID | Number | 8 | | N |
| | Creation Date | Date | | | N |
| | Quantity | Number | 10 | 3 | N |
| | Expiration Date | Date | | | Y |
| Market Interest | From Date | Date | | | N |
| | Thru Date | Date | | | Y |
| | Comment | Varchar | 240 | | Y |
| Note Status Type | Status Type Code | Varchar | 10 | | N |
| | Description | Varchar | 40 | | N |
| Order | Order ID | Number | 8 | 0 | N |
| | Order Date | Date | | | N |
| | Entry Date | Date | | | Y |
| Order Line Item | Line Item Seq | Number | 4 | 0 | N |
| | Comment | Varchar | 240 | | Y |
| | Outside Purchase Order ID | Number | 4 | | Y |
| Order Line Item Dependency Type | Dependency Type Code | Varchar | 10 | | N |
| | Description | Varchar | 40 | | N |
| Order Requisition | Quantity | Number | 10 | 3 | N |
| Order Role | From Date | Date | | | N |
| | Thru Date | Date | | | Y |
| | Percent Contribution | Money | 6 | 2 | Y |
| Order Role Type | Role Type Code | Varchar | 10 | | N |
| | Description | Varchar | 40 | | N |
| Order Shipment | Quantity | Number | 10 | 3 | N |
| Order Status | Status Date | Date | | | N |
| Order Status Type | Status Type Code | Varchar | 10 | | N |
| | Description | Varchar | 40 | | N |
| Order Term | Term Value | Varchar | 240 | | N |
| Organization | Name | Varchar | 40 | | N |
| | Federal Tax ID Num | Varchar | 15 | | Y |
| Organization Gl Account | From Date | Date | | | N |
| | Thru Date | Date | | | Y |
| Party | Party ID | Number | 8 | 0 | N |
| | Credit Rating | Varchar | 10 | | Y |

**TABLE A.1**  *Continued*

| Entity Name | Attribute Name | Datatype | Length | Prec | Optional |
|---|---|---|---|---|---|
| Party Account | Primary Responsibility Flag | Varchar | 1 | | N |
| | From Date | Date | | | N |
| | Thru Date | Date | | | Y |
| Party Address | From Date | Date | | | N |
| | Thru Date | Date | | | Y |
| | Comment | Varchar | 240 | | Y |
| Party Address Role | From Date | Date | | | N |
| | Thru Date | Date | | | Y |
| | Comment | Varchar | 240 | | Y |
| Party Address Role Type | Role Type Code | Varchar | 10 | | N |
| | Description | Varchar | 40 | | N |
| Party Allocation | From Date | Date | | | N |
| | Thru Date | Date | | | N |
| | Comment | Varchar | 240 | | Y |
| Party Asset Assignment | From Date | Date | | | N |
| | Thru Date | Date | | | Y |
| | Comment | Varchar | 240 | | Y |
| Party Asset Assignment Status Type | Status Type Code | Varchar | 10 | | N |
| | Description | Varchar | 40 | | N |
| Party Benefit | From Date | Date | | | N |
| | Thru Date | Date | | | Y |
| | Cost | Number | 9 | 2 | Y |
| | Actual Employer Paid Percent | Number | 6 | 3 | Y |
| | Available Time | Number | 9 | 2 | Y |
| Party Contact Mechanism | Party Cont Mech Seq | Number | 4 | 0 | N |
| | From Date | Date | | | N |
| | Thru Date | Date | | | Y |
| | Comment | Varchar | 240 | | Y |
| Party Contact Mechanism Role | From Date | Date | | | N |
| | Thru Date | Date | | | Y |
| | Comment | Varchar | 240 | | Y |
| Party Contact Mechanism Role Type | Role Type Code | Varchar | 10 | | N |
| | Description | Varchar | 40 | | N |

**TABLE A.1** *Continued*

| Entity Name | Attribute Name | Datatype | Length | Prec | Optional |
|---|---|---|---|---|---|
| Party Definition | From Date | Date | | | N |
| | Thru Date | Date | | | Y |
| | Comment | Varchar | 2000 | | Y |
| Party Priority | Priority Code | Varchar | 10 | | N |
| | Description | Varchar | 40 | | N |
| Party Relationship | From Date | Date | | | N |
| | Thru Date | Date | | | Y |
| | Comment | Varchar | 240 | | Y |
| Party Relationship Status | Status Code | Varchar | 10 | | N |
| | Description | Varchar | 40 | | N |
| Party Relationship Type | Description | Varchar | 30 | | N |
| Party Role Type | Role Type Code | Varchar | 10 | | N |
| | Description | Varchar | 40 | | N |
| Party Skill | Years Experience | Number | 3 | 1 | N |
| | Rating | Varchar | 10 | | N |
| Party Type | Party Type Code | Varchar | 10 | | N |
| | Description | Varchar | 40 | | N |
| Party Work Order Role | From Date | Date | | | N |
| | Thru Date | Date | | | Y |
| | Comment | Varchar | 240 | | Y |
| Pay Grade | Grade ID | Number | 8 | | N |
| | Name | Varchar | 40 | | N |
| | Comment | Varchar | 240 | | Y |
| Pay History | From Date | Date | | | N |
| | Thru Date | Date | | | Y |
| | Amount | Number | 9 | 2 | N |
| | Comments | Varchar | 240 | | Y |
| Pay Type | Pay Type Code | Varchar | 10 | | N |
| | Description | Varchar | 40 | | N |
| Paycheck | Account ID | Number | 8 | | N |
| | Check No | Number | 4 | 0 | N |
| | Check Date | Date | | | N |
| | Amount | Number | 9 | 2 | N |
| | Comment | Varchar | 240 | | Y |
| Payment | Effective Date | Date | | | N |
| | Payment Ref No | Integer | 5 | | N |
| | Comment | Varchar | 240 | | Y |

**TABLE A.1**   *Continued*

| Entity Name | Attribute Name | Datatype | Length | Prec | Optional |
|---|---|---|---|---|---|
| Payroll Preference | Preference Seq | Number | 4 | | N |
| | From Date | Date | | | N |
| | Thru Date | Date | | | Y |
| | Percentage | Number | 5 | 3 | Y |
| | Flat Amount | Number | 9 | 2 | Y |
| Payroll Preference | Routing Number | Varchar | 30 | | Y |
| | Account Type | Varchar | 10 | | Y |
| Period Type | Period Type Code | Varchar | 10 | | N |
| | Description | Varchar | 40 | | N |
| Person | Last Name | Varchar | 40 | | N |
| | First Name | Varchar | 40 | | N |
| | Middle Name | Varchar | 40 | | Y |
| | Personal Title | Varchar | 10 | | Y |
| | Suffix | Varchar | 3 | | Y |
| | Nickname | Varchar | 40 | | Y |
| | Sex | Varchar | 1 | | Y |
| | Birth Date | Date | | | Y |
| | Height | Varchar | 5 | | Y |
| | Weight | Integer | 3 | | Y |
| | Previous Last Name | Varchar | 40 | | Y |
| | Mother's Maiden Name | Varchar | 40 | | Y |
| | Marital Status | Varchar | 1 | | Y |
| | Social Security No | Varchar | 12 | | Y |
| | Passport No | Varchar | 20 | | Y |
| | Passport Expire Date | Date | | | Y |
| | Total Years Work Experience | Number | 5 | 2 | Y |
| | Personal Comment | Varchar | 2000 | | Y |
| Position | Position ID | Number | 8 | | N |
| | Estimated From Date | Date | | | N |
| | Estimated Thru Date | Date | | | Y |
| | Salary Flag | Varchar | 1 | | N |
| | Exempt Flag | Varchar | 1 | | N |
| | Fulltime Flag | Varchar | 1 | | N |
| | Temporary Flag | Varchar | 1 | | N |
| | Actual From Date | Date | | | Y |
| | Actual Thru Date | Date | | | Y |
| Position Classification Type | Position Class Type Code | Varchar | 10 | | N |
| | Description | Varchar | 40 | | N |

**TABLE A.1**  *Continued*

| Entity Name | Attribute Name | Datatype | Length | Prec | Optional |
|---|---|---|---|---|---|
| Position Fulfillment | From Date | Date | | | N |
| | Thru Date | Date | | | Y |
| | Comment | Varchar | 240 | | Y |
| Position Reporting Structure | From Date | Date | | | N |
| | Thru Date | Date | | | Y |
| | Comments | Varchar | 240 | | Y |
| | Primary Flag | Varchar | 1 | | N |
| Position Responsibility | From Date | Date | | | N |
| | Thru Date | Date | | | Y |
| | Comment | Varchar | 240 | | Y |
| Position Status Type | Position Status Type Code | Varchar | 10 | | N |
| | Description | Varchar | 40 | | N |
| Position Type | Position Type Code | Varchar | 10 | | N |
| | Description | Varchar | 40 | | N |
| | Title | Varchar | 240 | | N |
| | Benefit Percent | Number | 6 | 3 | Y |
| Position Type Class | From Date | Date | | | N |
| | Thru Date | Date | | | Y |
| | Standard Hours Per Week | Number | 5 | 2 | Y |
| Product | Product Code | Varchar | 10 | | N |
| | Name | Varchar | 40 | | N |
| | Introduction Date | Date | | | Y |
| | Sales Discontinuation Date | Date | | | Y |
| | Support Discontinuation Date | Date | | | Y |
| | Manuf Suggest Retail Price | Number | 9 | 2 | Y |
| | Comment | Varchar | 240 | | Y |
| Product Category | Category Code | Varchar | 10 | | N |
| | Description | Varchar | 40 | | N |
| Product Category Classification | From Date | Date | | | N |
| | Thru Date | Date | | | Y |
| | Primary Flag | Varchar | 1 | | N |
| | Comment | Varchar | 240 | | Y |
| Product Characteristic | Characteristic Code | Varchar | 10 | | N |
| | Description | Varchar | 40 | | N |

**TABLE A.1**  *Continued*

| Entity Name | Attribute Name | Datatype | Length | Prec | Optional |
|---|---|---|---|---|---|
| Product Component | From Date | Date | | | N |
| | Thru Date | Date | | | N |
| | Quantity Used | Number | 10 | 3 | Y |
| | Instruction | Varchar | 2000 | | Y |
| | Comment | Varchar | 240 | | Y |
| Product Definition | Conversion Factor | Number | 10 | 3 | Y |
| Product Invoice Line Item | Quantity | Number | 10 | 3 | N |
| | Unit Price | Number | 9 | 2 | N |
| Product Line Item | Quantity | Number | 8 | 2 | Y |
| | Unit Price | Number | 9 | 2 | Y |
| | Estimated Delivery Date | Date | | | Y |
| | Shipping Instructions | Varchar | 2000 | | Y |
| Product Obsolescence | Reason | Varchar | 240 | | Y |
| Product Price Component | Price Seq | Number | 4 | 0 | N |
| | From Date | Date | | | N |
| | Thru Date | Date | | | Y |
| | Price | Number | 9 | 2 | Y |
| | Percent | Number | 7 | 4 | Y |
| | Comment | Varchar | 240 | | Y |
| Product Price Component Type | Component Type Code | Varchar | 10 | | N |
| | Description | Varchar | 40 | | N |
| Product Substitute | From Date | Date | | | N |
| | Thru Date | Date | | | N |
| | Quantity | Number | 10 | 3 | Y |
| | Comment | Varchar | 240 | | Y |
| Product Supplier | Available From Date | Date | | | N |
| | Available Thru Date | Date | | | Y |
| | Comment | Varchar | 30 | | Y |
| Product Supplier Preference Type | Preference Type Code | Varchar | 10 | | N |
| | Description | Varchar | 40 | | N |
| Product Supplier Rating Type | Rating Type Code | Varchar | 10 | | N |
| | Description | Varchar | 40 | | N |
| Production Run | Quantity To Produce | Number | 10 | 3 | Y |
| Purchase Order | Purchase Order ID | Number | 8 | 0 | N |
| Purchase Order Invoice Xref | Amount | Number | 9 | 2 | Y |

**TABLE A.1** *Continued*

| Entity Name | Attribute Name | Datatype | Length | Prec | Optional |
|---|---|---|---|---|---|
| Quantity Break | Quantity Break ID | Number | 8 | | N |
| | From Quantity | Number | 10 | 3 | N |
| | Thru Quantity | Number | 10 | 3 | Y |
| Quote | Quote ID | Number | 8 | | N |
| | Issue Date | Date | | | N |
| | Valid From Date | Date | | | N |
| | Valid Thru Date | Date | | | N |
| | Description | Varchar | 40 | | Y |
| Quote Line Item | Line Item Seq | Number | 4 | | N |
| | Quantity | Number | 10 | 3 | N |
| | Quote Unit Price | Number | 9 | 2 | N |
| Quote Line Item Term | Term Value | Number | 9 | 2 | Y |
| Quote Role | From Date | Date | | | N |
| | Thru Date | Date | | | Y |
| Quote Role Type | Role Type Code | Varchar | 10 | | N |
| | Description | Varchar | 40 | | N |
| Quote Term | Term Value | Number | 9 | 2 | Y |
| Range Type | Range Type Code | Varchar | 10 | | N |
| | Description | Varchar | 40 | | N |
| Rate Of Pay | From Date | Date | | | N |
| | Thru Date | Date | | | Y |
| | Amount | Number | 9 | 2 | Y |
| | Comment | Varchar | 240 | | Y |
| Rate Type | Rate Type Code | Varchar | 10 | | N |
| | Description | Varchar | 40 | | N |
| Request | Request ID | Number | 8 | | N |
| | Request Date | Date | | | N |
| | Response Required Date | Date | | | N |
| | Description | Varchar | 40 | | N |
| Request Line Item | Line Item Seq | Number | 4 | | N |
| | Required By Date | Date | | | N |
| | Quantity | Number | 10 | 3 | Y |
| | Maximum Amount | Number | 9 | 2 | Y |
| | Description | Varchar | 40 | | Y |
| Request Role | From Date | Date | | | N |
| | Thru Date | Date | | | Y |

**TABLE A.1**  *Continued*

| Entity Name | Attribute Name | Datatype | Length | Prec | Optional |
|---|---|---|---|---|---|
| Request Role Type | Role Type Code | Varchar | 10 | | N |
| | Description | Varchar | 40 | | N |
| Requisition | Requisition ID | Number | 8 | | N |
| | Requisition Date | Date | | | N |
| | Description | Varchar | 40 | | Y |
| | Reason | Varchar | 240 | | Y |
| Requisition Line Item | Line Item Seq | Number | 4 | | N |
| | Required By Date | Date | | | N |
| | Quantity | Number | 10 | 3 | Y |
| | Description | Varchar | 40 | | Y |
| Requisition Request | Quantity | Number | 10 | 3 | N |
| Requisition Role | From Date | Date | | | N |
| | Thru Date | Date | | | Y |
| Requisition Role Type | Role Type Code | Varchar | 10 | | N |
| | Description | Varchar | 40 | | N |
| Requisition Status | Status Date | Date | | | N |
| Requisition Status Type | Status Type Code | Varchar | 10 | | N |
| | Description | Varchar | 40 | | N |
| Responding Party | Responding Party Seq | Number | 4 | 0 | N |
| | Date Sent | Date | | | N |
| Responsibility Type | Responsibility Type Code | Varchar | 10 | | N |
| | Description | Varchar | 40 | | N |
| Salary Step | Step Seq | Number | 4 | | N |
| | Amount | Number | 9 | 2 | N |
| | Date Modified | Date | | | N |
| Sales Order | Sales Order ID | Number | 8 | | N |
| Service Line Item | Estimated Start Date | Date | | | Y |
| Shipment | Shipment ID | Number | 8 | 0 | N |
| | Estimated Ship Date | Date | | | N |
| | Estimated Ready Date | Date | | | Y |
| | Estimated Arrival Date | Date | | | Y |
| | Estimated Ship Cost | Number | 9 | 2 | Y |
| | Latest Cancel Date | Date | | | Y |
| | Actual Ship Cost | Number | 9 | 2 | Y |
| | Handling Instructions | Varchar | 240 | | Y |
| | Last Updated | Date | | | Y |

**TABLE A.1**   *Continued*

| Entity Name | Attribute Name | Datatype | Length | Prec | Optional |
|---|---|---|---|---|---|
| Shipment Line Item | Line Item Seq | Number | 4 | 0 | N |
| | Quantity | Number | 8 | 2 | N |
| Shipment Method | Estimated Start Date | Date | | | Y |
| | Estimated End Date | Date | | | Y |
| Shipment Method Type | Shipment Method Type Code | Varchar | 10 | | N |
| | Description | Varchar | 40 | | N |
| Shipment Status History | Status Date | Date | | | N |
| Shipment Status Type | Shipment Status Type Code | Varchar | 10 | | N |
| | Description | Varchar | 40 | | N |
| Shipment Vehicle | Start Datetime | Timestamp | | | N |
| | End Datetime | Timestamp | | | N |
| | Start Mileage | Number | 8 | 1 | Y |
| | End Mileage | Number | 8 | 1 | Y |
| | Fuel Used | Number | 6 | 2 | Y |
| | Estimated Start Date | Date | | | Y |
| | Estimated End Date | Date | | | Y |
| Skill Type | Skill Type Code | Varchar | 10 | | N |
| | Description | Varchar | 40 | | N |
| Standard Time Period | Period ID | Number | 8 | | N |
| | From Date | Date | | | N |
| | Thru Date | Date | | | N |
| State | State ID | Varchar | 10 | | N |
| Task Assignment Status Type | Status Type Code | Varchar | 10 | | N |
| | Description | Varchar | 40 | | N |
| Telecom Number | Area Code | Number | 3 | 0 | N |
| | Contact Number | Varchar | 7 | | N |
| | Country Code | Number | 3 | 0 | Y |
| Term Type | Term Type Code | Varchar | 10 | | N |
| | Description | Varchar | 40 | | N |
| Time Entry | From Date | Date | | | N |
| | Thru Date | Date | | | N |
| | Hours | Number | 5 | 2 | N |
| | Comment | Varchar | 240 | | Y |

**TABLE A.1**  *Continued*

| Entity Name | Attribute Name | Datatype | Length | Prec | Optional |
|---|---|---|---|---|---|
| Transaction Detail | Detail Seq | Number | 4 | 0 | N |
|  | Amount | Number | 9 | 2 | N |
|  | Debit Credit Flag | Varchar | 1 |  | N |
| Unit Of Measure | UOM Code | Varchar | 10 |  | N |
|  | Description | Varchar | 40 |  | N |
| Valid Responsibility | From Date | Date |  |  | N |
|  | Thru Date | Date |  |  | Y |
|  | Comment | Varchar | 240 |  | Y |
| Vehicle Type | Vehicle Type Code | Varchar | 10 |  | N |
|  | Description | Date |  |  | N |
| Work Effort | Work Effort ID | Number | 8 |  | N |
|  | Name | Varchar | 40 |  | N |
|  | Description | Varchar | 2000 |  | N |
|  | Scheduled Start Date | Date |  |  | Y |
|  | Scheduled Completion Date | Date |  |  | Y |
|  | Total Dollars Allowed | Number | 9 | 2 | Y |
|  | Total Hours Allowed | Number | 5 | 0 | Y |
|  | Estimated Hours | Number | 5 | 0 | Y |
|  | Special Terms | Varchar | 240 |  | Y |
| Work Effort Type | Effort Type Code | Varchar | 10 |  | N |
|  | Description | Varchar | 40 |  | N |
| Work Order | Work Order ID | Number | 8 |  | N |
|  | Work Order Creation Date | Date |  |  | N |
|  | Required By Date | Date |  |  | N |
|  | Description | Varchar | 2000 |  | N |
|  | Quantity Required | Number | 10 | 3 | Y |
|  | Last Update | Date |  |  | Y |
|  | Estimated Cost | Number | 9 | 2 | Y |
| Work Order Budget Allocation | Amount | Number | 9 | 2 | N |
| Work Order Role Type | Role Type Code | Varchar | 10 |  | N |
|  | Description | Varchar | 40 |  | N |
| Work Order Type | Work Order Type Code | Varchar | 10 |  | N |
|  | Description | Varchar | 40 |  | N |
| Work Task | Task Seq | Number | 4 |  | N |
|  | Scheduled Start Date | Date |  |  | N |
|  | Scheduled End Date | Date |  |  | Y |
|  | Estimated Hours | Number | 6 | 1 | Y |

**TABLE A.1**   *Continued*

| Entity Name | Attribute Name | Datatype | Length | Prec | Optional |
|---|---|---|---|---|---|
| Work Task Assignment | Start Date | Date | | | N |
| | End Date | Date | | | Y |
| | Comment | Varchar | 240 | | Y |
| Work Task Dependency Type | Dependency Type Code | Varchar | 10 | | N |
| | Description | Varchar | 40 | | N |
| Work Task Fixed-Asset Requirement | Estimated Quantity | Number | 12 | 3 | N |
| | Estimated Duration | Number | 6 | 0 | N |
| Work Task Inventory Requirement | Estimated Quantity | Number | 12 | 3 | N |
| Work Task Rate | From Date | Date | | | N |
| | Thru Date | Date | | | Y |
| | Rate | Number | 9 | 2 | N |
| Work Task Role Type | Role Type Code | Varchar | 10 | | N |
| | Description | Date | | | N |
| Work Task Skill Requirement | Estimated Number Of People | Number | 6 | 0 | N |
| | Estimated Duration | Number | 6 | 0 | N |
| Work Task Type | Task Type Code | Varchar | 10 | | N |
| | Description | Varchar | 40 | | N |
| | Standard Work Hours | Number | 5 | 2 | Y |

# TABLE STRUCTURES FOR THE DATA WAREHOUSE DATA MODEL

Listed here are the table and column definitions for the data warehouse data model that was presented in Chapter 10. The **table name** and **column name** columns are those shown on the diagram and are presented in alphabetical order. The **datatype** column indicates the database data type for a column. The **length** column indicates the size of the column and **nulls** indicates if the column is required ("not null") or optional ("null").

The column sizes presented here are only *recommendations*. These should be adjusted to fit actual business requirements. The actual SQL code to build these tables (along with foreign and primary key constraints) can be found on the CD-ROM product, which can be purchased separately.

**TABLE B.1**    *Table Structures*

| Table Name | Column Name | Datatype | Length | Nulls |
|---|---|---|---|---|
| BUDGET_DETAILS | BUDGET_ID | NUMBER | 8 | NOT NULL |
| | REVISION_SEQ | NUMBER | 4 | NOT NULL |
| | LINE_ITEM_SEQ | NUMBER | 4 | NOT NULL |
| | BLI_TYPE_CODE | VARCHAR | 10 | NOT NULL |
| | BLI_TYPE_DESCRIPTION | VARCHAR | 40 | NOT NULL |
| | ORGANIZATION_ID | NUMBER | 8 | NOT NULL |
| | ADDRESS_ID | NUMBER | 8 | NOT NULL |
| | BUDGET_PERIOD | VARCHAR | 10 | NOT NULL |
| | LOAD_DATE | DATE | | NOT NULL |
| | BUDGET_AMOUNT | NUMBER | 9 | NOT NULL |
| | EXPENDITURES | NUMBER | 9 | NOT NULL |
| | PRODUCT_CODE | VARCHAR | 10 | NULL |
| CUSTOMERS | CUSTOMER_ID | NUMBER | 8 | NOT NULL |
| | SNAPSHOT_DATE | DATE | | NOT NULL |
| | CUSTOMER_NAME | VARCHAR | 40 | NOT NULL |
| | AGE | NUMBER | 2 | NULL |
| | MARITAL_STATUS | VARCHAR | 1 | NULL |
| | CREDIT_RATING | VARCHAR | 10 | NOT NULL |
| CUSTOMER_ADDRESSES | CUSTOMER_ID | NUMBER | 8 | NOT NULL |
| | ADDRESS_ID | NUMBER | 8 | NOT NULL |
| | ADDRESS_LINE1 | VARCHAR | 35 | NOT NULL |
| | ADDRESS_LINE2 | VARCHAR | 35 | NULL |
| | POSTAL_CODE | VARCHAR | 9 | NULL |
| | SALES_REP_ID | NUMBER | 8 | NOT NULL |
| | GEO_CODE | VARCHAR | 10 | NOT NULL |
| | LOAD_DATE | DATE | | NOT NULL |
| CUSTOMER_INVOICES | INVOICE_ID | NUMBER | 8 | NOT NULL |
| | LINE_ITEM_SEQ | NUMBER | 4 | NOT NULL |
| | INVOICE_DATE | DATE | | NOT NULL |
| | CUSTOMER_ID | NUMBER | 8 | NOT NULL |
| | BILL_TO_ADDRESS_ID | NUMBER | 8 | NOT NULL |
| | SALES_REP_ID | NUMBER | 8 | NOT NULL |
| | MANAGER_REP_ID | NUMBER | 8 | NOT NULL |
| | ORGANIZATION_ID | NUMBER | 8 | NOT NULL |
| | ORG_ADDRESS_ID | VARCHAR | 35 | NOT NULL |
| | PRODUCT_CODE | VARCHAR | 2 | NOT NULL |
| | QUANTITY | NUMBER | 10 | NOT NULL |
| | UNIT_PRICE | NUMBER | 9 | NOT NULL |
| | AMOUNT | NUMBER | 9 | NOT NULL |
| | PRODUCT_COST | NUMBER | 9 | NULL |
| | LOAD_DATE | DATE | | NOT NULL |

**TABLE B.1** *Continued*

| Table Name | Column Name | Datatype | Length | Nulls |
|---|---|---|---|---|
| EMPLOYEES | EMPLOYEE_ID | NUMBER | 8 | NOT NULL |
| | SNAPSHOT_DATE | DATE | | NOT NULL |
| | LAST_NAME | VARCHAR | 40 | NOT NULL |
| | FIRST_NAME | VARCHAR | 40 | NOT NULL |
| | SEX | VARCHAR | 1 | NOT NULL |
| | EEOC_TYPE_CODE | VARCHAR | 10 | NOT NULL |
| | EEOC_DESCRIPTION | VARCHAR | 40 | NOT NULL |
| | AGE | NUMBER | 2 | NOT NULL |
| | YEARS_EXPERIENCE | NUMBER | 5 | NOT NULL |
| | SOCIAL_SECURITY_NO | VARCHAR | 12 | NULL |
| GEOGRAPHIC_BOUNDARIES | GEO_CODE | VARCHAR | 10 | NOT NULL |
| | CITY_NAME | VARCHAR | 40 | NOT NULL |
| | STATE_NAME | VARCHAR | 40 | NOT NULL |
| | COUNTRY_NAME | VARCHAR | 40 | NOT NULL |
| | CITY_ABBRV | VARCHAR | 10 | NULL |
| | STATE_ABBRV | VARCHAR | 2 | NULL |
| | COUNTRY_ABBRV | VARCHAR | 3 | NULL |
| INTERNAL_ORG_ADDRESSES | ORGANIZATION_ID | NUMBER | 8 | NOT NULL |
| | ADDRESS_ID | NUMBER | 8 | NOT NULL |
| | ORG_TYPE | VARCHAR | 10 | NOT NULL |
| | ORGANIZATION_NAME | VARCHAR | 40 | NOT NULL |
| | ADDRESS_LINE1 | VARCHAR | 35 | NOT NULL |
| | ADDRESS_LINE2 | VARCHAR | 35 | NULL |
| | POSTAL_CODE | VARCHAR | 9 | NULL |
| | GEO_CODE | VARCHAR | 10 | NOT NULL |
| | PARENT_ORG_ID | NUMBER | 8 | NULL |
| | LOAD_DATE | DATE | | NOT NULL |
| POSITIONS | ORGANIZATION_ID | NUMBER | 8 | NOT NULL |
| | ADDRESS_ID | NUMBER | 8 | NOT NULL |
| | EMPLOYEE_ID | NUMBER | 8 | NOT NULL |
| | POSITION_ID | NUMBER | 8 | NOT NULL |
| | FROM_DATE | DATE | | NOT NULL |
| | THRU_DATE | DATE | | NOT NULL |
| | POSTION_TYPE_CODE | VARCHAR | 10 | NOT NULL |
| | TITLE | VARCHAR | 30 | NOT NULL |
| | ANNUAL_PAY | NUMBER | 9 | NOT NULL |
| | SALARY_FLAG | VARCHAR | 1 | NOT NULL |
| | EXEMPT_FLAG | VARCHAR | 1 | NOT NULL |
| | FULLTIME_FLAG | VARCHAR | 1 | NOT NULL |
| | TEMPORARY_FLAG | VARCHAR | 1 | NOT NULL |

**TABLE B.1** *Continued*

| Table Name | Column Name | Datatype | Length | Nulls |
|---|---|---|---|---|
| PRODUCTS | PRODUCT_CODE | VARCHAR | 10 | NOT NULL |
| | PRODUCT_DESCRIPTION | VARCHAR | 40 | NOT NULL |
| | CATEGORY_CODE | VARCHAR | 10 | NOT NULL |
| | CATEGORY_DESCRIPTION | VARCHAR | 40 | NOT NULL |
| PRODUCT_SNAPSHOTS | PRODUCT_CODE | VARCHAR | 10 | NOT NULL |
| | SNAPSHOT_DATE | DATE | | NOT NULL |
| | MSRP | NUMBER | 9 | NOT NULL |
| | UOM | VARCHAR | 3 | NOT NULL |
| | PRIMARY_SUPPLIER_NAME | VARCHAR | 40 | NOT NULL |
| | SUPPLIER_CITY_NAME | VARCHAR | 40 | NOT NULL |
| | SUPPLIER_STATE_ABBRV | VARCHAR | | NOT NULL |
| | SUPPLIER_COUNTRY_NAME | VARCHAR | 40 | NOT NULL |
| PURCHASE_INVOICES | INVOICE_ID | NUMBER | 8 | NOT NULL |
| | LINE_ITEM_SEQ | NUMBER | 4 | NOT NULL |
| | INVOICE_DATE | DATE | | NOT NULL |
| | SUPPLIER_ID | NUMBER | 8 | NOT NULL |
| | ADDRESS_ID | NUMBER | 8 | NOT NULL |
| | BUDGET_ID | NUMBER | 8 | NOT NULL |
| | REVISION_SEQ | NUMBER | 4 | NOT NULL |
| | BUDGET_LINE_ITEM_SEQ | NUMBER | 4 | NOT NULL |
| | PRODUCT_CODE | VARCHAR | 10 | NOT NULL |
| PURCHASE_INVOICES | QUANTITY | NUMBER | 10 | NOT NULL |
| | UNIT_PRICE | NUMBER | 9 | NOT NULL |
| | AMOUNT | NUMBER | 9 | NOT NULL |
| | LOAD_DATE | DATE | | NOT NULL |
| SALES_REPS | SALES_REP_ID | NUMBER | 8 | NOT NULL |
| | LAST_NAME | VARCHAR | 40 | NOT NULL |
| | FIRST_NAME | VARCHAR | 40 | NOT NULL |
| | MANAGER_REP_ID | NUMBER | 8 | NULL |
| SUPPLIER_ADDRESSES | SUPPLIER_ID | NUMBER | 8 | NOT NULL |
| | ADDRESS_ID | NUMBER | 8 | NOT NULL |
| | SUPPLIER_NAME | VARCHAR | 40 | NOT NULL |
| | POSTAL_CODE | VARCHAR | 9 | NULL |
| | GEO_CODE | VARCHAR | 10 | NOT NULL |
| | LOAD_DATE | DATE | | NOT NULL |

# TABLE STRUCTURES FOR THE SALES ANALYSIS STAR SCHEMA

Listed here are the table and column definitions for the departmental data warehouse data model that was presented in Chapter 11. The **table name** and **column name** columns are those shown on the diagram and are presented in alphabetical order. The **datatype** column indicates the database data type for a column. The **length** column indicates the size of the column and **nulls** indicates if the column is required ("not null") or optional ("null").

The column sizes presented here are only *recommendations*. These should be adjusted to fit actual business requirements. The actual SQL code to build these tables (along with foreign and primary key constraints) can be found on the CD-ROM product, which can be purchased separately.

**TABLE C.1**   *Table Structures*

| Table Name | Column Name | Datatype | Length | Nulls |
|---|---|---|---|---|
| Addresses | Address_Id | Number | 8 | Not Null |
|  | Address_Line1 | Varchar | 35 | Not Null |
|  | Address_Line2 | Varchar | 35 | Null |
|  | City_Name | Varchar | 40 | Not Null |
|  | State_Abbrv | Varchar | 10 | Null |
|  | Postal_Code | Varchar | 9 | Null |
|  | Country_Name | Varchar | 40 | Null |
| Customers | Customer_Id | Number | 8 | Not Null |
|  | Customer_Name | Varchar | 40 | Not Null |
| Customer_Demographics | Customer_Id | Number | 8 | Not Null |
|  | Snapshot_Date | Date |  | Not Null |
|  | Credit_Rating | Varchar | 10 | Not Null |
|  | Marital_Status | Varchar | 1 | Null |
|  | Age | Number | 2 | Null |
| Customer_Rep_Sales | Product_Code | Varchar | 10 | Not Null |
|  | Sales_Rep_Id | Number | 8 | Not Null |
|  | Customer_Id | Number | 8 | Not Null |
|  | Customer_Snapshot_Date | Date |  | Not Null |
|  | Ship_To_Address_Id | Number | 8 | Not Null |
|  | Invoice_Date | Date |  | Not Null |
|  | Gross_Sales | Number | 9 | Not Null |
|  | Quantity | Number | 10 | Not Null |
|  | Product_Cost | Number | 9 | Not Null |
| Customer_Sales | Product_Code | Varchar | 10 | Not Null |
|  | Sales_Rep_Id | Number | 8 | Not Null |
|  | Customer_Id | Number | 8 | Not Null |
|  | Customer_Snapshot_Date | Date |  | Not Null |
|  | Address_Id | Number | 8 | Not Null |
|  | Invoice_Id | Number | 8 | Not Null |
|  | Line_Item_Seq | Number | 4 | Not Null |
|  | Invoice_Date | Date |  | Not Null |
|  | Quantity | Number | 10 | Not Null |
|  | Amount | Number | 9 | Not Null |
|  | Product_Cost | Number | 9 | Null |
| Geographic_Boundaries | Geo_Code | Varchar | 10 | Not Null |
|  | City_Name | Varchar | 40 | Not Null |
|  | State_Name | Varchar | 40 | Not Null |
|  | Country_Name | Varchar | 40 | Not Null |
|  | City_Abbrv | Varchar | 10 | Null |
|  | State_Abbrv | Varchar | 2 | Null |
|  | Country_Abbrv | Varchar | 3 | Null |

**TABLE C.1**   *Continued*

| Table Name | Column Name | Datatype | Length | Nulls |
|---|---|---|---|---|
| Monthly_Time_Periods | Month_Code | Varchar | 10 | Not Null |
|  | Fiscal_Year | Number | 4 | Not Null |
|  | Quarter | Number | 1 | Not Null |
|  | Month | Number | 2 | Not Null |
| Products | Product_Code | Varchar | 10 | Not Null |
|  | Product_Description | Varchar | 40 | Not Null |
|  | Category_Code | Varchar | 10 | Not Null |
|  | Category_Description | Varchar | 40 | Not Null |
| Product_Sales | Product_Code | Varchar | 10 | Not Null |
|  | Geo_Code | Varchar | 10 | Not Null |
|  | Month_Code | Varchar | 10 | Not Null |
|  | Gross_Sales | Number | 9 | Not Null |
|  | Quantity | Number | 10 | Not Null |
|  | Product_Cost | Number | 9 | Not Null |
|  | Load_Date | Date |  | Not Null |
| Sales_Reps | Sales_Rep_Id | Number | 8 | Not Null |
|  | Last_Name | Varchar | 40 | Not Null |
|  | First_Name | Varchar | 40 | Not Null |
|  | Manager_Rep_Id | Number | 8 | Null |
| Sales_Rep_Sales | Sales_Rep_Id | Number | 8 | Not Null |
|  | Customer_Id | Number | 8 | Not Null |
|  | Address_Id | Number | 8 | Not Null |
|  | Month_Code | Varchar | 10 | Not Null |
|  | Gross_Sales | Number | 9 | Not Null |
|  | Load_Date | Date |  | Not Null |
| Time_Periods | Invoice_Date | Date |  | Not Null |
|  | Fiscal_Year | Number | 4 | Not Null |
|  | Quarter | Number | 1 | Not Null |
|  | Month | Number | 2 | Not Null |
|  | Week | Number | 2 | Not Null |

# TABLE STRUCTURES FOR THE HUMAN RESOURCES STAR SCHEMA

Listed here are the table and column definitions for the departmental data warehouse data model that was presented in Chapter 12. The **table name** and **column name** columns are those shown on the diagram and are presented in alphabetical order. The **datatype** column indicates the database data type for a column. The **length** column indicates the size of the column and **nulls** indicates if the column is required ("not null") or optional ("null").

The column sizes presented here are only *recommendations*. These should be adjusted to fit actual business requirements. The actual SQL code to build these tables (along with foreign and primary key constraints) can be found on the CD-ROM product, which can be purchased separately.

**TABLE D.1**   *Table Structures*

| Table Name | Column Name | Datatype | Length | Nulls |
|---|---|---|---|---|
| Eeoc_Types | Eeoc_Type_Code | Varchar | 10 | Not Null |
| | Description | Varchar | 40 | Not Null |
| Employees | Employee_Id | Number | 8 | Not Null |
| | Last_Name | Varchar | 40 | Not Null |
| | First_Name | Varchar | 40 | Not Null |
| | Social_Security_No | Varchar | 12 | Null |
| Monthly_Time_Periods | Month_Code | Varchar | 10 | Not Null |
| | Month | Number | 2 | Not Null |
| | Quarter | Number | 1 | Not Null |
| | Fiscal_Year | Number | 4 | Not Null |
| Organizations | Organization_Id | Number | 8 | Not Null |
| | Level1_Name | Varchar | 40 | Not Null |
| | Level1_Org_Type | Varchar | 10 | Not Null |
| | Level2_Name | Varchar | 40 | Null |
| | Level2_Org_Type | Varchar | 10 | Null |
| | Level3_Name | Varchar | 40 | Null |
| | Level3_Org_Type | Varchar | 10 | Null |
| | Level4_Name | Varchar | 40 | Null |
| | Level4_Org_Type | Varchar | 10 | Null |
| | Level5_Name | Varchar | 40 | Null |
| | Level5_Org_Type | Varchar | 10 | Null |
| Pay_History_Details | Organization_Id | Number | 8 | Not Null |
| | Employee_Id | Number | 8 | Not Null |
| | Position_Id | Number | 8 | Not Null |
| | Month_Code | Number | 8 | Not Null |
| | Eeoc_Type_Code | Varchar | 10 | Not Null |
| | Sex | Varchar | 1 | Not Null |
| | Age | Number | 2 | Not Null |
| | Years_Experience | Number | 4 | Not Null |
| | Years_Employed | Number | 4 | Not Null |
| | Annual_Pay | Number | 9 | Not Null |
| Pay_Summaries | Organization_Id | Number | 8 | Not Null |
| | Position_Type_Code | Varchar | 10 | Not Null |
| | Eeoc_Type_Code | Varchar | 10 | Not Null |
| | Sex | Varchar | 1 | Not Null |
| | Month_Code | Number | 8 | Not Null |
| | Ave_Age | Number | 2 | Not Null |
| | Ave_Years_Experience | Number | 4 | Not Null |
| | Ave_Years_Employed | Number | 4 | Not Null |
| | Ave_Annual_Pay | Number | 9 | Not Null |

**TABLE D.1**   *Continued*

| Table Name | Column Name | Datatype | Length | Nulls |
|---|---|---|---|---|
| Positions | Position_Id | Number | 8 | Not Null |
| | Position_Type_Code | Varchar | 10 | Not Null |
| | Title | Varchar | 240 | Not Null |
| Position_Types | Position_Type_Code | Varchar | 10 | Not Null |
| | Title | Varchar | 240 | Not Null |

# How to Use the CD-ROM Product

## Contents of the CD-ROM

The accompanying CD-ROM product, which is sold separately, provides all the SQL scripts needed to implement the data models described in this book. SQL scripts are provided that can be run in Oracle, Sybase SQL Server, Informix, and Microsoft SQL Server. ANSI standard SQL scripts are also included for use with other relational database management systems (RDBMSs). In addition to the scripts, reports are also included that detail the definitions for the tables and columns. These SQL scripts may be used to either build a database or reverse-engineer the models into a CASE tool for further analysis and modifications.

Each of the databases has its own directory on the CD-ROM. Scripts for Oracle are found in the \oracle directory; Informix in the \informix directory; Sybase in the \sybase directory; MS SQL Server in the \mssqlsrv directory; and ANSI scripts are in the \ansi directory. Within each of these directories can be found four subdirectories. Each of these subdirectories corresponds to a model described in this book. The \common subdirectory contains the scripts to implement the models that are part of the corporate data model described in Chapters 2 through 8. The \dwenter subdirectory contains scripts to build the sample enterprise data warehouse described in Chapter 10. The \dwsales subdirectory has the scripts to build the sales data mart described in Chapter 11. Finally, the subdirectory **\dwhr** contains the scripts needed to build the human resources data mart described in Chapter 12.

Within each of the subdirectories can be found several files which contain the actual SQL code needed to build the described models. The files with a **.tab** extension can be used to build all the tables for the model. The files with a **.con** extension contain the SQL code to build all the primary and foreign key constraints for a given model. For example, in the **\informix\common** subdirectory there are two files: **common.tab** and **common.con**. **Common.tab** has all the SQL to build the tables needed to implement the normalized corporate data model while **common.con** has the SQL to build all the constraints needed to enforce referential integrity on that model.

In each subdirectory there are files with a **.doc** extension. These are Microsoft Word documents which contain detailed column definitions and descriptions for the columns built with the corresponding SQL. In the **\common** subdirectory there is an additional file called **tabdsc.txt** which contains detailed table descriptions for the corporate data model. These documents could be converted to ASCII and used to load definitions into any CASE tool that has ASCII import facilities.

There is one additional file found in the **informix** directory. It is a Microsoft Word document called **ifmxabrv.doc**. It contains a list of abbreviations used in building the table and column names for implementation with an Informix database. Informix has a limit of 18 characters for all names. The standard used in this book was 30, so many of the names had to be shortened in order to be built in Informix (length was not a problem for the other databases). This list shows the original word used in the models in the book and is followed by the abbreviation for that word that was used in the Informix SQL scripts. This cross-referencing will be useful when trying to match the SQL code to the diagrams in the book.

## USING THE SCRIPTS

Using the scripts provided on the CD-ROM is quite simple. They can be used immediately if no changes are going to be made or they could be copied to a working directory on a hard drive or file server so they can be edited before execution. In either case, the scripts are ASCII files that can be loaded and executed from the standard SQL interface for the database selected (e.g., SQL*Plus for Oracle, ISQL/w for MS SQL Server). Be sure to execute the **.tab** files (to build tables) before the **.con** file (which builds constraints).

Most modeling tools have a reverse-engineering feature which allows the extraction of object definitions from the database into the CASE tool. So once the models have been built in the target database, tools such as Oracle Designer/2000, Erwin, or StarDesignor can be used to reverse-engineer the definitions for further analysis or reengineering. Many popular CASE tools even have the ability to reverse engineer directly from the SQL scripts.

If the target database is Oracle, there is a slightly different method that can be used. In all the subdirectories under **\oracle**, there is a **.sql** file. This file when executed in SQL*Plus will call all the other files to build that model, in the correct order. For an Oracle database, *comment* statements are also included in the scripts to build table and column descriptions directly into the data dictionary. Note too that in **\oracle\common** there is a **.ind** file. This file contains additional SQL code for building various indexes for the Oracle database. It is left up to the end user or database administrator as to whether or not to use these indexes. They are suggestions only and may or may not help performance. Note that all the primary key constraints are already created with an index.

# INDEX

Logical data model entities are in all-capitals. Sorting is word-by-word, as in telephone books.

attribute listings for, 307–323
creating physical database design, 301–302
customizing, 300–301
purposes of, 299–300
LOT entity, 121–122
attribute listing, 313

## M

MAINTENANCE entity, 149
mandatory relationships, 10
many-to-many relationships, 10–11
MARKET INTEREST entity, 47
attribute listing, 313
measures, using as dimensions, 291–292
merging table, 251–252, 263
Microsoft SQL Server, 16
MISCELLANEOUS CHARGE entity, 78, 80
multidimensional analysis, 269–270

## N

NON-EMPLOYEE entity, 21
NOTE entity, 184, 185
NOTE STATUS TYPE entity, 36–37
attribute listing, 313

## O

OBLIGATION entity, 183, 184, 185
one-to-many relationships, 10–11
one-to-one relationships, 10–11
online transaction processing (OLTP) systems, 236
optional relationships, 10
Oracle, 16
ORDER entity, 71–73
and AGREEMENTs, 106–108

attribute listing, 313
and PARTY ADDRESS, 71–72, 82–86
ORDER LINE ITEM DEPENDENCY entity, 76, 78, 80–82
ORDER LINE ITEM DEPENDENCY TYPE entity, 78, 81
attribute listing, 313
ORDER LINE ITEM entity, 71, 73–74, 76–78, 81, 82, 198, 199–200, 202
and AGREEMENTs, 108
attribute listing, 313
and PARTY ADDRESSes, 83
and QUOTE LINE ITEMs, 99–100
and REQUISITION LINE ITEMs, 88, 91
and SHIPMENTs, 116, 118, 123–124
and WORK EFFORT INVOICING, 170–172
ORDER LINE ITEM TERM entity, 78, 82
ORDER REQUISITION entity, 91
attribute listing, 313
ORDER ROLE entity, 88
attribute listing, 313
ORDER ROLE TYPE entity, 88
attribute listing, 313
ORDER SHIPMENT entity, 123–124
attribute listing, 313
ORDER STATUS entity, 74–76
attribute listing, 313
ORDER STATUS TYPE entity, 74–75
attribute listing, 313
ORDER TERM entity, 74, 76
attribute listing, 313
orders, 67. *See also* invoices; requisitions; shipments
adjustments, 80
header, 74–75
in high-level data models, 241
model definition, 69, 71–74
model summary, 110
and party address, 82–86
person roles for, 86–88